BEASTLY BRITAIN

BEASTLY BRITAIN

An Animal History

KAREN R. JONES

YALE UNIVERSITY PRESS
NEW HAVEN AND LONDON

Copyright © 2025 Karen R. Jones

All rights reserved. This book may not be reproduced in whole or in part, in any form (beyond that copying permitted by Sections 107 and 108 of the U.S. Copyright Law and except by reviewers for the public press) without written permission from the publishers.

All reasonable efforts have been made to provide accurate sources for all images that appear in this book. Any discrepancies or omissions will be rectified in future editions.

For information about this and other Yale University Press publications, please contact:
U.S. Office: sales.press@yale.edu yalebooks.com
Europe Office: sales@yaleup.co.uk yalebooks.co.uk

Set in Adobe Garamond Pro by IDSUK (DataConnection) Ltd
Printed in the Czech Republic by Finidr

Library of Congress Control Number: 2025930628
A catalogue record for this book is available from the British Library.
Authorized Representative in the EU: Easy Access System Europe, Mustamäe tee 50, 10621 Tallinn, Estonia, gpsr.requests@easproject.com

ISBN 978-0-300-26447-0

10 9 8 7 6 5 4 3 2 1

For the Beasts

Contents

List of Illustrations	*viii*
Animals and Us: An Entangled History	1
Woodland Wanderers	
1 Hedgehog	13
2 Fox	45
Farmed and Fancy	
3 Sheep	89
4 Pigeon	116
From Stream to Sea	
5 Newt	145
6 Herring	169
What Lies Beneath	
7 Stag Beetle	199
8 Flea	222
Ghosts and Monsters	
9 Black Dog	251
10 Plesiosaur	273
Epilogue	303
Animal Tracks: A Select Bibliography	*307*
Index	*315*

Illustrations

1. The front and back of a dog, illuminations in a Book of Hours (c.1485), KMN15002910, Foundation XX, pp. 469–70. The Princes Czartoryski Library, National Museum in Krakow. — 4
2. 'Erinaceus: The Common Hedgehog', coloured etching by J. Pass after H. Meyer (1803). Wellcome Collection. — 17
3. Table spread from Ladybird's *Learn About: Cooking*, Cooking © Ladybird Books Ltd (1977) pp. 50–1. — 24
4. Hedgehogs sticking fallen fruit to their quills and carrying it back to their burrow, detail of a miniature in the Rochester Bestiary (c.1230), Royal MS 12 F. xiii, f. 45r. From the British Library archive / Bridgeman Images. — 25
5. *A Crowned Fairy King Seated on a Hedgehog Drawn by a Girl Holding a Giant Daisy, Accompanied by Dancing Fairies*, watercolour by Charles Altamont Doyle (nineteenth century). Wellcome Collection. — 31
6. 'Seven Different Specimen of the Families of Wolves and Foxes (*Canis lupus* and *Vulpes*)', coloured etching by John Miller (eighteenth century). Wellcome Collection. — 49
7. A hunting fox, Hayden Valley, Yellowstone National Park (2016). National Park Service / Neal Herbert. — 63
8. 'A Huntsman at the Death, Surrounded by Horses and Hounds, Holding Up the Body of the Fox', coloured etching by J. Mackrell after J.F. Herring (c.1846). Wellcome Collection. — 69

ILLUSTRATIONS ix

9. Soay sheep, East Kent (2019). Author's photograph. — 93
10. Brasses depicting Thomas and Joan Bushe with their feet placed on woolpacks and sheep, Church of St Peter & St Paul, Northleach (c.1525). Jules & Jenny, Lincoln, UK, CC BY 2.0. — 98
11. 'A South Down Ram Viewed in Two Positions', etching by H. Beckwith after W.H. Davis (c.1849). Wellcome Collection. — 109
12. 'A pigeon Perched on the Branch of a Dead Tree', etching by C.M. Fessard (1767). Wellcome Collection. — 119
13. A miner releasing pigeons at Unicorn Head Colliery (1954). © National Coal Mining Museum for England / Harold White Collection. — 131
14. An inspection of RAF pigeons at a Scottish Coastal Command station (c.1939–45). Imperial War Museum. — 136
15. Families feeding pigeons in Trafalgar Square (1920s). Leonard Bentley from Iden, East Sussex, UK, CC BY-SA 2.0. — 140
16. 'The Waves – Their Inmates', colour line block (c. nineteenth century). Wellcome Collection. — 150
17. 'De saura serpente; Of the Serpent Called the Saura', miniature in the Aberdeen Bestiary (c.1200), MS 24, f. 70r. University of Aberdeen Special Collections, CC BY 4.0. — 158
18. 'Salamandar', illustration in Conrad Gessner, *Icones Animalium* (1560). Reproduced by kind permission of the Syndics of Cambridge University Library. — 160
19. 'Herring, Ling, Sole, Flounder Fish', hand-coloured print by Adam White (1859). Wellcome Collection. — 171
20. A group of Pittenweem 'herring lassies' knitting in Great Yarmouth (c.1900). Courtesy of the Scottish Fisheries Museum. — 189

ILLUSTRATIONS

21. Postcard from Great Yarmouth, produced by Alfred William Yallop (c.1919). Alfred William Yallop, Great Yarmouth. — 194
22. 'Twelve Beetles (Insects of the Order *Coleoptera*)', coloured etching (1787). Wellcome Collection. — 202
23. 'The Beetle Map', coloured etching in George Edwards, *A Natural History of Uncommon Birds* (c.1746). Wellcome Collection. — 211
24. A girl playing with a kitten and a stag beetle, illustration from Reverend John Wood, *Episodes of Insect Life* (1879). — 214
25. 'Haymakers Resting', etching by David Deuchar (eighteenth–nineteenth century). Wellcome Collection. — 227
26. 'The Flea', illustration in Robert Hooke, *Micrographia* (1665). Wellcome Collection. — 232
27. 'Les animaux savants', wood engraving by Gilbert Randon (nineteenth century). Wellcome Collection. — 244
28. *Shadows of the Shuck*, illustration by Lauren Sharples (2024). Image courtesy of Lauren Sharples. — 264
29. Wistman's Wood, Dartmoor (2021). Author's photograph. — 268
30. Autograph letter concerning the discovery of plesiosaurus, by Mary Anning (26 December 1823). Wellcome Collection. — 287
31. Plesiosaurs, illustration in Henry De la Beche, *Duria Antiquior, or, a More Ancient Dorset* (1830). — 289
32. 'The Crystal Palace from the Great Exhibition, installed at Sydenham', print by George Baxter (c.1864). Wellcome Collection. — 293
33. 'The Effects of a Hearty Dinner After Visiting the Antediluvian Department at the Crystal Palace', *Punch* (2 March 1855). Look and Learn / George Collection / Bridgeman Images. — 294

Animals and Us:

An Entangled History

I suppose I have always been drawn to the beastly.

When my newborn brother was brought home from hospital, Mum and Dad asked me what I thought of him. 'He's quite nice,' I (in)famously said, 'but can we take him back and swap him for a dog?' This tiny human, wrapped in a blanket, bleary-eyed and gurgling seemed a lot less exciting to my two-year-old self compared to a canine playmate.

As time went on, I forged a sort of peace with my brother (except when playing Monopoly or football). I also tried a different approach to my beastly conundrum. Why not become a beast myself? Birthday on birthday, then, I blew out the candles on my cake and wished for a canine metamorphosis. Sometimes, a monkey tail. Flight-ready wings. Or, best of all, the ability to transform into any creature I wanted. It was probably too much of an ask. Better to try for a Britains farm tractor or a space hopper. Luckily, the community of the four-leggeds beckoned anyway. Sequestered in a makeshift den, fashioned from an old bedsheet draped over living-room chairs, I communed with a lively creaturely complement. A white Playmobil dog, a plastic Charolais bull, a stuffed bear called Growly, especially. Animals were friends and fellow travellers. Occasionally, they could be foes – as in the case of 'the Bays', imaginary beings who lived in the curtain pelmet (ingenuously named by me as the 'wee angle', for reasons unknown). Beyond the great indoors, the critterly potential was immense: a leaping, whooping and chewing ensemble of small furries – rabbits, guinea pigs and hamsters – snails, earwigs, starlings and wasps (always so many wasps, who dived into beer tankards and chanced a steal of ice cream). Further afield, Longleat and Bristol Zoo offered each holiday a heady dose of exotic animaldom: white tigers, car-aerial-stripping monkeys, a sorrowful polar bear and the ever-elusive red panda.

Stop for a moment. What are *your* animals? Those seared into your memory. Formative encounters and imaginary friends. A long-suffering cat who you dressed in doll's clothes? A fiery dragon who flew into your bedroom on command? The snuffling presence of a farmyard pig (this, as it happened, was my brother's kindred spirit)? A majestic swan along the river who someone said would break your arm? We all have a beastly past, if we think hard enough. And so do these isles.

Beastly Britain takes a fresh look at the history of this country with an animal-centred view, showing how a vibrant menagerie of furred, feathered and flippered creatures enlivened the historical world with their presence. Animals are all around us – in our environment and our culture. We tell stories about them, use them, are entertained by them and claim their spaces. They affect our lives in profound ways, just as we do theirs. What follows is somewhere between a natural history and a human history, a journey into an entangled past that explores the lifeways of a number of species and, at the same time, takes a wander through their long (and often convoluted) relationships with us. Often what we think we know about an animal is not the same as what the animal *is* or *does*. Instead, our perceptions are drawn from a cognitive tapestry made up of hearsay and memory, story and science. Some of the species which we are most familiar with have remarkable abilities hiding in plain sight. The way we see them, as it turns out, says rather a lot about ourselves.

How is an animal history different from any other history? Does it tell us anything new about the past? For a start, history has been overwhelmingly focused on humans (some would say dead white men) and has often ignored the many encounters our ancestors had with other species, every single day. Instead, when we choose to look at the past through a beastly lens – by which I mean a critter-centred optic rather than a 'horrible history' – animals creep into view everywhere. Beavers chew through the history of fashion, falcons dive through the history of medieval heraldry and donkeys loudly bray the history of the beach holiday. *Beastly Britain* celebrates the fact that the landscape and identity of these isles have been made by the four-, eight- and no-leggeds as well as the two-. From the Ice Age to the Machine Age, the Black Death to the Second World War, the transformative moments in British history come to life with an injection of beastly presence. Leave animals out of the picture and the past suddenly seems very empty.

How do you go about writing the history of other species? Historian Erica Fudge claims that the history of animals is actually the history of human attitudes towards other species. After all, we can't speak nightingale or natterjack. We can't read the diary of a badger or a basking shark. To tell their story is impossible on one level. However, the historical record is full of animal traces: in law, poetry, literature, legislation and the landscape itself. Animals scamper across the illuminated texts of medieval manuscripts (see Fig. 1), the sketches of

1. A wonderfully evocative image showing an animal (in this case a dog) literally bursting out of the margins of a medieval manuscript. The author of this Book of Hours (c.1485) found time for humour amid the moral instruction – overleaf was a view of the dog's bottom, back legs and tail.

soldier diarists and the journals of amateur naturalists. We can reconstruct a version of the animal past using these sources, as well as archaeology, GPS, scientific reports and DNA trails. Which is all history can ever do of any past. The material matter of the archive is itself alive with animality – much to the curator's dismay sometimes – tiny insects in old papers, moths in the spine of learned books, not to mention the calf-leather bindings and cattle-hoof glue. Animals may not have crafted legal treatises, run for political office or traded in commodities, but they did leave plenty of tracks across the landscape: ones which we can follow with a bit of imaginative detective work and an intellectual curiosity.

The path of animal history requires a move away from the familiar ground of anthropocentrism. However, take a glimpse into the creaturely past and it is not long before we find ourselves back in the human camp. Anthropogenic forces have irrevocably shaped the landscapes and the lives of Britain's fauna in powerful and decisive ways. This makes for uncomfortable reading at times (I don't mean just the flea chapter). However, the past is not just a troubled trail of exploitation, loss and endangerment. Neither is it a nostalgic den to hide away from the realities of our environmental predicament or to lament the passing of the good old days. Instead, history is served up here as a kind of desire path – a choice to walk through the historical world with our eyes open to other species, to understand how we got here and to champion the unique and fascinating relationship we have with other animals on these isles. Charismatic and amazing creatures are not only to be found in distant places. They are here. In our everyday spaces. And our collective memory. The story of these isles may be told by human voices, but it is fully brought to life by listening to the squawks, bellows and howls that make Beastly Britain what it is. Our history couldn't be told without them.

When I started thinking about this book, the cast of animals was epic: a veritable ark of critters jostling to represent the four nations. Narrowing the field was tough, but necessary for the book to ever get finished. In the end, the animals here got their place through a mixture of impulses – taxonomical, ecological, cultural, sentimental – based loosely on the slippery question of what is a British animal. As a starting point, it seemed important to represent different habitats, hence the sections divided into woodland wanderers, farmed and fancy, from stream to sea and what lies beneath. A group of islands in the North Atlantic covering close to 95,000 square miles, the ecology of the United Kingdom is diverse and supports an array of species. It encompasses four main terrestrial ecoregions (Celtic broadleaf forest, Caledon conifer forest, English lowlands beech forest and North Atlantic moist mixed forest) and in the span of several hundred miles – or a cross-country, longitudinal thirteen-hour train trip from Aberdeen to Penzance – moves from subarctic tundra through to a temperate oceanic climate. Prevailing south-westerly winds and the mild currents of the Gulf Stream keep temperatures fairly warm, despite the northerly latitude. The place is famous for its rain, its verdant gardens and its countryside.

From this grounding in place, I got to thinking about our most-loved species, the ones which we declare an affinity and particular affection for. Hedgehog and fox typically come top in polls of 'the nation's top animal', hence their placement. We 'know' them from our gardens, yet perhaps understand rather less about their biological and historical tracks. Equally, there are many unusual species – newt, stag beetle – who deserve a bit of flag waving on their behalf, as well as those – herring, flea – which have shaped the national story in profound and astonishing ways. As humans, we typically favour forms of life which are biologically or behaviourally similar (often charismatic mammals), as well as those with which we share a strong historical or cultural bond. It felt important to try to tip the scales in the favour of the creatures we struggle to connect with – the overlooked and the strange, the marginal and the misunderstood – as well as to acknowledge the aquatic and subterranean contours of Beastly Britain as well as more customary terrestrial haunts.

On hearing the word 'beast', you might think of wild creatures – this was what the term described when it first appeared in Middle English (c.1200) – and these kinds of animals certainly stand centre stage here. However, *Beastly Britain* also takes a step outside the theatre of the wild to consider other beastly traces, linguistically speaking. The first of these acknowledges the world of the domesticated – a space where animals are proximate to us but are not always noticed or appreciated. This brings farm livestock into the fold – animals of utility which were often described as 'beasties' in the familiar language of the eighteenth-century countryside – as well as fancy breeds kept for show or sport. Enter sheep and pigeons. Lastly, in a nod to deep time and to the importance of folklore in conjuring up our creaturely visions, the final section playfully turns from the flesh-and-blood animals of the British present to embrace a couple of fabulous (and fabular) types. In other words, beasts as monstrous apparitions. Some might baulk at stretching the boundaries of the animal guest list to include legendary and spectral beings in the form of phantom dogs and sea monsters. However, rubbing shoulders with such entities is not so much of a leap when you consider Britain's animal emblem is a lion: an exotic species that roams freely over heraldic flags and sports kits, but is scarcely to be found stalking British fields and woodlands (Longleat excepted). Sightings, somewhat bizarrely, of canine cryptids and phantasmagorical plesiosaurs are far more likely – these isles being particularly famed for both.

As a bestial corpus, *Beastly Britain* tries to share space with different kinds of species: the favourites and the forgotten, the feted and the feared. All told, the ten creatures who earned a chapter here offer striking historical profiles that more than substantiate their claim to be iconic British animals. All are vibrant carriers of identity and meaning, boast unique and interesting connections to people and place; and – across land, sea and air – transformed the historical landscape in powerful and enduring ways.

In 1963 the Bronx Zoo launched a new exhibit called 'the most dangerous animal in the world'. A sign painted in red above a sturdy cage signalled the hazardous nature of what lay inside. When people peered in, they saw themselves reflected in a mirror. Before too long, many other zoos (including Bristol, as I recall) installed similar features. *Homo sapiens* may well be the most dangerous animal in the world. It is also one of the most curious.

As a species, we have become more and more estranged from our environment. Doctors and psychologists talk about a 'nature deficit disorder' where lack of contact with the natural world stunts sensory and learning opportunities and impairs physical and mental well-being. In a 2016 survey for the Canal and Rivers Trust, 76% of British parents felt themselves to be less knowledgeable about the natural world than their forebears. Our society is taking more and more to the great indoors. How many of us could identify the boisterous tik-tik of a wren? The cannily camouflaged comma caterpillar, with its orangey-brown body and white 'saddle' designed to fool predators into thinking it is a bird poo? Instead, we choose to spend our time plugged into a virtual world, shop at supermarkets for food we probably don't stop to think about the provenance of and live in spaces where traces of green are distant or, in one way or another, uninviting. And yet, at the same time we are mesmerisingly, unequivocally captivated by nature. In *Biophilia* (1984), biologist Edward O. Wilson argued that humans, as a species, have an inbuilt compulsion to 'explore and affiliate with life'. Health psychologists and sports scientists measure this 'nature-connectedness' in terms of reduced cortisol and heightened endorphins, improved cognitive functions and energy levels. Have a rummage beneath the dead digital foliage which dominates our culture and you find a rich humus of nature fancy – garden rewilders, wandering artists and memoirists celebrating their beastly encounters on seashore and in wildwood, camera snappers capturing kingfishers in flight, volunteers counting bitterns and beetles – a vibrant, creative delight in the living world around us.

We need green space and wild things. Restoratively. Instinctively. But we get easily distracted. Enticed by the shiny and the new. We have short memories. And we definitely forget what is good for us. If we want a biodiverse Britain to survive and thrive in the twenty-first century, we need to find a way through this dense thicket of natural and cultural entanglement. To (re)connect with nature, understand our complicated past with other animals and learn some lessons for the future. From a feeling of biophilia, Wilson said, came a desire to know more and, from that, a greater valuation of other species and of ourselves. He was thinking principally in terms of biological knowledge, but *Beastly Britain* champions the role of history, culture and story in this process. Understanding the physical and imaginary entanglements we have had with other species helps to 'join the dots' on that all-important journey from care to concern and conservation. By throwing light on the amazing attributes of the creatures who roam these isles, we can take a fresh look at the place we all call home. If the animals in the following pages could talk (to us), their message might be this. Notice us in the past and share space with us now. What is good for our future is also good for yours.

A final word on my own beastly story. I did eventually get the dog of my dreams. The Terrier. Choreographer of the everyday and (with full disclosure) pretty much a co-author of *Beastly Britain*. Writing stopped when she demanded a walk (morning) or garden time (afternoon). She called me to heel when the prose became boring and scampers through these chapters as an ever-present personality. Her 'animal voice' mostly said: 'Stop writing about nature and let's get out in it. NOW.' Beyond the realms of human–canine relations (what Donna Haraway nicely described as a 'significant otherness'), as each chapter came to be written, its lead animal grabbed my attention in captivating and often unanticipated ways. Each stalked my imagination like Ted Hughes's *The Thought Fox* (1995), a creaturely presence that animated the dark recesses of my mind. Some have described the writing of animal history as a lonely path, but this was not my experience. All along, I've been very happy in the company of animals. Like a pig in the proverbial. I may never have turned into a beast (at least, not so far), but it was a delight to wander with them through Beastly Britain. I hope it is for you too.

Woodland Wanderers

CHAPTER I

Hedgehog

Is it because of their cute faces and spiny bodies? The nostalgic glint of Beatrix Potter's Mrs Tiggy-Winkle? Their nocturnal presence in our gardens? Whatever the reason, the hedgehog is consistently awarded the accolade of Britain's favourite animal. It has the most Google searches and Instagram tags of any native species, topped a Royal Horticultural Society/Wildlife Trusts 'Wild About Gardens' survey (2005) and won a whopping 35% of 5,000 votes cast in a Royal Society of Biology poll (2016) asking what the nation's favoured mammal from a shortlist of ten was. The fox came second, trailing behind with 15% of the vote, followed by the red squirrel. Another poll (2013), organised by the *BBC Wildlife Magazine*, saw the 'hog fell oaks and trample on bluebells to be crowned as Britain's national emblem. It won by an even greater margin – 42% of 9,000 votes cast – though critics accused the pollsters of 'institutional vertebratism' in not including butterflies, bees or amphibians on the shortlist. The stag beetles, newts and fleas of *Beastly Britain* might yet demand a rerun.

That takes nothing away from the hedgehog, which befits its placement at the top of the charts. It seems entirely appropriate that an animal to which many of us are accustomed has been (semi)democratically selected as our national, natural symbol. This little critter has a reputation for being industrious and friendly, both qualities 'we might like to associate with Britishness', says the *Guardian*. Poet Pam Ayres, of 'I wish I'd looked after my teeth' fame, remarks there is something 'sweet and homely' about its 'rounded prickly body'. Many will envy the fact hedgehogs sleep (mostly) through the winter, though some of their other traits are perhaps less likely to be ones we aspire to. Noisy copulators, known for their prickly exteriors, and able to eat 10% of their bodyweight in a single night: remind you of anyone?

Being the national animal is no guarantee of having a secure place to live, however. Hedgehogs have experienced a sharp decline in numbers over the last twenty-five years, due largely to habit loss and fragmentation, a food desert of overly tidy and tightly enclosed gardens, a gauntlet of busy roads and the negligent use of pesticides. Numbers are 50% down in rural areas and 30% in towns since 2000. This status as vulnerable on the UK Species Red List means they now, sadly, have another identity the British are drawn to championing: that of the underdog.

Spiny, Sleepy Spheres: The Anatomy of a 'Hog

Britain's native 'hog, labelled by Linnaeus in 1758 as *Erinaceus europaeus*, the European hedgehog, also known as the West European hedgehog, is one of seventeen species worldwide, a family that contains spineless varieties from the Far East and spiny ones from Africa, the Middle East, Central Asia, the Mongolian steppe and China. Originally classified with the *Insectivora* – typically long-snouted, often nocturnal, sharp-toothed insect-scoffers – hedgehogs were rehomed in the late twentieth century (along with shrews and moles) into a new category of *Eulipotyphla*: part of a taxonomical tidy-up of a 'catch-all' category that naturalists had created for a bunch of creatures they didn't quite know what to do with.

Hedgehogs, in fact, are one of the oldest genera of mammals. One of their earliest ancestors, the recently unearthed *Spinolestes xenarthrosus*, was a 2-foot-long shrew-like animal with a mohawk of prickly bristles down its back which lived 125 million years ago. Around 70 million years ago, hedgehogs split from shrews, solenodons and moles (their closest modern relatives) and fossilised remains have been found at various sites across Asia, Africa and Europe. One of the most striking of these was *Deinogalerix*, a formidable, supersized beast that stomped across the Mediterranean in the late Miocene period. Weighing in at 9 kilograms, the so-named 'terrible shrew' was about the size of a small dog (roughly the same weight as the Terrier when she spent a summer gorging on pears).

Hedgehogs of the size and shape we know and love have been around for the last 15 million years. They scurried beneath sabre-toothed tigers, witnessed the demise of the woolly mammoths and saw the first humans arrive in Europe. Archaeological evidence places them in the UK at least 10,000 years ago, where they thrived courtesy of a warming climate and new opportunities for species colonisation as the ice sheets receded. 'Hogs crossed into southern England from the continent and spread north and west across the lowlands. Abetted by Neolithic farmers transforming forests into mixed grasslands and early medieval open field systems, these denizens of rural 'edge' environments became familiar sights in woodland margins and hedgerows.

The average hedgehog is somewhere between 18 and 28 centimetres long and weighs 0.8–1.2 kilograms. Males are generally larger and all animals put on an extra 20–30% of body mass before hibernation. They are predominantly brown in colour, with dark snouts and buff-coloured underbellies. At first glance, hedgehogs have stubby legs but, when they pick up their bodies to run, this reveals a short, bald tail and four well-proportioned pins that are capable of a remarkable turn of speed – up to 4 metres a minute and 9 kilometres an hour. Take a nocturnal stroll through a suburban estate in the balmy nights of late spring and you might well see this park-run phenomenon in action as males go in search of paramours. Mating season is definitely the best time to see (and hear) 'hogs, a part of the year when these usually shy and retiring animals spend their evenings scrapping and shuffling with rival males, butting bodies and biting legs, before trying to win over females with circular shimmies and urgent snorts in a vocal and sometimes violent mating performance. The collective noun for a group of hedgehogs is an 'array'.

A species that has changed little since the time of the dinosaurs, hedgehog anatomy remains beautifully simple. Zoologist Pat Morris includes in these 'basic' mammalian attributes blunt-clawed fingers and toes, flat feet, small collarbones, undescended scrotums in the males, senses attuned to smell over sight and small brains. What sets them apart is their trademark prickles, wonderfully described by John Maplet in *A Greene Forest* (1567) as a 'sharp and quickthorned garment on his backe'. Despite their antediluvian aesthetic, this animal's spines are actually remarkably sophisticated in design: made of super-strong keratin and mostly hollow, with cross-ridges that allow them to flex easily. When they are born, hedgehogs begin to grow white spines under the skin, which emerge in a few hours and are replaced by brown ones after a few days. As they grow, they sprout more to suit, and moult them almost constantly. Juveniles have about 3,000 and an adult 5,000. Seniors might boast up to 7,000. On a full-grown animal, they are typically brown with a white or cream band, which gives a

2. A nineteenth-century coloured etching showing the hedgehog in prostrate and balled forms.

mottled or brindled look to the body, and are bent where they enter the skin. Echidnas and porcupines – species that hedgehogs are most likened to – sport a similarly spiky armour, but these egg-laying mammals and rodents (respectively) developed their defensive attributes along a separate evolutionary path.

The special move the hedgehog plays which makes their spiny defences all the more effective is to roll into a ball – something which is particularly handy given the fact their underside and head is not protected by prickles but covered in buff-coloured hair. Other than armadillos and pangolins, 'hogs are the only species to do this and the way they do it is remarkable. Many have wondered at this special ability, described by M. Peter Viret in *The School of Beastes* (1585) as 'rowleth him selfe . . . within his prickles, as the Chestnut is enclosed within his hull . . . so that he cannot be any whit hurted'. The special move starts above the eyes, where the animal crinkles its brow to activate two special muscles that draw the spines securely over the face. A set of similar muscles does the same with its bottom. In between, the *panniculus carnosus* – a sheet of muscle which encircles the torso – activates the spines across the back and the *orbicularis* muscle draws together like a purse-string to enclose the animal in a prickly protective barrier. A baggy skin and flexible spine assist with the overall effect.

The manoeuvre doesn't take much energy, hence the animal can stay in a balled-up state for a long time. The spines deter would-be attackers from biting the 'hog and also act as shock absorbers, the latter particularly useful when canny foxes try discombobulation tactics by rolling them around the floor or tossing them down banks. As Greek philosopher and poet Archilochus put it (later popularised by essayist Isaiah Berlin): 'the fox knows many things, the hedgehog knows one important thing' – namely to roll up in a ball when under attack. Writing in *The Historie of Four-footed Beasts* (1607), Edward Topsell described this 'one great thing' as an 'admirable instinct of nature'. Badgers – with the advantage of sharp claws able to prize open a 'hog ball – and owls – enabled by a silent and stealthy night dive – are harder to fend off.

Hedgehogs do most of their business at night and, when encountered, tend to adopt the ball response and sit tight – which is why, even today, not a great deal is known about their life habits. Largely solitary animals, they are omnivorous, munching on beetles, caterpillars, worms, earwigs and millipedes. They will feast on snails and slugs, though this is not always their preference. Snails are a bit tough to consume due to their hard shells and (along with slugs) run the risk of parasitic or lung worm infection. 'Hogs have also been known to eat young voles, mice and chicks, as well as frogs and bird's eggs. They spend a lot of time each night seeking forage and tend to follow a two-sitting pattern, roving in the hours after twilight, digesting and resting for a few hours, and then resuming the search once more. Come sunrise, they retreat to summer nests, meticulously constructed retreats of grass and leaves which are typically located in hedges, tree stumps, bramble bushes and shrub cover. 'Hogs don't just have one, instead they construct a number of resting places, nest-surfing night by night across several sites. As a species they aren't especially territorial, though they do range over surprisingly large areas (between 10 and 50 hectares) and often cover 1 or 2 miles on their nightly foraging trails.

Aside from the odd food squabble, hedgehogs only really interact for the purposes of mating. The rut takes place in May and June, when males extend their nightly activities from food hunting to courtship. Maurice Burton, one of the first observers to see the nuptials in action (1965), described the huffing noises and circular movements of the male as having a mesmerising quality (at least to a female hedgehog). The species is polygamous/polygynous, making the whole experience something of a lottery. Biologist Amy Haigh recorded thirty-nine courtship performances between sixteen animals, lasting from an hour to 2 hours 20 minutes (none of these ended in a successful mating, with the male sloping off to look for food). It is not uncommon for one female to have hoglets by different boars. When the female does decide the time is right, she presses her body to the ground and flattens her spines to allow the male to mount from behind (earlier natural histories surmised a belly-to-belly position, based purely on the idea of prickly discomfort). After a thirty-day gestation, the young emerge – usually four or five – which are born in a special nursery nest that is more robust than the day-to-day summer ones. The hoglets are born blind and hairless. At two or three weeks they have fur and the beginnings of milk teeth and, at a month old, can roll into a ball.

The female stays in the nest until the litters are weaned (six weeks) and they head out on their own at two months old.

Another distinctive feature of the hedgehog is hibernation, an aspect of its life habits which we have been eternally intrigued (and some would say envious) about. The dormouse and bat are the only other British mammals which do this. Come late autumn, our native 'hogs, fattened with a summer surfeit of arthropods, take to the wonderfully named *hibernaculum*. This winter nest is 30–60 centimetres in diameter, strategically located to make the most of sheltering structures in the form of log piles, brambles, burrows or sheds, and is carefully constructed using leaves, sticks and grass to create a safe, dry home for overwintering. A new one is made every autumn. The timetable for adopting residency is still relatively mysterious, but experts suspect it has something to do with sex, size, age and hormonal and temperature changes. Hedgehogs don't *need* to hibernate to recharge their bodily systems. They do so primarily as a mechanism to avoid the full force of the cold (and depleted food reserves), hence the different lengths of hibernation in different habitats. In New Zealand's temperate North Island – where 'hogs were introduced by acclimatisation societies in the 1870s to eat creepy-crawlies and make settlers feel more at home – some don't hibernate at all. Slight fluctuations in the hibernation timetable are found between populations in south-western England and northern Scotland.

Typically, the slumber clock activates when the mercury drops in autumn (the optimum temperature to snuggle into hibernation is 4°C), which in the UK is late October or early November. Males enter first, having had the benefit of fattening themselves up without childcare responsibilities. Females are usually a week later. Once inside, the hedgehog spins round and round, agitating the loose material to create a layered leafy insulation, a woody-mass duvet to protect it from freezing temperatures. The heating controls of the *hibernaculum* have to be finely tuned – warm enough to keep out the cold but not too hot to cause the animal to wake up. It then hunkers down to lie half curled up on its side and enters a period of suspended animation where the body temperature dips from the mid-30s to 10°C and the heart rate from 280 to 5 beats a minute. A hedgehog often holds its breath for an hour in this state, breaking the pause with a series of rapid panting breaths to propel oxygen through its system.

In this metabolic hiatus, the animal draws mainly on reserves of white fat (slow-burn snoozing fuel) as well as brown fat (ignition fuel to kickstart it into awakeness), which together amount to 25% of the animal's body weight. Most animals actually get up several times during the hibernation cycle and stay awake for a few hours, possibly (Morris suggests) because of a need to pee or to refresh the circulatory system. When springtime temperatures rise above 10°C, usually late April in the UK, the hibernation alarm goes off, hedgehogs slowly wake up, shiver to warm themselves and stumble around to get their bearings. Males often go out into the world first.

Shining a Garden Torch on 'Hogly Supernatures

Hedgehogs manage the unique combination of being familiar and somehow extraordinary. They are a neighbourly garden mammal, and yet, at the same time, a creature of the night that looks quite unlike any other species. In common with newts or stag beetles (more on them later) they carry with them a sense of the otherworldly and have long enticed us with their difference. Proximate peculiars. Everyday agents of the fantastical. Perhaps this helps explain how they have been decorated with many weird and wonderful attributes. This section looks at a few of these – the ability to milk cows, scrump fruit on their spines, forecast the weather and safely chew on toxic toads – all of which appeared as natural truths in the countryside almanac.

The first 'hogly supernature to blur the boundaries of biology and mythology involved their reputation for milking cattle. According to local lore, these animals were often found hanging around cows, keenly exploring how to get their next dairy fix. Writing 'Notes on the Hedgehog' for the *Zoologist* magazine in 1858, Major John Spicer ruminated on the industriousness of the species (and the chirping habit of young hoglets) before relating a friend's anecdote that 'hogs were able to mimic the noise of a calf expressly to invite the herd to approach them. 'I confess', he said, to 'not see the great improbability of it.' For one thing, Spicer noted, 'the hedgehog has the power of stretching its neck a long way out from its body'. Meanwhile, from a bovine perspective, he pondered, might it be that a cow could 'bear a little punishment from its prickles for the pleasure of having her milk drawn from her?'

This manoeuvre seems biologically improbable given the average size of even the largest hedgehog in relation to the distance between the ground and a cow's udders. Rural chroniclers, however, had an answer to the naysayers: the diminutive lacto-hunters simply waited until cattle lay down in the grass. T. Buxton from Leytonstone, Essex, reported in November 1853 how his stable boy went out into the field one evening after hearing a banging noise and spied two 'hogs suckling from a prostrate cow. When she got up, they tightened their grip and were only dislodged from her teats after much poking with a stick. Buxton says he watched his employee's lantern flailing across the field as he prised the animals free. In another case, printed in the *Zoologist* of July 1821, a gentleman from Thickleby, Yorkshire, keenly reported an 'unsuspicious' anecdote from years gone by in which a workman heading out at dawn found a hedgehog attached to the udder of a sleeping cow. Ever the empiricist, the author planned to test the hypothesis by presenting a stick crafted to resemble a cow's teat to the mouth of the next 'hog he came across.

In a May 1921 editorial, *Nature* deemed the 'hog milking phenomenon as a 'manifest impossibility'. According to the Board of Agriculture, it was nothing more than the idle fancy of irresponsible antiquarians and naturalists who reported the orations of country folk as facts and never stopped to think about the evidence. That said, hedgehogs do have a sweet tooth and a particular liking for dairy products. Turning to bovine physiology, it is also the case that cows sometimes secrete milk from their teats when they get up or lie down. However, as WRD noted in the journal *Folklore* (1934), the fact that hedgepigs were seen around cattle dung was scarcely surprising given their customary diet of invertebrates. This vignette of the pastoral fantastic was whimsically appealing, but highly implausible. As WRD put it, 'more picturesque than trustworthy'.

Aside from milk stealing, these animals were also said to indulge in another capricious foraging activity: that of using their spiny armour to spear a range of culinary delights, including apples, berries and grapes. Hedgehogs were said to do this in a novel way: rolling on the ground to impale fallen fruits before shuffling off to their nests in the fashion of *Eulipotyphlan* kebabs. John Clare's poem 'The Hedgehog' (c.1841) painted an endearing image of the scrump in action: an animal emerging from a hedgerow to 'fill his prickles full of crabs', before perambulating homeward with a whistling tune.

Attendees of 1970s children's parties might recall an inspired salute to this countryside practice in which an orange (or in the Jones's household, a potato, as it could be easily reused) was covered with silver foil, spiked with cocktail-stick delights of cheese and pineapple and placed on the table for all to fight over. This modish party piece sits, pride of place, on a table spread in the Ladybird book *Learn About: Cooking* (1977), where young eyes and fingers are drawn to the 'hogly spikes (see Fig. 3). An altogether more distinguished illustration of the prickly practice can be found in the Rochester Bestiary (c.1230), a medieval manuscript which famously pictured

3. A feast of a party, 1970s style, as shown in the Ladybird book *Learn About: Cooking* (1977). The cheese-and-pineapple hedgehogs are clearly the culinary stars of the show.

'hogs joyously rolling on their backs to spear fruity spoils (see Fig. 4). A deliciously irreverent comparison, there is a certain symmetry between these two images. Compared to the frivolous airs of the kids' party (where the 'hog was a clear hit), however, the medieval manuscript traded in a more serious message. Observe, it noted, those heretical hedgehogs processing into the vineyard, climbing up the stems to shake free the juiciest of grapes, shimmying back down to the ground for a fruitful roll and returning triumphantly to their burrows. Beware, likewise, it urged, the wily ways the Devil might employ to seize the spiritual fruits of even the most devout.

By the time of the Rochester Bestiary, this particular habit was well known. Pliny the Elder was the first to mention the phenomenon in his *Natural History* (AD 77–79), eagerly copied in medieval bestiaries in the centuries after. Edward Topsell's *Historie of Four-footed Beasts* offered the following description: 'His meat is apples, wormes, or grapes; when he findeth apples or grapes on the earth, hee rowleth himselfe upon them, until he haue filled all his prickles, and then carrieth them home to his den . . . so forth hee goeth, making a noyse like a cart wheale.' Once back home, the young ones greeted their parent with great enthusiasm – Topsell noted they 'pull of his load where withall he is loaded, eating thereof what they please' – rather like the kids at the party table.

Given its 2,000-year provenance, why have so few of us seen this amazing feat? Simple, said Miller Christy, who reported on the matter for the Manchester Literary and Philosophical Society newsletter in 1918 – hedgehogs only ever performed their stealthy sweep of local orchards at night. The other reason is that hedgehogs do *not* eat fruit, favouring instead a diet of beetles, worms and the like. The manoeuvre would also require them to keep their spines erect (or else the fruit would fall off) – something impossible for their muscular system to do in an uncurled state. *Nature*

4. A delightful image from the medieval Rochester Bestiary (c.1230), a richly illustrated manuscript containing depictions of all manner of beasts, with accompanying Christian lessons. Here, heretical hedgehogs are shown scrumping fallen fruit from the Lord's orchard, before hot-footing it back to their nests to feed their young. The message: beware the canny ploys the Devil might use to steal the spiritual fruits of even the most pious.

accepted 'there must have been ... some substratum of actual observed fact, renewed from time to time, to keep any legend of the kind alive', but saw this as the product of an overactive countryside imagination perpetuated by 'persons of little education'.

Next on the list of 'hogly supernatures was an even more spectacular ability: one where hedgehogs predicted the weather. Topsell writes that: 'when they hide themselves in their den, they have a natural understanding of the turning of the wind ... The wild ones have two holes in their cave, the one North, the other South, observing to stop the mouth against the wind.' Viret's *School of Beastes* described how the animals could open and close each door, depending on the direction of prevailing gusts. Others, too, commented on the species's forecasting savvy. Aristotle described the simple 'hog as a weather prophet of 'great renowne' and Plutarch spoke of a man from Constantinople who kept one as a pet for the purposes of foretelling climatic conditions. Lawrence Price in the *Shepherds Prognostication* (1652) described them as 'witty and wise' in matters of meteorology, while *Poor Robin's Almanak* (1733) celebrated their 'secret art' which was better at predicting the weather than a good many humans.

This is clearly a stretch of astronomical credulity, though we are talking about an animal whose internal body clock is set to wake up when the mercury gets to a certain level. Also, in the rural calendar, it made sense to think about the planting cycle when the annual exodus from the *hibernaculum* took place. The first two days of February – the Celtic festival of Imbolc – was traditionally seen as the start of spring. At the centre of the celebration was the fertility goddess (and later Christian saint) Brigid, who represented seasonal rebirth and was honoured in fire rituals, cleansings of the home (a spring clean) and blessings of the sheep herds and fisheries. On Brigid's Day, she was said to travel round the land to check all was as it should be. Villagers left a meal of bread and milk out for her to sup on and looked out for various animal signs to indicate the shape of the coming season.

Snakes, badgers and cats all featured as meteorological guides but, particularly, this was an occasion to see what hedgehogs were doing. If they emerged from their winter nests, it was a portent of milder conditions, otherwise inclement weather was likely to continue. European settlers to North America transplanted the tradition, and recruited the groundhog as stand-in weather prophet. Today, on Gobbler's Knob, Pennsylvania, an eager crowd still gathers every February to see Punxsutawney Phil, first seen in 1886 and reputedly sustained by a special elixir, emerge from his subterranean lair. If he casts a shadow, winter remains in force. If he doesn't, spring has officially sprung.

Finally, the last wildly sensational hedgehog behaviour: munching on toxic toads. Like the milking, spearing and forecasting, this is also not true. But it does combine various behavioural quirks. Hedgehogs *are* resistant to the toxins produced by the skin of these amphibians (and also to snake venom). They also have a habit of biting random objects – stray tufts of fox fur, carpet, cigarettes, leather, anything with a strong and pungent flavour. The purpose of this is unclear, but it perhaps serves as a masticatory trigger for a peculiar behaviour known as self-anointing, which involves the hedgehog flicking saliva from the underside of the tongue onto its back and sides. Typically practised by juveniles and males, the activity takes from a few minutes to an hour, during which the animal writhes about in a series of contortions to spread the frothy substance across its spines, splaying its legs out and twisting its neck with frenzied determination.

'Hogs are not the only creatures to self-anoint. Capuchin monkeys do it with millipede secretions to protect themselves against mosquito bites (captive animals are known to use limes or onions for similar functions) and red deer cover themselves in urine from their wallows as a lure for females. In the hedgehog's case, the function is not fully understood.

Some speculate that self-anointing might serve as a form of parasite repellent. These animals are renowned as carriers of fleas (*Archaeopsylla erinaceid*, a species with long legs and thin bodies specially adapted to life between the spines and which won't jump onto humans, cats or dogs as permanent hosts). A healthy individual supports around 100 and an ailing animal probably several times that. Others ponder whether it might be used to deter predators. The idea of spiking your spines with something foul-tasting or even poisonous seems like a handy thing to do when faced with a badger attack. Neither of these theories really stands up to scrutiny, though.

The most plausible theories suggest self-anointing might relate to sexual competition, with young animals deploying it as a sort of olfactory camouflage to render themselves invisible to larger, older males. Alternatively, it may operate as a form of scent-marking or communication. As Morris saw it, this scently adornment could say many things: 'I'm here, come and say hello', 'Do I know you?' or 'Stay right away'. Whatever is going on, this is a habit 15 million years in the making and must have had a useful function at some point in the hedgehog's evolutionary past. Suffice to say, it has confounded many a homeowner who has spied their garden favourite sitting in a frothy daze next to the pond.

Of Urchins and Vermin:
The Prickly Past of Hedgehogs and People

Derived from the Middle English *heyghoge*, 'hedgehog' first appeared in popular usage around 1450. The name was self-explanatory: a mash-up of the animal's favourite habitat combined with its pig-like attributes. Hedgehogs have snouts, the young look very similar to wild boar and their meat was said to taste rather like pork. Topsell put it bluntly: 'when the skin is off, it is in all parts like a Hog.' The *heyg* part of the name also had an etymological connection to the Middle German word *hage*, which translates as thorn.

Before the fifteenth century, a different phrase was often used to describe this creature – urchin. A corruption of the Old Northern French *herichon* (hedgehog), it found its way into Scottish and Northern English dialect in a local word for the creature, *hurchin* or *hurcheon*, and also related to a popularly held belief that this creature of the British countryside was related to the sea urchin.

Beyond that, a wealth of regional names communicated the sense of a rich and lively interaction between people and 'hogs over a long span of time. They could be *furze-man-pigs* in Gloucestershire (shortened to *vuz-pigs* across the west of England), *pochins* in Somerset, *pricky back ochuns* in Yorkshire, *prickle back urchins* in Sussex, *zarts* in Cornwall, *hootchi-withci* in Cumbria. In Gaelic, their linguistic label carried a negative tone – in Irish they were *grainneog*, meaning little ugly one, in Scottish *craineag* or *graineag*, bristly and short-tempered. In Welsh, the animal was known as the *draenog*, meaning prickle or thorn, while tight-fisted individuals were *cadw draenog yn boced un* (said to keep a hedgehog in their pocket).

The hedgehog has snuffled its way into British cultural life for hundreds if not thousands of years. In classical times, hedgehogs were revered as representatives of Artemis, the Greek goddess of hunting. Aesop mentioned them in his tale of a fox stuck in a river who turned down a kindly 'hog's offer to eat the insects biting him for fear more would appear. The moral of the story: put up with discomfort, because remedying it could bring worse fortune. At Stonehenge, excavations of a Bronze Age burial site revealed the remains of a young child who had been interred with a small chalk hedgehog, perhaps a beloved toy or a companion for the world beyond. In Romany legend, the demonic 'hog or the *Xagrin* was somewhat less affable. A huge yellow creature, half a yard long, it was known to hurt cattle and wrangle horses at night, urinating on their backs and giving them sores.

In literature, an otherworldly tint, spiny countenance, ability to roll into a ball and shuffling habit seemed to be common reasons for adding a 'hog to the story. Shakespeare hurled one – linguistically speaking – from Anne to the King in *Richard III* as a term of derision; in *A Midsummer Night's Dream* grouped the animal with a whole bunch of assumed-to-be-nasty critters: snakes, newts, blindworms; and invoked them in *Macbeth* as part of the witches' incantations. Frequent associations with magic and mysticism reflected the popular belief that witches could turn into and talk to hedgehogs and that fairy folk regularly used them as an albeit prickly form of transit (see Fig. 5). 'Hearts delight', an Easter sermon from sixteenth-century Cambridge divinity don Thomas Playfere, deployed the animal in a morality tale about the dangers of worldly temptations, 'likened to a hedgehogge' because they seemed unassuming at first but were 'full of bristles or prickles' and thus needed to be resisted. Earthly pleasures, he said, needed to be dealt with 'as a man would handle a hedgehogge': grab it by the hind leg and toss it to one side.

The Brothers Grimm used the humble 'hog as a rather more endearing figure in a story which substituted one for Aesop's tortoise in a race with a hare (1857). British versions of the tale saw the spiny wanderer successfully face off against the Devil. In Rudyard Kipling's *Just So* story, 'The Beginning of the Armadillos' (1900), one with the wonderful name of Stickly-Prickly lived in the Amazon with Slow-Solid Tortoise and came up with the idea of combining their biological attributes to fend off the painted jaguar. Lewis Carroll's *Alice's Adventures in Wonderland* (1865) favoured a more surreal, playful image, using the animals' curling-up habit to employ them as croquet balls in the game played by the Queen of Hearts. With flamingos twisting their necks round and hedgehogs un-balling to shuffle off the field of play, Alice found it 'a very difficult game indeed'.

In terms of uses, the hedgehog has proved surprisingly versatile. Its prickles were used in medieval times to create rough

5. A fantastical nineteenth-century watercolour by Charles Altamont Doyle (father of Arthur Conan Doyle), which paid heed to the idea of hedgehogs as magical animals that consorted with fairies and witches. In this image the Fairy King rides a spiny steed, surely quite an uncomfortable experience.

brushes and Romans repurposed their spine-adorned skins as combs for the processing of raw wool. They also provided a whole host of medicinal benefits. The Romans applied their oil as a cure for earache, while Topsell detailed a great many medical applications. Mixed with laurel, pepper, gum resin and water, dried ribs could alleviate colic (men had to use the bones of males and women female), while burned ashes could be used to reduce swelling and heal boils. Powder from the skin and head might be mixed with honey (and sometimes bear's grease) to cure hair loss (as could faeces, if mixed with vinegar, sandarac and pitch) or added to wine to reduce fluid retention or fever and expel kidney stones. Hedgehog flesh was said to be good for leprosy, cramp, sickness and digestive complaints (stale flesh even took away madness). Gargling with hedgehog fat, honey and warm water cured a sore throat, and a liquid made from the left eye fried in oil aided sleep if dropped into the ear canal (the right eye improved vision at night). The gall bladder – when mixed with the milk of a dog and brain of a bat – alleviated kidney complaints. The wonderfully titled *Panzooryktologia. Sive Panzoologicomineralogia. Or A compleat history of animals and minerals* (1661) by Robert Lovell recommended them for ague, belly pain, ruptures, colic, colds, convulsions, leprosy, ringworm, ulcers, snake bites and warts, while John Keogh's *Zoologia Medicinalis* (1739) noted their value in treating skin rashes, ulcers, herpes and colic.

Aside from this function as spiny medicine cabinets, hedgehogs also found themselves on the menu. They were eaten by the Romans and featured on the medieval table. *Le Ménagier de Paris* (1393), a famous French recipe book, contained a recipe for cooking the animal, which it recommended should have its throat cut before being gutted and trussed like a pullet, and pressed in a towel to dry it off. It could then be roasted with carmeline sauce (made from bread and wine) or put into a pastry with wild duck sauce (a spicy-sour mixture which contained no actual duck). Would-be chefs struggling to get their main courses to unroll from a ball might, the cookery book suggested, toss the animals into hot water. Topsell recorded it as a culinary fare in the early fifteenth century, describing how the animal might be skinned, blanched in wine and vinegar before being roasted. If the head was not cut off with one cleave, he noted, the meat did not taste good.

Hedgehog largely disappeared from the menu thereafter, though still remained a recourse for poor, rural folk, itinerants and Romany communities, which traditionally ate the animal they called *hociwici* by covering it with clay and baking it in a fire. When the baked case was removed, the animal's spines peeled off with it, leaving roasted meat which was wrapped in sorrel leaves or added to a stew with country herbs. Hedgehog was said to taste sweet, and similar to pork, though John Clare was less complementary of the 'black and bitter and unsavoury meat'. *Romano Lavo-Lil: Word-Book of The Romany; Or, English Gypsy Language* (1874) by George Borrow talked of children bringing home the animals for their mothers to cook, while *Gipsy Life* (1880) described an elderly Romany woman who lived near Notting Hill and tempted the author with her signature recipe, promising it would be 'nicer than the finest rabbit or pheasant I had ever tasted'.

That is not to say that hedgehogs were particularly appreciated as faunal British residents. In fact, they were the subject of extraordinary levels of persecution in early modern times. Spiny armour and the ability to roll into a ball may have offered good protection from owls and foxes, but these creatures were pretty easy to find and kill when it came to human hunters. As Roger Lovegrove writes in *Silent Fields* (2007), 'the slaughter was of almost unimagined proportions'. In Bunbury, Cheshire, parish records from the late 1600s indicate that 8,585 hedgehogs were despatched over a 35-year period. Sherbourne, Dorset, another hotbed of killing, counted 3,344 animals in the period between 1662 and 1799. Why? The simple answer is that these unassuming beasts were regarded as vermin – berated, especially, for stealing poultry eggs and cow's milk. As such, the whimsical tales of 'hogly supernatures served an ominous social function, one in which negative images of animals were used to sanction their killing. Founded on what nineteenth-century naturalist James Knapp called an 'ancient prejudice', the hedgehog became a countryside criminal courtesy of its fabular (and erroneous) reputation as dairy junkie. For John Clare, there was a direct line of ascent between the milking myth and the hunting of these animals with 'savage force'.

The abuse was both casual and targeted. Many anecdotes that peddled the cow-suckling story saw their human protagonists kick hedgehogs across fields following their discovery. Legislation, meanwhile, mandated local parishes to hunt them down with impunity. Critical here were a series of Vermin Acts, passed 'for the preservation of grayne' – legislated by Henry VIII (1532) and extended by Elizabeth I (1566) – which required that every citizen should kill as many so-called noxious animals as possible. The act was prompted by a confluence of ecological and social challenges, a run of severe winters (the so-called Little Ice Age), epidemics and failed harvests, set against a rapidly growing population which needed feeding. All parishes had to raise funds for the bounty from local landowners and tenants to administer the scheme, or face stiff penalties from the Crown.

The hit-list included some 30 species, such as kite, rook, hawk, sparrow, kingfisher, raven, fox, badger and hedgehog, the latter commanding a bounty payment of 2d per animal (half a day's work for a rural labourer), the same as an otter and twice as much as a polecat, stoat or weasel. Tracking the impact of the law is complicated by patchy records and regional variations – Lovegrove found the South-West, Kent and the Midlands to be particularly high kill-zones – though the law seemed to be prosecuted by churchwardens and taken up by many parishioners as a financial and community good. Hedgehogs, which were among the easiest critters to catch on the list, suffered significant losses. The act was finally repealed in 1863, but not before an estimated 2 million bounty payments were paid out in exchange for dead hedgehogs. This didn't mean an easy ride for the species, however. The Enclosure Acts (1750–1850) that appropriated common lands into private estates, and the rise of game bird shooting as a vocation of the gentry, saw hedgehog persecution continue under the (dubious) auspices of egg protection well into the twentieth century. As Pat Morris notes, records from the royal estate of Sandringham listed the killing of 5,904 'hogs between 1938 and 1950.

The Travails of the Modern Hedgehog: A Tale of Washerwomen and Motorways

Writing in the mid-1800s, poet John Clare bemoaned the fact that nobody cared about the hedgehog. The fortunes of this small mammal, however, changed radically during the course of the twentieth century. From verminous dairy fiend, it emerged from the *hibernaculum* of history to become the nation's favourite animal. What happened?

A certain fictional washerwoman had no small part to play in rescuing the animal's reputation. *The Tale of Mrs Tiggy-Winkle* (1905), a children's book written and illustrated by Beatrix Potter, featured a bustling, busy hedgehog as its titular character. This book, in common with others in the Peter Rabbit series, featured creatures of the British countryside in anthropomorphic guise, amiable, everyday 'persons' who presented a romantic, nostalgic lens on rural life. In this story, a wandering child Lucie seeking lost handkerchiefs and a pinafore wandered up the hill to find a secret doorway behind a rock, behind which lay a home in miniature, inhabited by a singing washerwoman busily starching away. There, alongside a pile of beautifully laundered garments (including Peter Rabbit's fine sky-blue jacket) were her own missing hankies and apron. The two took tea and headed off down the hill, Lucie to home and the laundress to deliver her clothes. However, when the girl looked back to say thanks, she saw not a bonneted washerwoman but a prickly hedgehog.

Combining a gentle instructional along the lines of Aesop's fables with a rosy conjuring of a British arcadia, Potter mixed plain speech and imaginative charm, simple prose and pastel-precise illustrations to bring her characters to life. Her protagonists were entertaining because they were both in and out of place, little people in fur and feathers, and yet their ways were familiar and their animal natures still visible under the rustic clothing. In the case of *Tiggy-Winkle*, the story was infused with a sense of 'proper' female household duties (and designed to apprise young girls) and thus struck as much more indoors than some of Potter's other titles. It also lacked the existential threats or 'nature red in tooth and claw' dangers of some of the other stories. Here there was no villainous Mr McGregor, duplicitous Mr Tod or rats with designs for a Tom Kitten banquet (though as I child I remember finding the illustrated face of Mrs T in a bonnet quite disturbing). The trick in this yarn's tail was a puzzle: was this a dream or was it real? The narrator of the tale insisted on the latter, being a good friend of Tiggy-Winkle and having seen the door by the rock on Catbells hill.

A close observer of nature and someone keen in her writing to communicate 'reality and wonder akin, the fact and strangeness like each other,' Potter took inspiration from her home in the Lake District (where her critterly characters were placed) and from personal experience. In the case of Tiggy-Winkle, that came from recollections of a diminutive Scottish laundrywoman she encountered as a young woman on holiday in Perthshire, a child Lucie, who (as in the book) was inclined to lose things, and her own pet 'hog (named Mrs T), which she adored as if a 'fat rather stupid little dog'. The initial print run was 20,000 copies, followed by another 18,000 soon after. Tiggy the elderly pet sadly didn't survive long enough to see the runaway success of her namesake in print. Potter euthanised her in spring 1906 as her health deteriorated – the product, she said, of 'an unnatural diet and indoor life'. Generations of children, however, read and adored the simple tale (my grandfather gave me *The Tale of Benjamin Bunny* as my first ever book).

Underneath its quirky countryside costuming, Potter's book spoke to many things – class lines, gender politics, social norms – and offered life lessons on surviving (and thriving) under adversity, thrift, humility, industriousness, fair play and pretension. It also suggested an important role for storytelling in creating positive imprints of Britain's beasts. Ecologist, writer and self-confessed 'hedgehog man' Hugh Warwick attributed a monumental role to Potter's washerwoman in changing popular attitudes towards her species. Prior to the book's publication, he noted, 'pretty well every reference' in literature involved 'hogs being 'discarded, dismissed'. Thereafter, Warwick pointed out, 'everybody loves the hedgehog'.

This twentieth-century explosion in literary 'hogs as folksy and precious residents of the British countryside was particularly evident in the genre of children's fiction. Following in Potter's footsteps, interwar authors wrote them into romantic romps across rural Britain. Alison Uttley's *The Story of Fuzzypeg the Hedgehog* (1932) told of a year-and-a-half-old hoglet and the occasion of his birthday. As mother pottered around the domestic realm, father (a milkman) did his rounds to encounter various neighbours offering culinary gifts for the young 'un, all with an egg theme – boiled from rabbit, poached from rat, scrambled from mole. After adventures of adder-wrangling and hill-rolling, the yarn culminated in a stand-off with a dog, a benevolent human placing Fuzzy under a flowerpot for safe-keeping, a daring rescue led by owl and mole and a hearty ending meal of baked acorns and blackberry pie. Enid Blyton's *Hedgerow Tales* series (1935) also drew on 'hogly folk tales of egg-stealing to present a 'factitious' take that emphasised predatory threats from badger and fox to hedgely families of various shapes and sizes.

An avalanche of titles from the 1960s onwards, meanwhile, conjured with 'hogs that were untidy and hungry, helpful and shy, adventurous and naive. 'Mr Hedgehog's Christmas Present' in *Richard Scarry's Best Storybook Ever* (1963) – a title crammed full of didactic animal characters from Pierre Bear (my personal favourite, despite the mildly traumatic image of his ursine family clothed in spotty seal-fur coats) to the Polite Elephant – traded in 'hogly supernatures to suggest the best gift a mother hedgepig could wish for was an apple, all ready for baking into a festive pie. Hedgerow heroes for a youthful audience, it seemed, almost always sported names starting with H or ones relating to their most famous attributes. Enter Spike, Prickles, Roly and the like.

A key part in this new-found affection for the animal – one which grew more pronounced as the century wore on – was a sense of precarity. From the 1950s, population numbers experienced a decline in rural areas, precipitated by the result of habitat loss and degradation (especially the grubbing out of hedgerows, uprooting of woodlands and cultivation of edgeland space), the intensification of agriculture and widespread use of chemicals. Running parallel to this was an explosion in road building that spanned the completion of the first major motorway, the M1 (1959), to the pro-car policies of the Thatcher government, exemplified by the controversial routing of the M3 through Twyford Down (1993). From a mere 8,000 in 1900, there were 21 million cars in Britain a century later. While freeway fanciers were taking a day trip to Watford Gap Services to buy a postcard and marvelling at concrete cantilevered car parks and the entangled modernism of Spaghetti Junction (1972), Britain's 'hogs navigated home territories criss-crossed by tarmac and nocturnal foraging trips with an extra predator careering into view: the automobile.

With Beastly Britain under attack, its complement of critterly characters needed defenders. Championing the cause was a new genre of environmental(ist) fiction – dating from the 1970s – which offered a bucolic lament to a world now lost and presented a visceral critique of the rise of urban industrialism and agribusiness. Hedgehog versus road emerged as a common theme. In Dick King Smith's *Hodgeheg* (1987), a young 'hog called Max was clipped by a car as he crossed a busy road, one which separated the family home from the halcyon grounds of the park and had claimed the lives of a good number of his relatives. Comic relief was provided in the form of a concussed Max mixing up his words (hence the novel's title). All ended happily ever after when the resourceful youngster enlisted a team of humans (policeman, lollipop lady) to help him cross the tarmac safely.

In *The Animals of Farthing Wood* (1979), Colin Dann's bleak eco-refugee tale, hedgehogs were among the band of animals fleeing from their soon-to-be-bulldozed ancestral home to seek solace in White Deer Park. Two of the older 'hogs were killed on a motorway, though the rest of the contingent made it to the nature reserve. Richard Adams's powerful animal fable *Watership Down* (1972), though famously dominated by rabbits, contained a hedgehog trace in the form of the mythic character *Yona*, who serenaded the Moon to provide a surfeit of slugs and loved to gossip. On one occasion the rabbits ventured across the road, they found a decayed prickly corpse, bloody, flattened and covered with flies. 'What harm does a *Yona* do to anything but slugs and beetles?' Blackberry queried.

Endearment towards the 'hog also manifested itself in a conservationist impulse that sought to protect and rehabilitate native species. In 1981 the species was named under the new Wildlife and Countryside Act as one requiring partial protection. Legislation under Schedule 5 made it illegal to catch them with snares or poison, chase them down using a vehicle or hunt them using automatic weapons, crossbow, gassing or lamping. This was all well and good, but it scarcely offered respite from the things which were causing the species most trouble: modern farming techniques and car culture. Concerned citizens, meanwhile, turned to advocate for this garden favourite that needed help at the roadside. The British Hedgehog Preservation Society was founded in 1982 by Major Adrian Coles (aka Major Hedgehog), who was inspired to form a dedicated group for 'hogly protection after finding a marooned animal under a cattle grid on his land in

Shropshire and hoofing it to safety with a handy saucepan. Today, the society boasts 11,500 members and remains an active campaigner for the species. At almost exactly the same time, Sue and Les Stocker from Aylesbury began to take in sick and injured wildlife (their first patient was a wood pigeon), animals 'left behind' by domestic veterinary provision. With demand rocketing, they registered as a charity in 1983. The drought of 1984 saw a flood of hedgehogs arrive at the facility, which prompted them to create a specific hedgehog 'ward'. The shed soon became colloquially known as St Tiggywinkles and, as more and more animals came across the threshold, they built a dedicated wildlife infirmary. The facility was the first of its kind in Europe and has since become the world's largest wildlife hospital, treating a whopping 300,000 critters over its forty-year history.

A look at the modern 'hog cannot fail to notice some strange manifestations in popular culture. Some of these turned the idea of the harmless, twinkly-eyed garden familiar on its head for the purposes of surrealistic humour. For instance, Monty Python's giant predator Spiny Norman who stomped over a tiny London, haunting and hunting crimelord Dinsdale Piranha. Also prevalent as comic staple in the 1970s and early 1980s was a gallows humour that revolved around roadly misfortunes. This sat within a broader obsession with amusement and the animal-macabre – for example, Simon Bond's hit cartoon book *101 Uses of a Dead Cat*, which spent twenty-seven weeks on the *New York Times* bestseller list in 1981 – that seemed to take a ghoulish delight in the two-dimensionality of squashed hedgehogs. *Not the Nine O'Clock News* (1981) offered their take on the genre with the song 'I Like Trucking', an of-its-time skit in which lorry driver stereotypes Mel Smith and Rowan Atkinson mowed down cyclists, drank petrol, cut up other motorists and hurled chauvinistic remarks at Pamela Stephenson's hitchhiker. The sketch ended with them notching up hedgehog kills on a squash-tally and Smith tucking into a hedgehog sandwich.

These small mammals, it seemed, were the flavour of the month. Harking back to old tales of hedgehogs on the menu and hoping to harness the commercial potential of a good laugh, Welsh publican Philip Lewis developed a line of 'Hedgehog-Flavoured Crisps' in 1981. The idea was apparently inspired by pubgoers and drew on the traditional flavourings used by the Romany to bake hedgehogs, with added pork fat to make them taste authentic. As the crisps did not contain any actual hedgehog, there was a problem under the Trade Descriptions Act. After lengthy negotiations with the Office of Fair Trading, they were relaunched as 'Hedgehog Flavour Crisps' in 1984. My brother and I had a passing obsession with them as 'shock food', as I recall. Lewis's Hedgehog Foods counted profits of $3.6 million in 1991 (a portion of which was donated to St Tiggywinkles). 'Savour all the flavour of traditional country fare cooked the old-fashioned way without harming a single spike of a real hedgehog', went the tagline. The novelty allure didn't last long, however: Lewis's cash-cow disappeared from supermarket shelves in 1994. Cheese and onion lived to fight another day.

Alien or Endangered:
The Curious Island Lives of the Hedgehog

On Alderney, in the Channel Islands, most of the wild 'hogs are blonde. How so? Biologically speaking, it was pretty simple to explain: these animals all had a leucistic gene that affected their pigment. But why so many here? This is where the story gets interesting. Historical accounts of the island in the 1800s do not feature hedgehogs, though some residents recalled seeing regular brown ones (likely introductions from Guernsey) in the early twentieth century, but these had disappeared by the interwar period. Instead, this novel population of blonde beach bums is said to be descended from several animals imported onto the island as pets in the 1960s that escaped their garden homes. Some of these, the story goes, were bought from Harrods Pet Kingdom, a department of the famous store that operated until 2014. Until the Dangerous Wild Animals Act (1976) forbade the sale of exotics, the Knightsbridge emporium traded in beasts of all shapes and sizes. A gorilla was shipped to a country house in Gloucestershire, a lion to some Aussies living in a flat on the King's Road (the animal moved on, rather swiftly, to Kenya, apparently), an elephant to President Ronald Reagan and (evidently) four 'hogs to Alderney.

Sixty years and much prickly copulation later, there are around 500–600 of the animals roaming free on the island, of which 60% are blonde. It remains the only place in the world to boast this genetic anomaly: an unintended consequence of someone with designs on taking these critters to their heart. That is, until they left the array in a Harrods bag and the little beasts escaped. Alderney's 'hogs are thriving – the result of the island's lack of ground predators, perhaps their striking coloration which acted as a de facto 'hi-vis' on roads at night and also, arguably, the place's relatively undeveloped state.

A very different story played out in the western isles of Scotland, several hundred miles further north. Here, in the Outer Hebrides, hedgehogs were also non-native species which created something of a prickly dilemma. In 1974 seven animals escaped from gardens in South Uist where they had been introduced by householders to solve a slug and snail problem. However, over the next couple of decades, they spread across the Hebridean islands, enjoying the lack of predators, the quiet roads and the eggs of endangered nesting birds such as lapwing, curlew, dunlin and redshank. In 2001 the RSPB and NatureScot were so concerned about declining bird numbers, they ordered a cull on North Uist, which pleased ornithologists but angered many locals who were rather fond of these small mammals. Facing intense opposition from the newly formed Uist Hedgehog Rescue, the kill order was rescinded but a thorny issue remained.

When were British animals 'in place' and 'out of place', especially when it came to a clash between sentimentally favoured and ecologically important populations? In the end, a compromise was reached and, since 2002, a translocation project has been in place which captures the animals and relocates them to sites in Ayrshire. At a cost of £2.1 million, nearly 2,500 'hogs have been apprehended at night using sniffer dogs, traps and a dedicated group of volunteers armed with torches and sturdy gloves.

It is on mainland Britain where the hedgehog is in trouble. In 2018 Pam Ayres wrote a short poem which was part eulogy, part call to arms about the one remaining hedgepig to exist on the planet. *The Last Hedgehog* was poignant, disturbing and conjured with a scenario not as far into the future as you might imagine. In 1950 there were 30 million hedgehogs in Beastly Britain. Today, there are fewer than 1 million. The biggest decline has been in the rural environment, where intensive agricultural production, mechanisation and more and ever-busier roads have seen a catastrophic decline in numbers. The 'hog fared a little better in semi-urban spaces, assisted by garden cover and the relative paucity of their main predator, the badger, but they are still struggling. Overly manicured gardens, slug pellets and weedkillers, plastic lawns and hermetically sealed fence lines leave little forage and limited movement opportunities in suburbia. As Philip Larkin mused in his 1979 poem 'The Mower', the blades of this ubiquitous piece of garden machinery slice through grass and spines at will, mauling all in its path.

Larkin ended his poem by advising readers to be kindly to our 'hogs while we still have them. Ayres's 'endling' 'hog told readers to quit their crocodile tears and take action. And, actually, we *can* make a huge difference by taking small steps in our gardens to help *Erinaceus Europaeus*. Have fun making a makeshift *hibernaculum* from old logs or dig a wildlife pond (with ramps to allow animals to exit). Be lazy! Grow to love that bramble in the hedge, resist the urge to tidy leaf litter, keep the grass long, plant wildflowers and leave the mower in the shed sometimes. Say no to pesticides, take care when you dig into a compost heap and always check a bonfire before lighting it. Lastly, make sure your 'hogly paradise is not a prison: a few 5-inch square holes cut in the fence are all you need to enable their nocturnal perambulations to operate effectively. Dale Road in Keyworth, Nottinghamshire, is the street to beat – crowned in 2022 as Britain's most 'hog-friendly road, its thirty back gardens connected by a whopping forty snuffleways: a spiny spaghetti junction to be proud of.

If you want to offer sustenance to your local 'hogs, you can leave out food: but don't fall into the milk trap. Like many of us, hedgehogs are not especially good at eating what is good for them and a combination of lactose intolerance and a capacity to eat massive quantities of food in a single sitting means there is a price to pay for culinary indulgence (as there usually is). So, ditch the gold top and instead buy hedgehog-specific food that is packed full of the nutrients they need and won't give them diarrhoea or a fatty liver. Alternatively, just leave them to sniff out the delightful buffet of invertebrates in your garden. In return, they will protect your prize hostas from munching molluscs. They won't take your blackberries or kebab-spear fallen apples. Neither will they milk your cows or give your dog fleas. But they will bring a certain wild charm to your garden. As Benjamin Zephaniah effused in his wonderful poem 'Luv Song' (1994), a friendly 'hog, living by the shed, animated the garden and warmed the heart.

CHAPTER 2

Fox

Foxes, legend has it, have been known to get hedgehogs to uncurl by urinating on them. A curious folk tale, documented examples of this behaviour are hard to come by. I'd wager very few (read none) of us have gazed, sleepy-eyed, out of a bedroom window at night to spy a fox lifting a leg to offer a targeted spray at a spiny-balled thing blissfully sequestered in the shrubbery. From a fox's-eye view, this strategy does have its merits. A startled 'hog, forced out of its armoured stance by a urinary intrusion, is much more biteable. Dinner seems a good enough reason to harness the call of nature, with the added benefit of getting one over on an animal that always beats you into second place in the wildlife popularity charts.

Wild conjecture aside, this scenario does bear witness to a few actual fox behaviours. They do interact with hedgehogs. Sometimes they nip them, sometimes they do find a way to eat them and, occasionally, they share a food bowl with them. They also dutifully mark their territory and are rather inclined to urinate on anything that strikes them as new or interesting on their nightly patrols. An unlucky 'hog could easily find itself in the line of fire, so to speak. What the yarn says most about, though, is how *we* see the fox. Think about this particular animal and a set of specific adjectives will almost certainly come to mind. Crafty. Cunning. Bold. Over centuries of storytelling, we have conjured the fox into a character with an extraordinary capacity for guile: ever artful, at times duplicitous, perennially quick-witted and endlessly ingenious. Even if it means peeing on a hedgehog.

What is it about the fox that sets it apart? Writer John Lewis-Stempel points out they 'captivate us like no other species'. *Vulpes vulpes* (the red fox) is striking in colour and, in gait, powerful and agile. At least some of its animal magnetism comes from the way it seems to vault effortlessly over binary categorisations. Mysterious and enigmatic, the fox patrols the boundaries of the wild and the domestic, the neighbourly and the exotic. It is recognisable, distinctive and yet, at the same time, a chimera of a beast. For one thing, foxes bark, smile and wag their tails in doglike fashion and yet, in their slinky movements and angular features, they have the way of the cat about them. Something about their way of being also seems to invite an anthropomorphic costume, which they pull off with great flair. Across medieval fable and modern fiction, foxes walk on two legs, wear human clothes and speak our language (usually well-to-do English). Think Reynard the Fox, Mr Tod and, my personal favourite, Basil Brush: charismatic characters with a trick in their tail. Boom boom!

Set against all this fabular shapeshifting is a striking nonchalance, a feral and unruly quality which also sets the fox apart. Carrying themselves with a light-of-paw confidence, their penetrating stare looks right back at us (and sometimes through us) if not from another plane, then certainly from a secret, other place. Foxes are what Lewis-Stempel calls 'the untameable fido', living on the boundaries of our world, distant but somehow homely. Most of us have probably encountered one, at least fleetingly. Naturalist Mary Colwell aptly describes them as living 'among us, but not with us – wild beauties hiding in plain sight'.

In the fashion of the 'what am I' riddle, the fox seems to be rolled up in a set of delicious oppositions – unknowable but not unknown, familiar but not fathomable. Its hold over the British imagination is powerful, visceral, tricky. We rarely think of this species in lacklustre terms. Instead, the fox is typically viewed through emotional extremes – adoration and abhorrence – which confer on it a striking identity as supreme hero and arch-villain of Beastly Britain. 'To love and loathe the fox', Lewis-Stempel argues, 'is a British condition.' Roger Lovegrove, in *Silent Fields*, sees no animal with which we have a more 'schizophrenic relationship'.

A dive into the historical realm provides a clue as to the roots of this dualistic bind. Foxes and humans have negotiated one another on these isles for century on century, rival predators embroiled in a clash both material and existential, and one which played out in the arenas of subsistence and sport, farming and fashion, landholding and leisure. Significant here is the fact that the fox is Britain's only (surviving) wild canid, which confers on it both a special allure and a special burden. After all, it eats things we have kept for our own food. It also moves across spaces we claim for ourselves. A signal of the polarised gaze through which we see the species, *The Wild Life of the Fox* (2020) lambasts its subject for stealing poultry yet champions its magnificence.

The other thing to note about *Vulpes vulpes* is its tenacity and resilience. For Colwell, 'to see a fox is to behold one of the greatest all-rounders and survivors on the planet'. An opportunistic omnivore, it moves through the changing landscape of Britain in a fashion not unlike our own, carving out territory in a range of diverse habitats, armed with an array of sensory and dietary attributes. This adaptability allowed a further sleight of paw, one which saw this animal installed not only as bucolic emblem of Merrie England, but also as edgy icon of the urban jungle. Accordingly, as the twentieth-century fox loped from pasture to asphalt, covert to cul de sac, it added wild redeemer and furry delinquent to its older identities as sporting pest and vagabond outlaw.

A fox remained a fox, of course, wherever it wandered, yet to the human eye it inspired radically different feelings. Sniffing around the henhouse, running full pelt from huntsmen in the pink, lazing on a woodland bank with tumbling cubs, screaming atop a bin at the back of the local shops: these are a few of the common vignettes in which we picture the fox. Except that we don't see it, not really. Instead, over successive generations, our encounters have often involved an imaginative snare, one that turned fox bodies into spectral signifiers through which we chewed over ideas about landscape, history, power, freedom, the wild and our complex relations with it. The problem was this didn't happen in a vacuum. Instead, the various clothes we garbed the fox in – from tweed jacket to hoody – shaped their treatment in the real world and made Beastly Britain a pretty challenging space to navigate. This chapter takes a trot through the complicated and colourful history of the fox to consider the changing fortunes of an animal icon quite unlike any other.

Taxonomical Tussles: What's in a Name?

The red fox is one of the most widely distributed land mammals on Earth and roams diverse environments from Alaska to Algeria, Jutland to Japan. Equally at home on the tundra or in the desert, this wild canid occupies somewhere in the region of 70 million square kilometres of territory. A small, adaptable carnivore, it has become one of the most successful species on the planet. Given this, one might assume the fox's evolutionary story to be relatively easy to trace. Instead, a delve into the world of vulpine genealogy

6. An etching by John Miller, a noted illustrator from Germany who worked in London from 1744. Many of his subjects were botanical, but this one depicts the canid family, including the fox (fourth animal down, on the right-hand side).

throws up a series of complicated and cryptic puzzles. As Martin Wallen, author of *Fox* (2006), notes, this animal, above all others, is the one 'whose most defining feature is its ambiguity'.

What's in a name? When Linnaeus formally named *Canis vulpes* (the 'dog fox') in the tenth edition of his *Systema Naturae* (1758), that was only the beginning of the story. As new canine species joined the taxonomical pack, all sporting wildly different habits and habitats, the logic of universal classification based on morphological traits and a bionominal signature (a two-word name containing species and genus) got rather unwieldy. This was not a conundrum exclusive to the doglike beasts. As more and more animals were discovered, natural historians found it hard to find spaces for them in what historian of science Stephen Gould calls 'a glorified filing system' overflowing with new biological data. Various solutions were adopted: moving animals into different classifications, placing them in a 'catch-all' group (as in the hedgehog) or creating new sub-categories.

German naturalist Just Leopold Frisch is credited as the first to use *Vulpes* as the species prefix for the red fox (rather than *Canis*) in his work on animal classification in 1775, though there were other names and variants in circulation through the 1800s. Frisch's model emerged as the nomenclature of choice by the early twentieth century, but the International Commission on Zoological Nomenclature had other ideas. This organisation, which rigorously policed the line of animal classification from the time of its formation in 1895, engaged in a comprehensive sort-out of the taxonomical rules of engagement in the 1950s. *Vulpes* was thrown out as species classifier because, experts said, Frisch had not followed proper notation procedures. *Canis vulpes* was instead favoured. Humans, being less adaptable than foxes, nonetheless found it hard to get used to the fact that what had become customary scientific terminology was now colloquialism and, as a result of campaigning from biologists at the Natural History Museum, *Vulpes vulpes* was reinstated as appropriate nomenclature in 1979.

It was no wonder the taxonomical landscape was confusing. A few centuries of classification hijinks and a view of the world approached firmly from a European vantage had created a beastly family tree full of twists and contortions, stunted boughs and curious splices. When it came to the canine family, the binary ordering of the fox types (*vulpini*) and the dog/wolf types (*canidi*) presented an illusion of intelligibility beyond which things got pretty messy. The *vulpini* category – where one might expect to find *all* of the foxes – thus contained bat-eared foxes, arctic foxes, racoon dogs and what were known as true foxes. This latter group houses ten species, including the Bengal, Cape, fennec and red fox, each of which was said to share a common root ancestor. To complicate things further, various foxes, including four South American species, the maned wolf, the Falkland Island fox and the crab-eating fox, were housed in the *canidi* section. Elsewhere, there were various species with the common name 'fox' which weren't actually foxes at all. What's in a name, taxonomically speaking? Best not to ask.

When it came to evolutionary history, the story was equally convoluted. The genealogical trail starts, somewhat speculatively, around 50–60 million years ago, when the order *Carnivora* evolved from small, forest-dwelling carnivores known as miacids (think marten or civet). Fast-forward to somewhere in the region of 42 million years ago and the *Carnivora* split into distinct canine and feline lines. About 10 million years ago, the foxes split off from the *Caniform* (dog) grouping and the first true foxes spread from their origin point somewhere in the American South-west to occupy range across the North American continent. A couple of million years later, the descendants of these animals spread eastwards (presumably using the Bering Land Bridge) to claim territory in Eurasia and North Africa. Fossilised remains of *Vulpes riffautae* discovered in Chad and dating to 7 million years ago present the earliest imprint of any canine animal in the Old World.

We know that recognisably foxlike animals were roaming the Mediterranean at the end of the Pliocene (somewhere in the region of 2.5 million years ago), though the fossil record from Europe in this period is pretty sparse. What exists are a variety of genealogical markers, all of which have respectable provenance, but none of which present a definitive ancestral track leading to the modern red fox. As such, the evolutionary story of *Vulpes vulpes* remains fragmentary, hard to decipher and maddeningly entrancing. Characteristically foxy, one might say. This list included *Vulpes alopecoides*, a species first identified by Italian archaeologists in the late 1800s, which lived an estimated 2 million years ago. In appearance, it looked very like the modern red fox, but was smaller in size (about the size of a desert grey fox today). Also in the frame was *Vulpes chikushanensis*, a Chinese species which some saw as ancestor material because of its migration pattern across Asia and physical similarity to the modern red fox. Lastly, *Vulpes praeglacialis* and *Vulpes praecorsac*, discovered in Greece/Spain and Bulgaria/Ukraine, spoke to the existence of fox-type animals in central and southern Europe some 1.8 million years ago.

The prehistoric world – ancient, immense and (literally) set in stone – is surprisingly malleable when it comes to the matter of knowledge. This was certainly true of fox ancestry which, courtesy of new fossil finds and the application of novel technologies, offered a fast-moving landscape of genealogical reveals. In 2010 scientists on an expedition in southern Tibet unearthed a new species, *Vulpes qiuzhudingi*, which inhabited the region 3–5 million years ago. This Himalayan dwelling species with super-sharp teeth was identified as the closest-known relative of the arctic fox, a discovery which suggested a new evolutionary picture of adaptation and migration in which ancestors honed their cold-climate skills on the Tibetan plateau rather than in Ice

Age Europe, which had previously been thought. Equally revealing were excavations at a 16,500-year-old burial site at Uyun-al-Hammam, northern Jordan, which contained a grave of a woman and the bones and skull of (what was deemed to be) a pet fox. This discovery, around 4,000 years older than the previously oldest-known human–dog grave, suggested ancient human communities experimented with vulpine animals as pets, before moving on to the more compliant *Caniforms* as companion species.

Perhaps the most significant genetic revelation of all, however (at least for the foxes of Beastly Britain), was announced in 2020 by a team of earth scientists working at the University of Florence. Using cutting-edge morphological and biometric techniques, they revisited teeth and bone material from fossil specimens scattered across a number of European research institutions (including the best-preserved example of a fox cranium dating to the Pleistocene and found in Villány, Hungary). Weighing in on the vulpine family tree in decisive fashion, they proclaimed 'the ancestor of the European fox has only one name'. That was *Alopecoides*.

Island Life, Foxly Migrations and the 'British' Fox

The earliest-known fossils belonging to the living red fox, Wallen notes, suggested the species was thriving in Europe somewhere in the region of 230,000 years ago. When did *Vulpes vulpes* first set paw in Britain itself? The conventional wisdom has been that it arrived at the end of the Pleistocene, the era characterised by successive waves of glaciation from 2.5 million to 11,000 years ago, which covered Scotland, Ireland, Wales, northern England and the Midlands in a thick sheet of ice. Having taken refuge in the relatively temperate climes of the southern Mediterranean, foxes supposedly made the journey northwards when the ice sheets receded, to take advantage of a new temperate habitat and its woody cover. *Vulpes vulpes* readily extended across the northern hemisphere and, in Britain, found a profitable ecological niche pretty much everywhere aside from the Scottish islands (excepting Skye), the Isles of Scilly and the Channel Islands.

The post-glacial migration theory is a neat hypothesis, but not water-tight, especially given the scattered fragments of geological and archaeological evidence suggesting foxly presence much earlier in what would become Beastly Britain. Micro-palaeontological analysis of Wolstonian glacial sediment suggested they may well have been roving over the steppe landscape of Warwickshire as far back as 135,000 years ago. Fast-forward a bit and foxes could be found on the English Riveria in Torbay, where fossil remains in Kents Cavern located them holed up in a cave system some 23,000 years ago. Not a bad place to make camp. In the early 2010s teams of researchers based at the University of London and Trinity College Dublin added an important piece to this puzzle courtesy of mitochondrial DNA analysis of more than 500 British and European fox remains dating from the Pleistocene period. Their corroborative findings established scant evidence of 'genetic drift' (which happens when populations are isolated from one another and thus develop a distinctive genetic signature through in-breeding) and concluded that a contiguous population may well have remained active here during the Ice Age, interacting, breeding and associating with other foxes across an expansive, chilly European theatre.

This finding not only produced an evocative image of *Vulpes vulpes* rubbing shoulders with glacial megafauna including the musk ox, woolly mammoth, cave bear and giant elk, but it also reflected powerfully on the fox's place in Britain's natural heritage. What is a native animal? Somewhat expectedly, there is a combination of specificity and abstraction when it comes to such things. To be categorised as a bona fide British animal, applicants needed to be able to prove residency before the end of the last Ice Age *or* to have made it to this country without human assistance (which, for terrestrial animals, effectively meant getting here before the flooding of Doggerland, which physically separated Britain from Europe, around 8,000 years ago). Significantly, this new slice of foxy DNA provided a critical piece of evidence in the first category.

Why did this matter? How could a fox *not* be a British animal? Jump into the heated debates between pro and anti lobbies as to the efficacy of fox hunting in twenty-first-century Britain and we see why. Here, in one angry corner of social media chatter, an idea began circulating that the fox was not part of Britain's natural wildlife complement and needed to be removed. In common with most nuggets of fake news, this allegation had enough of a seed of plausibility to attract those looking for a reason to character-assassinate Mr Reynard. The argument went as follows: the fox is an illegal alien which had effectively been saved from extinction in the nineteenth century by imports of European animals designed to swell the number available for sport (more on this later). The allegation was problematic for all kinds of reasons and (thankfully) never really made it beyond the online fringe. However, it did highlight an important point. For human and non-human residents alike, the contours of residency, nationality and identity on a small island were complicated, contested and far from immutable.

Zooming in on island life, meanwhile, the genealogical trail throws up a few micro-mysteries. Speculation remains as to whether *Vulpes vulpes* ever made it to the Isle of Man, Brownsea Island or the Orkneys, where a spate of modern sightings, engineered hoaxes and artificial introductions/escapes neither confirms nor denies the possibility that foxes made it across the waters from the mainland in historical times. A mammoth question also lurked in the taxonomical shadows: was there one British fox species or might there be many? According to Anglo-Irish novelist Oliver Goldsmith, writing in *The History of the Earth and Animated Nature* (1774), there were three different kinds of fox on these isles. These included the greyhound (or Scottish) fox – the largest and fiercest of the bunch; the mastiff fox – a sturdy and powerful mid-sized animal; and the smallest variety, the cur fox – a lowland dweller which 'lurks about hedges and out houses'.

In the nineteenth-century natural history canon, foxes were described in terms of mountain, common or lowland varieties – a distinction, most authors agreed, that was explained by evolutionary development in pockets of territory whose habitat types were wildly different and thus favoured the development of specific attributes. Lowland, or English, foxes were typically presented as red in pelage and smaller in stature, whereas upland foxes appeared darker, heavy-coated and larger – feistier customers all round. According to Charles Darwin in 'Natural Selection' (1858) – a lengthy manuscript which delineated his views on evolution and formed the basis for *On the Origin of Species* (1859) – the highland fox could easily be distinguished from 'the small fox of the low grounds; he stands higher, his head broad, nose not so pointed, his coat more shaggy . . . he is much more powerful and preys on young sheep and rears his young, not in holes, but in clefts in the rocks . . . altogether more like a wolf, than a lowland fox.'

Genealogical commentary on the fox illustrated cultural striations of place, culture and identity across the four nations. In the linguistic tradition of Welsh hill farmers, the *corgi* (or mongrel) lowland fox dwelt in the valleys while the *milgi* (greyhound) fox, an elusive grey-silver beast, lived in the hills. Often, the flavour of regional reportage on the upland fox was distilled into a hagiography of borderlands resistance and appreciation for a 'one true original' – wild, tenacious and uncontaminated by either English or French fox-blood. Writing in *Sport on Fell, Beck and Tarn* (1924), Richard Clapham mused, 'in the old days there were some very big foxes on the fells, but now the breed has somewhat deteriorated owing to the admixture of outside blood', while Colonel J.S. Talbot, a profligate huntsman and author of *Foxes at*

Home and Reminiscences (1906), described the greyhound fox as a 'splendid specimen . . . the largest and stoutest member of his race, long, limber, and grey – a wolf on a small scale'. Sometimes, this North–South divide could be pretty fierce, as Oliver Pike's *Wild Animals in Britain* (1950) illustrated: 'If a fox from an English county was transferred to the wild mountains of Scotland, I doubt very much if he would survive.'

Only in the last few years have the genetic threads of fox heritage been teased out. Writing in *Mammal Research* (2015), a team of scientists led by Helen Atterby of the UK Food and Environment Research Agency noted the lack of published reports on the population genetics of Britain's foxes in a groundbreaking study of vulpine lineage. Their findings, along with a swathe of companion research from Europe, established a mixture of local distinctiveness and familial links across the red fox diaspora. British foxes were indeed different to their continental cousins. Several thousand years had created a kind of genetic island mentality, within which there were granular variations between foxes, say, in Kent, London, Leicestershire and the Scottish Borders. That said, despite these regional differences, all belonged to the same species. All British. All European. All Eurasian, even. *Vulpes vulpes* was a beast of northern hemispheric proportions.

Skulks and Stories: The Fox in Its World and Ours

Today, a combination of technology and a shared urban habitat allow us to get up and close with Britain's foxes. Many people will have taken to the sofa, armed with a cup of tea or something stronger, to watch the mesmerising night-vision footage of foxes going about their business on BBC's *Springwatch*, while a quick wander through the landscape of social media reveals an extravagant capture of amateur reels showing cubs gambolling on garden lawns and nonchalant adults tripping doorbell cameras on their nocturnal patrols.

Interestingly, this sense of the fox as a familiar animal obscures the fact that, until comparatively recently, it was somewhat understudied as a biological subject, mainly as a result of its nocturnal and secretive nature. This most enigmatic of beasts can be hard to track, is seen only momentarily and doesn't tend to use a singular home den or earth except in cubbing season. They are usually seen alone and rarely spotted in a 'skulk' (the collective noun for a group of foxes). In 1965 popular naturalist and writer Brian Vesey-Fitzgerald (who wrote a regular column in the *News of the World* on cats and dogs) authored a short study called *Town Fox, Country Fox*, in which he pointed out the relative lack of knowledge about the species. In a pioneering study, Roger Burrows spent three years surveying a local population in Gloucestershire. Published as *Wild Fox* (1968), this closely observed study lifted the lid on ecology and social life, combined with a lyrical style that talked about the animal's 'music and movement'. In general, however, it has been Britain's urban-dwelling foxes that have received the most attention, particularly Bristol's famous community, which has been the subject of a long-term genealogical study since the late 1970s.

Set against its fragmentary presence in biological fieldwork is the fact that the fox is one of our most storied animals. A charismatic trickster, the fox roves far and wide across Beastly Britain in speech, sculpture and stone. We talk of being 'outfoxed', of the 'foxtrot' and, respectively, the amorous charms of the 'foxy lady' and the 'silver fox'. *Vulpes vulpes* is the animal after which most places are named in England (206 says Lewis-Stempel) and sports a raft of regional nicknames. In Suffolk it is a *rinkin*, a *roplaw* on the Scottish Borders, a *tod-tyke* or a *faws* in northern England. In Dartmoor one might be referred to as a *Hector* on the moor and (in common with many folkloric traces) comes with a hint of devilish collusion, especially if it has a black tail. Witches, it was said, could turn into fox forms, while in

Scotland their heads were nailed onto stable doors to scare others away. On the Isle of Man a 'fox day' is used to describe a period of squally weather, while our countryside favourite, the foxglove, is so apparently named after an Anglo-Saxon yarn which alleged that canny animals used the flowers as mittens for their pads: an extra floral silencer to their already light-footed gait. Continuing on the theme of the charming killer, St Mary Redcliffe Church in Bristol features a misericord wood sculpture of two foxes engaged in deep conversation with two geese, while in Ely Cathedral a stunning stained-glass panel depicts a fox dressed up as a pastor and waiting for his goose parishioners to come close enough to bite them.

A glimpse into the natural history of the fox both grounds the animal in its own lifeways and helps to contextualise the cultural misalignment of the fabled Mr Reynard. A particularly compelling example of the fox as a physical and imaginative presence, *The Darkness is Light Enough* (1986), offered a charming and intimate glimpse into the twilight world of the fox and other countryside denizens. The author, self-described 'night naturalist' Chris Ferris, wrote up the account after a four-year-long nightly ramble through the environment of Chantry Wood, where she walked the 'fox ways' of a non-human landscape and confronted beauty, wonderment and the ambiguous relationship our 'strange nation' has with the natural world. Sentimental, she said, yet also brutal, especially when it came to middle-aged men with snares and rifles.

Our stories conjure the fox as a particularly expressive animal, smiling and serenading at us through centuries of yarns. Biologically speaking, there is some truth to this picture. The anatomy of a fox's head, with its long muzzle and angular cheeks, indeed gives the impression they are grinning, either with mouth closed, or open in panting stance, revealing a set of powerful teeth. Foxes also have highly developed systems of communication: speaking to one another through an array of call signs, tail movements, facial expressions, body stances and somewhere in the region of twenty-eight different sounds, including squeaks, yips and barks. Most evocative of all orations is the sound of a vixen calling for her mate, what Lewis-Stempel describes as 'the eeriest sound of the British night'.

Take a proper look at *Vulpes vulpes* and you will find it is surprisingly small. Many will probably think of the fox as medium-doglike in size but, actually, under all that fur, they are small-boned and slight of stature. What makes them look larger is their famous brush (tail), which, at approximately 40 centimetres long, is nearly two-thirds the length of the entire body. In March 2012 the *Daily Mail* reported on the killing of a 'monster' dog fox on farmland near Moray, Aberdeenshire, that weighed in at a whopping 17 kilos, the biggest ever recorded in the UK. The previous holder of the record was a 'giant' caught earlier that same year in East Grinstead, whose 15-kilo stature, the *Mail* said, resulted from town residents embracing environmentally friendly compost heaps and providing rubbish-bin takeaway meals. Putting these sensationalised examples to one side, the average British fox usually weighs somewhere between 5 and 6 kilograms.

The other distinguishing feature about this animal is its colour – red – something which gives it its name and makes it instantly recognisable. In fact, foxes are not one single colour and that isn't even red. Their pelage is typically orange, yellow or reddish brown, and varies considerably across individuals. Some are white, while rarest of all are black foxes, the product of a melanistic gene which both parents have to carry, and regarded as signs of bad luck in Gaelic folklore. Only five have ever been seen in the UK – in Chorley (2008), Hertfordshire (2012), Dorset (2016), Hounslow (2016) and Halifax (2016–17), which boasted the most famous of all black foxes, Bob, a regular roamer of the town's gardens in the mid-2010s which was crowned by the *Sun* newspaper as 'Britain's rarest animal' and stuffed for posterity after his death by a local super-fan.

In the version of Aesop's fable 'The Leopard and the Fox', as told by eighteenth-century Northumbrian naturalist and engraver Thomas Bewick, Leopard was a proud beast, swaggering through the forest and treating all other animals with contempt based on his stunning good looks. Most creatures gave him a wide berth, except Fox, who, with a 'great deal of spirit and resolution', took Leopard to task. The merit of a person, he pointed out, derived not from their physical appearance but the 'quality and endowments' of their mind. A look at the biological attributes of *Vulpes vulpes* helps explain why this species earned such a reputation. Foxes are indeed smart and they possess an armoury of sensory abilities which help them successfully negotiate their world.

Through vulpine eyes, Beastly Britain appears a rather different place. In daylight, foxes' ocular ability is most suited to noticing objects in motion. They don't see things at distance nor do they have a particularly wide field of observation. Vesey-Fitzgerald pointed out they tended to use their eyesight more to avoid obstacles than to identify prey. Like dogs, they possess a dichromatic vision, which essentially means they see red and green as shades of brown and grey. After dark, however, the situation is transformed. This is due to a couple of special ocular abilities which the fox possesses. The first of these is enabled by an organ called the *tapetum lucidum*, literally an 'extra carpet' of reflective cells in the eye which allows light to travel across the light-sensitive parts of the retina twice. This is why the eyes of *Vulpes vulpes* glow green whey they are captured in torchlight.

The second is a 'visual streak', the technical term used to describe the alignment of the fox's pupil. In common with domestic cats, crocodiles and snakes, this animal has a vertical slit rather than a round pupil: a shape which has greater functionality across different light conditions as it allows the iris to expand and contract more effectively and also maximises the amount of light that can reach the lens. Humans, sheep, lions, tigers and most dog species have round pupils; horses and goats have horizontally aligned slits; frogs' are heart-shaped. The reason? It all has to do with the size of the animal and where it sits in the predator–prey universe, according to recent research from scientists at the University of California, Berkeley. A round eye is good for daylight hunters chasing down lunch, a horizontal slit for panning the horizon for threats without getting blinded by the sun, and a vertical one for nocturnal specialists looking to ambush small critters.

The fox hears the world as much as it visualises it. Its large, mobile ears can move independently to capture an array of sounds and direct them into the ear canal, where a bony, air-filled cavity, the *tympanic bulla*, protects the inner ear and serves as a second echo chamber providing extra amplification. These abilities, combined with the expertise of hearing across low frequencies, are the main enablers of the fox's legendary hunting acumen. This is perhaps most dramatically depicted in the spectacular leaping technique – captured in slow-mo glory in countless wildlife documentaries – which involves this animal standing motionless, except for its flicking ears, making a 'boing-tastic' take-off into the air and diving head first into the long grass or snow to trap unsuspecting rodents (see Fig. 7).

Assisting this acrobatic hunting technique is a particularly amazing ability, first documented in 2011 by Czech wildlife biologist Jaroslav Červený and a team of scientists who followed eighty-four foxes around and reported more than 600 leaps. They found that these animals typically leapt in either a north-easterly or a south-westerly direction, the reason for which became clear when success rates were taken into account: 73% and 60% of these manoeuvres were successful, compared to a lowly 18% from all other directions. And this is the amazing part. The reason for this better accuracy is due to the fox's comprehension of geomagnetic

7. An action shot taken in the Hayden Valley, Yellowstone National Park (2016), which shows a fox making its trademark 'Attenborough leap' (as the Terrier calls it) in pursuit of rodents under the snow.

physics. This animal gauges the location of its prey according to a complex calculation that compares the sound bouncing off its ears with the downward slope of the Earth's magnetic field. Other species use geomagnetic markers for navigation (for instance, pigeons) but no other has perfected this pinpoint pouncing ability.

What must it feel like to harness such a power? For American journalist Robert Krulwich, it inspired not only admiration but an ardent desire to leap across the species boundary: 'I wanted to be a fox. Very badly. Not forever. Just for the time it would take to sense a magnet, to leap into the sky, to plunge down into a snowbank and land on my lunch.' The Terrier, incidentally, has also perfected what she calls the 'Attenborough leap': in her view, far and away the best strategy for stopping a toy bone escaping across the lawn. I'm not sure a magnetic calculation comes into the equation, though.

If that wasn't enough, the sensory armoury of the fox also includes an ability to 'feel' its way through the environments it moves through courtesy of tiny hairs called *vibrissaie* or whiskers (located on the face, muzzle, chin, above the eyes and on the front legs). These are found in all mammals aside from the great apes and communicate an array of information to facilitate navigation, hunting and interpersonal relationships. The fox also has a fine sense of smell, which performs an important function in its daily routines and social world. An individual's 'signature' is released by scent glands on the face and neck (these are released by rubbing, like a cat) and by sweat glands in their foot pads. Glands on the tail and the anus also mean that a personal calling card is placed on deposits of urine and faeces. Foxes are profligate scent markers, which they do liberally on their nightly patrols to indicate the limits of territory, acknowledge the appearance of something new in their world or show where food has been stashed. Their urine contains a cocktail of chemical compounds uncommon to any other animals (aside from skunks) and has a particular olfactory signature. Most humans recoil from it, though Martin Hemmington, author of *Foxwatching* (1997), described it as akin to 'a freshly opened jar of Nescafé'. Dogs go wild for it. *Eau de Reynard*, the Terrier says, is the finest scent in the land.

Across the landscape of natural history writing and popular fable, the smartness of the fox is often referenced in terms of its predatory nature: intellect and hunting acumen combining in devastating and innovative ways. In the Greek *Physiologus*, a second-century work of natural history, the fox was said to come from the ground, damaging the earth with its digging, much like the Devil rooting into the human soul. The animals were said to steal grapes (though not as sensationally as the hedgehog) and to play dead on the ground with their tongues lolling out in order to catch curious birds. Medieval clergyman Olaus Magnus alleged that foxes commonly immersed themselves in rivers, holding pieces of wool in their mouths to allow fleas to jump on, before casting the ball into the current (foxes, incidentally, do not carry many fleas). Meanwhile, according to famous French naturalist the Comte de Buffon, the fox was famously stealthy: 'Acute as well as circumspect, ingenious, and patiently prudent, he diversifies his conduct, and always reserves some art for unforeseen accidents.'

Similar themes played out in the stories attached to the two most famous of all vulpine villains, Reynard the Fox and Mr Tod. A character from the twelfth-century poem, first published in English by William Caxton in 1481, the former was a 'craftie' outsider 'well knowne' for 'wit and pollicie' who alienated the other animals with his outrageous behaviour. Isengrim the Wolf claimed Reynard urinated on his children (it was not only hedgehogs, evidently). Chanticleer the cockerel claimed he masqueraded as a monk to kill eleven chicks. And Corbant the Rook complained his mate, Sharpbeck, was taken courtesy of the play-dead ruse. The king of the beasts, Lion, didn't really know how to tackle Reynard, not least as he had many hiding places, all with twisting passageways that provided multiple escape routes. The story ended when Badger managed to convince Fox to see Lion and he was sentenced to death by hanging by the royal court.

Mr Tod, likewise, performed the role of charming marauder with aplomb. The creation of Beatrix Potter, he was a cunning country gent who was instantly recognisable (with his tweed jacket, cravat and stick) and partial to a 'wandering habit'. He first appeared in *The Tale of Jemima Puddle-Duck* (1908) to play a 'foxy whiskered gentleman' in a modern parable about stranger danger that would have seen the titular goose-heroine end up in the pot with the herbs she was collecting for supper, were it not for the quick-witted interventions of a collie dog. In the *Tale of Mr Tod* (1912), meanwhile, he kidnapped the flopsy bunnies with designs on them for dinner, prompting a daring rescue from Tommy Brock, Peter Rabbit and Benjamin Bunny.

A glance at the hunting behaviour of the fox throws light on these yarns. *Vulpes vulpes* is indeed an accomplished apex predator. A small and adaptable hunter, it can range over long distances, has a body built for agility and can muster an explosive turn of speed (30 miles per hour over short distances). Add an expansive sensory skillset and this animal is especially well placed to successfully capture its prey, which includes a wide array of species, including small mammals (mice and other rodents), birds (from small fledglings to pigeons), insects, worms, frogs, beetles and berries. Aligned to its omnivorous habit is a highly opportunistic one. Foxes will kill what they can get their paws on and stash the spoils for later. This is a hugely advantageous survival strategy, but one which has got the fox into a lot of trouble, especially when they make multiple kills in the henhouse. Our storied landscape communicates the idea, very vividly, that these animals slaughter for the sheer fun of it. It remains a popular assumption, even today. There's no doubt that the sight of a clutch of hens with their throats ripped out is distressing to see. And might well have significant economic implications for those raising those animals for eggs or meat. However, from a fox's-eye view, this is not sporting butchery but strategic food shopping.

Though they often hunt alone, foxes are extraordinarily social animals. At the heart of a family group are the alpha dog and vixen, which bond for life unless mortality intrudes on the romance (as it sadly often does). In the wild, the average British fox lives for eighteen months to two years, as compared to a possible lifespan of up to fourteen years. Other adults exist in the group, usually cubs from previous years (often females) who chose not to disperse. Some of the larger collectives in Bristol sported as many as ten adult animals together with cubs, though rural habitats tend to feature smaller groupings. For half the year, the fox family is loose and nomadic, individuals resting up in ditches or under hedges, with no fixed den. After the mating season, which takes place once a year in January, however, the vixen starts to scout out possible earths in which to birth her young. These take many forms – abandoned badger setts or rabbit warrens, thickets, wood piles and tree stumps – somewhere draught-free, secure and dark. Foxes can squeeze themselves into tight spaces, so a 10-centimetre square of hollowed earth will do. In urban habitats, that is often under the garden shed or, as in the case of two Bristolian families, the corner of a room in an abandoned office block and beneath the floorboards of a residential house (accessed via the cat-flap).

In March, a few days before her cubs are due, the pregnant vixen makes a final choice out of several would-be earths and hunkers down. The male is refused entry to the den just before the pups emerge. The litter contains from three to six animals, which are born deaf and blind, measure just 10 centimetres long and boast a crop of short, black fur. For about a fortnight, they are unable to heat themselves and remain entirely reliant on their mother for warmth, protection and sustenance. She stays in the den for a month, supplying her young with milk, while her mate (and others) provide food at the den entrance, announcing their arrival with a woof. After two weeks, the pups open their eyes (which are bright blue) and begin to totter around the underground den. Around one in seven die in the first month of life, a combination of predation from badgers and dogs, cold weather, flooding or the death of the vixen. They emerge above ground at six weeks, at which point they start feeding on regurgitated solid food. The adults bring them objects to play with, of all shapes and sizes. Evident in the Bristol study was a penchant for shoes, gardening gloves, tennis balls and dog chews: anything that might be easily pilfered. Aged six weeks, the cubs have almost shed their baby fur and look much more like miniature foxes, complete with characteristic red-orange pelage. May is a time for exploration and experiment, with the pups left on their own to perfect the 'Attenborough leap' or tagging along on hunting excursions. Aged two months, the cubs are weaned and, by the end of September, fully grown and ready to make their own way in the world.

Rituals and Rights in the Countryside: Hunting and the Fox

Think about a fox and invariably thoughts turn to the matter of hunting, a topic which has inspired, and continues to inspire, passionate and heated debate about the role of this animal in countryside ecosystems, our ethical responsibilities towards other species and the relationship between sport, landscape, class and British identity. There is a history of fox hunting in various other countries (the USA, where it was a favoured pursuit of George Washington and Southern plantation owners; Australia, where it was introduced by settler-colonists in the 1830s), but nowhere else in the world has a stronger historical association with this field sport than Britain.

The art and literature of these isles resound with the 'thrill of the chase', from the comic adventuring of Robert Surtees's sporting novels to Henry Alken's visual vignettes of all-action pursuit. Rudyard Kipling's poem 'Fox-Hunting: The Fox Meditates' (1933) combined romantic and historical threads to track the hunt from the Roman invasion and Norman Conquest, by way of the Civil War and Cromwell, to the nineteenth-century 'march of progress' – hunting foxes emblazoned as the quintessence of this country. Similar themes featured in Siegfried Sassoon's *Memoirs of a Fox-Hunting Man* (1928), where the youthful George Serston (a not very carefully concealed Sassoon) learned the ways of the sport and its 'kindly country scene' in a rose-tinted conjuring of an English past(oral) smashed to pieces in the trenches of the Somme. In his take on *Reynard the Fox* (1919), John Masefield described 'the bright colour and swift excitement' of the hunt as 'in the blood and the mind' of every Englishman, while Virginia Woolf saw the tradition so enmeshed in British cultural life that it shaped 'the very

8. A colourful scene (c.1846) showing a huntsman victoriously holding up the corpse of a fox, surrounded by mounted hunters and hounds. The engraving, by J. Mackrell, was based on a painting by J.F. Herring, a Victorian animal artist who specialised in equestrian and sporting subjects.

texture of English prose' and gave it its characteristic 'leap and dash'.

In fact, the lingua franca of the hunt is so imprinted onto daily life that we probably don't even think about where it comes from. We talk about being 'in the pink' (the scarlet uniform of the hunt's riders) and 'painting the town red' (a phrase first used to describe the antics of the 'Mad Marquis' of Waterford who, on a post-hunting bender in Melton Mowbray, Leicestershire, in 1837, decided to daub red paint on the White Swan Inn and other hostelries). Pilots in the Battle of Britain shouted 'tally ho' before engaging the enemy, while a nation of children galloped along on the parents' knee to the folk song 'A Hunting We Will Go', written by John Gay for *The Beggar's Opera* (1777). In Parliament, unruly MPs are still kept in line by the Chief Whip (the functional equivalent of the 'whipper' in a hunting party). Next time you go into a country pub, see how much hunting paraphernalia is hiding in plain sight: a horn over the fireplace, prints of hounds and horses on the walls and your Sunday roast served on sporting placemats.

There is a problem with this image, however. In fact, two problems. Firstly, the cultural presentation of fox hunting mostly focuses on people. Yes, there are foxhounds and equine steeds – the companion animals of the hunt – but, in the main, the story is a human one. The sport was nothing without the fox as quarry, but *Vulpes vulpes* was almost always out of sight or, at most, as Vesey-Fitzgerald puts it, 'a passing reference'. Instead, the culture of the hunt centred on pomp and performance, rules and etiquette, flashing anecdotes and the leisured swagger of a (predominantly) masculine elite. The other thing was, despite appearing to be an ancient practice written into the very fabric of British society, fox hunting was not actually that old. It was what historian Eric Hobsbawm calls an 'invented tradition', an eighteenth-century craze, like the ha-ha or the pouf, which saw the sport become wildly popular among landed gentry and nouveau-riche social climbers.

Prior to the 1700s, the fox was hunted largely as a nuisance animal. 'Nocturnal thieves' was how William Jago Edge-Hill described them in 1767. Based on a biological morality that condemned animals for their eating habits, foxes were routinely killed using snares, nets and traps, run down with hounds and hauled out of their earths using terriers, shovels and crooks. Of all beasts targeted in the Vermin Acts (1532, 1566), the fox was a prized capture and commanded the highest bounty price of all animals (equalled with badger): a shilling. As sporting quarry, meanwhile, their historical provenance was patchy. In the eleventh century, King Canute defined it as a 'beast of the chase', while *Le Art de Venerie* (c.1327) by William Twiti, huntsman to Edward II, noted that these animals were sometimes located by scent and then trailed using greyhounds.

However, the fox was not really seen as a game animal in the medieval and early modern period. Killing them didn't involve any mortal danger (and thus kudos) for the hunter, failed to provide a course for the table and wasn't especially interesting as a vocation. The heavy-set horses designed for deer hunting made for a slow pursuit, while the fox's proclivity to disappear into thick cover made it a frustrating target. The fourteenth-century romance poem *Sir Gawain and the Green Knight* told how Sir Reynard twisted and turned to take the 'woodland way', while *The Master of Game* (c.1413), one of the earliest English-language texts on hunting, authored by Edward of Norwich, illuminated a British hierarchy of huntable animals. Hare was top, followed by hart, buck, roe, wild boar and wolf. Only then did fox appear, closely followed by badger, wild cat and otter. The animal was described as a 'common beast' with 'venomous biting', 'cunning and subtle' and 'as malicious as a wolf'. It was said to dine on 'vermin and all carrion and on foul worms', though its favourites were 'hens, capons, duck and young geese and other wild fowls ... also butterflies and grasshoppers, milk and butter'. The book saw some value to the species as a fur animal, useful for adding to cuffs and lapels as a warming trim, but warned the pelt needed to be treated properly or else it would 'stink evermore'.

Things changed in the eighteenth century when the hunt became an altogether different beast. From a dawn raid against an everyday pest, it became a fast-paced gallop of approximately 20 miles over at least a few hours, where up to 300 mounted young 'thrusters' (as they were called) trailed foxes across open country. Meets started mid-morning, a time more conducive to social niceties, by which time the fox was less full of food and more likely to run. There were daring jumps to negotiate, competitive masculine jockeying and the ritualised killing of the fox at the end of play. Part of the reason for the new craze was sociopolitical. The economic boom of the 1700s brought great wealth to the landed elites, who were particularly drawn to outdoor leisure (landscape parks, hunting), as well as a burgeoning group of business interests keen to affirm their social status by rubbing shoulders with the gentry. The shape and power dynamics of land ownership also exerted an influence, with the new worlds of 'improvement' and enclosure encouraging the consolidation of informal commons and strip-farmed fields into large, well-drained pastures separated by hedges and fencing, what Surtees famously called 'grass, grass, and nothing but grass for miles and miles'. The other reason that fox made the leap from verminous animal to ultimate trophy related to issues of animal scarcity. Post-Civil War, there was a dearth of traditional quarries (hare, deer) and the other 'go-to' species (wild boar, wolf) were pretty much extinct. By contrast, *Vulpes vulpes* was found across the countryside and counted few defenders.

The Bilsdale Hunt in Yorkshire, established by the 2nd Duke of Buckingham in 1668, claims fame as the first to raise hounds specifically with fox hunting in mind, while the 5th Duke of Beaufort created a dedicated fox hunt in Gloucestershire in 1762. However, it was Leicestershire, Rutland and Northamptonshire which emerged as major centres of activity, places where the landscapes of enclosure were particularly evident and (later on) within easy railway reach from London. This was the stomping ground of Hugo Meynell, popularly regarded as the 'father of the modern hunt', who pioneered the new style with his dog-breeding and advocacy work. Others were also driving things forward using a combination of landed wealth, passion for the 'long-form' chase and the new science of agricultural improvement, but Meynell's striking contribution was his forty-seven-year tenure as Master of the Quorn Hunt (1753–1800) and his dog-breeding activities, notably the creation of the foxhound, which brought speed and stamina to the scent trail and drew inspiration from neighbour Robert Bakewell's sheep-breeding initiatives. Equally critical were equestrian innovations, especially the adoption of race-fit thoroughbreds which (literally) gave the hunt its legs and attracted the attention of a legion of horse fanciers enticed by a combination of lively riding and a social whirl that galloped seamlessly from the field to the evening ball.

In 1760 there were six registered foxhound packs in Britain. By century's end, thirty. In 1900 a whopping 153 in England and ten in Scotland. Fox hunting became wildly popular, not only for the rural aristocracy but for up-and-coming urban middle classes seeking upward social mobility. For some, it became nothing short of an obsession. The 10th Duke of Beaufort was said to hunt six days out of seven, given the chance. Meanwhile, as the hunt expanded in reach and gravitas, so did its performance codes. Borrowing from the medieval traditions of stag hunting, meets in the nineteenth century assumed the practice of 'blooding' (the smearing of blood on new hunters and children at their inaugural meet) and claimed various parts of the animal as trophies (brush, snout, head, feet). A range of customs carved out various ceremonial contours which gave the sport an air of grandeur and antiquity. Costuming was one key aspect: members of the hunt paid fastidious attention to looking the part, especially the scarlet tunics designed by Thomas Pink (hence 'in the pink'), which combined military regiment with gentlemanly fixings to affirm the pageantry of the experience.

Anthony Trollope praised the hunt as a levelling enterprise open to all-comers and, in as much as it was a public display, embedded in the rural economy; and, in pursuit of an animal which anyone could kill (vermin as opposed to game), it was more inclusive in comparison to the closed-door partridge shoots of the landscape park or gentrified adventures on the grouse moorlands. That said, the sociopolitics of fox hunting were still entrenched in class, race and gender hierarchies. To be accepted required a careful rehearsal of the proper ritual codes as well as a large bank balance – a master of hounds could expect to spend £2,000 a year on kennel fees alone.

Installed as trophy animals, foxes found themselves with a curious new status. No longer vermin, they were now sporting quarry and period chatter began to applaud their value as a faunal nemesis with a fine racing pedigree. Arthur Stringer, writing in *The Experienc'd Huntsman* (1714), noted the animal presented a 'brave, noble chace', while Colonel John Cook's *Observations on Fox Hunting* (1826) revelled in fox hunting as 'so very far superior to other sports' because of the 'wildness of the animal you hunt, and the difficulty in catching him'. That was not the only flip. Foxes were essential for the hunt to operate. Without them, the sport could neither thrive nor survive (or not least in its current form). Accordingly, and not without a sense of irony, hunt organisers adopted a swathe of measures designed to conserve the species, including the planting of coverts (wooded retreats protected with spiky and scrubby vegetation such as gorse and blackthorn), construction of artificial earths, population translocations, hand-rearing of pups and the waiving of rent for tenants who looked kindly on local foxes. Such measures caused friction with the shooting fraternity and local farmers, as did the practice of training the hounds to corner but not kill the fox. One famous animal from Devon was caught and released some thirty-six times, courtesy of what Reverend John Russell (the 'sporting parson' famed for breeding the Terrier's ancestors) called 'hard riding' and 'the obedience of the hounds'.

Others even took to rearing semi-captive populations. Peter Beckford, a prominent huntsman from Dorset and author of *Thoughts upon Hare and Fox Hunting* (1781), talked about how some of his peers captured young foxes and raised them in a 'fox court', a structure 'open at the top and walled in', which featured interior wooden shelters, freshwater and a ready supply of birds and rabbits. When the animals were old enough, they joined the hunt as quarry and were recaught at the end. The 'bagmen' (as they were called) were returned to their pen for another day and another chase. Traditionalists baulked at the strategy, seeing these animals as weedy and smelly (hence easier to track) compared to their wild cousins, but that didn't stop a run-away trade in fox imports from France, Germany, Holland and Sweden at the rate of 1,000 a year by the mid-1850s. These European animals were seen as inferior to properly British foxes in terms of stamina and tenacity, but still commanded up to 10 shillings each at London's Leadenhall Market.

While exponents proclaimed fox hunting as an embodiment of English liberty, fortitude and good breeding, the sport was not without its opponents. Oscar Wilde's quip in *A Woman of No Importance* (1893) – 'the unspeakable in full pursuit of the uneatable' – is perhaps the most famous evisceration of the sport, though criticism went back a lot further. Twelfth-century philosopher John of Salisbury criticised elites for spending too much time (and money) on hunting, a vocation which, he felt, stripped them of their humanity to leave them savage, 'nearly, as the very brutes they hunt', while Robert Pye complained to Thomas Cromwell in 1539 about those gentlemen who kept an 'ungodly hound population' and fed them with food that could be gainfully used for the rural poor. The nineteenth century, however, brought more of a substantive critique, one which first took on the hue of party politics as Whigs and Liberals used the fox hunt as a stick to beat gentry Tories, and later galvanised around issues of animal welfare and human cruelty. Historian E.A. Freeman, an Oxford don, emerged as a vocal critic, writing blistering articles on the brutality of an atavistic leisure pursuit which had nothing to do with rural utility, while Henry Salt, founder of the Humanitarian League (1891), campaigned against a 'blood sport' which revelled in the conjoining of pleasure and pain.

Also feeding off the hunting craze was a subversive costuming, one which played with the idea of the animal as a rebellious citizen of the rural everyday. As Nick Hayes, author of *The Book of Trespass* (2020), notes, an insurgent vulpine character roamed the popular imagination by the end of the eighteenth century, a 'peasant-hero . . . either gypsy or vagabond, outwitting the lords and gentry with his wily ways'. This identity was always lurking in the covert – notably with *Reynard the Fox* and its satirical poke at clergy and aristocracy – and now, firmly connected to the men in scarlet, the revolutionary romantic bolted out of the undergrowth to enact class war in story and song. In John Clare's poem, the eponymous fox survived attacks from shepherd and ploughman (by playing dead) to dive into an old badger sett and live on to 'chase the hounds another day'. Harangued and harassed by an entitled elite, *Vulpes vulpes* became loveable rogue, tragic victim and resilient survivor. *Gone to Earth* (1917) by novelist Mary Webb used the premise of the bolting fox as a stage for a romantic drama starring free-spirited nature lover Hazel Woodus, her staid pastor husband and obsessive suitor, the hunting squire, both of whom she fled from (with beloved pet fox in hand) by throwing herself down a mine, while David Garnett's *Lady into Fox* (1922) told the story of Silvia, a woman who metamorphosed into a fox only to be killed by hounds.

A better outcome was to be found in Hugh Lofting's *Doctor Dolittle's Circus* (1924), where the animal-loving lead successfully rescued a vixen and her cubs from the hunt. Equally so in *Wild Lone* (1938), D.J. Watkins-Pitchford's short story of intimate and hopeful resistance which focused on the life experience and landscape of a fictional Northamptonshire fox. 'Rufus', as the author named his lead, was orphaned as a cub (when his chicken-stealing mother was shot by the local farmer), raised by a kind-hearted dog-walker and released back into the countryside to wander through the 'scented tree aisles'. A glimpse into the countryside through a foxly lens (Watkins-Pitchford said the writing of the novel led him on a mystical and mysterious journey to 'become a fox'), this was not only a world of scent, movement and beauty, but also one of endless foraging, 'fury and fear' due to the frequent incursions of the 'sinister hunt'. The book ended with a climatic chase scene in which the old dog hid from his pursuers in the den where he had been born. The men went home to bed and the fox lived on to roam the night.

Cultural critique took longer to manifest itself as legislative action. The first concrete attempt to ban the sport came in a parliamentary private member's bill brought by the Labour MP for Ashfield, Seymour Cocks, in 1949, which gained only lukewarm support and was withdrawn on the proviso of a government investigative committee chaired by J. Scott Henderson. When that reported in 1951, it ruled – unsurprisingly given its rural and sporting membership – that hunting was less cruel than other animal control methods. By the early 1970s there were still 189 hunts in England, 50,000 active participants and many more on waiting lists to sign up. But things were changing. In 1963 the Hunt Saboteurs Association was formed and used direct action tactics (sonic/scent diversions, blocking gates) to disrupt hunting meets. The RSPCA came out against all hunting with hounds in 1976.

By the early 1980s more than 70% of the British public opposed the sport, according to an RSPCA survey (up from 53%, in the first survey by Gallup on the issue, in 1953). In popular culture, Richard Adams's *The Plague Dogs* (1977) saw two escaped animals from the Animal Research (Scientific and Experimental) lab (yes, ARSE) in the Lake District team up with a savvy Geordie fox to evade capture, while 'Reynard the Fox' (1984), Julian Cope's gloriously raucous take on the epic anti-hero, saw the hunt in starkly violent terms through vulpine eyes, a rain-sodden male fox, looking on in terror, as the men in scarlet invaded his den and murdered his mate and cubs. In the polarised landscape of Thatcherite Britain, the hunting meet emerged as a battleground, literal as well as figurative, where rival constituencies articulated wildly different views on the rituals and rights of the countryside. For the League Against Cruel

Sports, it was a 'senseless and cruel sport . . . dressed up as a noble effort to rid the countryside of a pest'; for advocates, a social and economic good and, in the words of a letter to *Horse and Hound* magazine (June 1978), a 'golden thread that runs through the tapestry of the countryside' under siege from leftie townies.

In the end, the fox earned a reprieve with the election of New Labour. There had been a handful of bills in the early 1990s, which threw the idea of a ban into mainstream political discourse, but it was the momentum of an energised and empowered Labour backbench which carried things forward. Starting with Michael Foster's Wild Mammals (Hunting with Dogs) Bill in June 1997, the wrangle to hunt or not to hunt played out over seven years and 700 hours of parliamentary debate. Outside Westminster, the public appetite for chewing over the issue was equally voracious (historian Emma Griffin remarks that, by the end, it was 'analysed to death'). There were tabloid and talk-show debates, in-your-face advertising campaigns, two massive pro-hunting rallies in Hyde Park (July 1997, March 1998) courtesy of the newly formed Countryside Alliance, animal rights vigils in Downing Street and even a forced invasion of the House of Commons from pro-hunt activists (the first since 1642).

The Burns Committee, which Tony Blair's cabinet commissioned to investigate the impact of hunting on British socioeconomic life and landscape, published its report in June 2000. That, remarkably, seemed to satisfy both sides, perhaps because it refused to take a view on the ban and instead shone a light on various aspects of the hunting world. It questioned the economic reach of the sport, acknowledged its role in rural identity, emphasised the importance of animal welfare and raised the time-old conundrum about rationale. The hunt, it said, killed 25,000 animals per year or 6% of the fox population, not exactly efficient as population control. Was this *really* about utility or was it more about the maintenance of an elite leisure activity?

When Labour won a second term in 2001 there was more time and space to flesh out the parameters of legislation. The leadership, as Emma Griffin notes, remained lacklustre in their resolve, but backbenchers had the scent of victory. More bills followed, more consultations, a list of options for Parliament to consider (self-regulation, government oversight or a total ban) and the promise of a free vote for MPs. After much fist-waving from the House of Lords and a High Court appeal by the Countryside Alliance, the Hunting with Hounds Act finally passed into law in November 2004 and came into force in February 2005. It banned the hunting of wild mammals with dogs in England and Wales (Scotland had passed similar legislation two years previously under the Protection of Wild Mammals [Scotland] Act), though built in exemptions allowing for the use of up to two dogs for rabbit hunting, an acknowledgement of accidental kills and full endorsement of drag hunting to preserve most of the usual contours of the meet (social, equestrian). Cynics saw the bill as a bargaining chip of the leadership to appease Labour backbenchers after the UK's invasion of Iraq in 2003 and secure their vote for university tuition fees, but, in any case, it was a landmark piece of legislation.

Traditionalists scarcely imagined the hunt would ever end. Opponents couldn't believe this countryside staple was now outlawed. Change came, arguably, because the fox became embroiled in many fights – between the Houses of Commons and Lords, the town and the country, between nostalgic constructions of an old pastoral Albion and the moral tone of a modern, progressive Brit-popping nation. These lines of contest were resolutely anthropocentric: identity, class, ethics, values. Not really about the fox at all. Nick Hayes even went as far as to argue that *Vulpes vulpes* was a 'red herring that leads you on a chase away from the real meaning of the hunt', namely the binds of 'possession, property, power and dominion' which shaped land rights and rituals on these isles. Griffin described it as 'not about animals, so much as about us ... a debate about ourselves and our society'. Somewhere along the way, however, the fox – often invisible in the cultural tracks of the hunt – trespassed its way into Westminster. And came out with the right to roam.

The Suburban Utopia: Beastly Fortunes in the Urban Jungle

Today, there are more foxes (or, more accurately, a higher density of foxes per square mile) in Britain compared to anywhere else in the world. How so? The hunting ban? Our temperate climate? The lack of other (larger) wild canids? The main reason is to do with where the fox has chosen to hang out in recent times. Surveys from DEFRA (2013) and Natural England/The Mammal Society (2018) estimate the UK population at somewhere between 357,000–430,000 animals, a third of which live in towns and cities. This last point is critical. Whereas many large carnivores across the world are in trouble from intensified agriculture, industrial development and urbanisation, there are some benefits to being a smallish, agile predator with a generalist appetite. Especially if you find a way to live successfully in urban and semi-urban habitats.

And that is exactly what *Vulpes vulpes* has done. In 1900 there were hardly any urban foxes in Britain. Fast-forward a hundred years and they were to be found in almost every town and city in the UK, denning under garden sheds, roaming city streets at night and finding rich dietary pickings in the form of rats, pigeons, (pesticide-free) worms, not to mention generously donated bowls of canned dog food supplied by animal-loving suburbanites. London, Brighton and Bristol emerged as particular hotspots of fox activity, though it was Bournemouth which served up the ultimate vulpine postcode. Here, in the leafy confines of Hampshire's county town, there were twenty-three of them per square mile (the UK average, for comparison, is two). That is one fox for every 300 humans.

Why did the fox come into the urban jungle? Firstly, there was the population pressure hypothesis, in which burgeoning countryside fox populations (precipitated by a decline in gamekeepers after the Second World War) struggled to find food in usual haunts due to an outbreak of rabbit myxomatosis (which spread from a Sussex estate in 1953, where it was deliberately used on the local warren, and killed up to 95% of British rabbits in two years) and moved into semi-urban spaces out of necessity. The second hypothesis, the urban island theory, posited instead that foxes moved from choice, finding good forage in the suburban districts that spread across southern England and the Midlands from the 1920s and 1930s. These privately owned residential areas were marked by low-density homes, large gardens, low levels of industry and quiet roads: the modern dream for thousands of Brits and what became known as the 'bourgeois' fox. During the 1960s, meanwhile, a 'second wave' of fox migrations saw the species move even further into city limits, following roads and railway lines into the very heart of the urban jungle. Many of these are canid commuters: coming into the city at dusk, working the nightshift looking for food, and retreating to the suburban edgelands at dawn.

Both of these theories overlooked an important element. Foxes were not moving *into* suburban space; suburbia was being built on *their* home turf. Hemmington's *Foxwatching* offered an evocative observation of this process in motion when a local earth was obliterated by a housing estate. The foxes did not vacate, rather they adapted to survive in a shared space. The irony was, as Hemmington bristled, 'Within a very short time the householders in this area started asking why foxes, which belonged in the countryside, had started to invade their streets and gardens.' Evocatively put by Adele Brand in *The Hidden World of the Fox* (2019), 'the fox is not an intruder into our world. We have simply laid our modern ambitions over the landscape it already knew.'

Significantly, as this species became a fixture of urban space, its dualistic identities – wily villain and wildly hero – gained a fresh twist. A historical profile as a nuisance animal easily transplanted to a new setting to craft the fox as a pestilent urban menace. Foremost in popular criticism was the idea of the animal as a profligate trash-raider, upturning rubbish bins and tearing open sacks whenever it found them: a monstrous marauder with an insatiable appetite for last night's leftovers. If the 'dustbin fox' wasn't bad enough, there was also the bone-chilling resonance of their nocturnal mating call, of a loud lothario polluting the night with screams. The *Daily Mail* (February 2024) warned: 'How foxes are taking over London: Urban menace keep people awake at night with their VERY amorous noises and ride public transport in daylight after being drawn to rubbish.' Fattened on junk food and decidedly street-smart, complainants argued, the urban fox was bold, swaggering and dangerous. Suburbanites feared for the welfare of their pampered kitties out after dark and, following the apparent fox attack on two young children sleeping in a residential house in Hackney in 2010, they were even called 'baby snatchers'.

Such was the concern about the 'red peril' that various municipalities adopted control programmes. In common with pigeons (more on them later), the success of animals in urban space seeped into issues of environmental health and civic order and tapped into a visceral fear of nature out of control. The Ministry of Agriculture, Fisheries and Food ran a shoot-and-trap programme in London from the 1940s to the 1970s, while a skulk in Plymouth came in for particular criticism when they killed geese and ducks at the zoo. Eight were tracked to a local city park by the Fowey foxhounds and two were shot. Elsewhere, civic authorities used snares, dogs and even cyanide guns to remove urban foxes. All these measures were scrapped, not least because they didn't really work. Remove a fox population from a local area and another one simply moves in to claim the vacant space, causing fights and more often attacks on pets. Deterrence measures, from secure wheelie bins and advice to households to keep their rubbish tidy and lock up their chickens at night, actually work pretty well. Wildlife biologists also usefully point out that fox populations are essentially self-regulating.

Is there such a thing as an 'urban fox'? The more sensationalist chatter on these animals certainly assumed them to be different, based on judgements of size (massive), aggression (high) and nerve (even more so). Such ideas played off rural/urban divides to position the metropolitan fox as a gobby scrounger as opposed to its well-bred country cousin. According to scientists at the University of Glasgow, there was some evidence to suggest city foxes had acquired a few biological adaptations, namely slightly longer snouts and smaller brains, both of which related to the logistical and intellectual requirements of hunting in a built environment. There was, however, little scientific ground to support claims they were monstrously bigger animals, supersized on junk food and spoiling for a fight. Even in urban space, foxes favour small mammals as a food source. Sure, they scavenge our leftovers (we throw away 7.3 million tonnes of it a year) and dine out on food placed out by fox fanciers, but rarely get into bins (especially wheelie varieties). They are in the habit of stealing a shoe or a glove and do defecate and urinate in inconvenient places (from their perspective, the most conspicuous, olfactorily speaking, the better). But they don't terrorise our neighbourhoods.

Set against the darkling vision of the fox as urban hoodlum is one of wild redeemer, a conduit through which we can connect with the magnetism of other beasts and a welcome sign of nature in the city. Many of us delight in hearing about the animal (dubbed Romeo) who climbed all the way to the top of the Shard looking for a mate, or the individual that took to travelling round the city on the upper deck of a London bus. I saw a dog fox recently trotting across the middle of a busy road in Aberdeen city centre, where it was heading home on the canid commute at 8 a.m. Cars stopped, schoolkids squealed and office workers shot a wry smile in the direction of the animal. The world stopped as the fox carried on with his business, highly attuned but entirely unperturbed by the human zoo: scent-marking a lamppost, momentarily pausing for a red traffic light, sniffing the air to check the news.

The notion of Reynard with rights to the city aligns the vagabond identity of the hedgerow with a streetwise swagger – as well as a dose of magical realism (think the 2017 John Lewis Christmas ad and its presentation of a charmingly playful fox leaping around on a trampoline and inviting other animals, including the local dog, to have a go). Whether we marvel at the fox because it is *in* place or *out of* place, it opens us to a wildly kind of scopophilia (visual theorist Laura Mulvey's term to describe our 'love of looking'). The presence of this animal brings to view a city not entirely under our command, one alive with critterly possibility. For artist Rachel Lockwood, there was joy to be had in this urban wilding and also a delicious smattering of foxly agency. 'The fox brings wildness closer to us,' she said; 'it entwines its life with ours, using us, feeding from us subtly.'

The power of a feral urban ecology, Matthew Gandy notes in *Natura Urbana* (2022), lies in its spontaneity, its subversiveness, its transgressive possibilities. It invites us to look at what is hidden in the cracks of the anthropogenic, between the wild and the domestic and to escape/find ourselves in a more-than-human world. This can happen in that thirty-second interruption, when *Vulpes vulpes* appears as a flash of biotic colour to enliven a mundane moment, or it might involve a deeper form of experimentation, transformation, even. Lorcan Finnegan's short film *Foxes* (2011), for instance, conjured with the idea of 'becoming fox' in an eerie story set in an abandoned housing estate in Dublin at the height of the 2008 financial crisis. Living with her partner in the only inhabited house on the development, Ellen, a photographer, became increasingly drawn to the local foxes she snapped during the day and heard calling in the night.

As thistles reclaimed the gardens around and the symmetrical boxes of the housing estate became more and more alienating, she vaulted over the back fence and left humanity to join the skulk. For Charles Foster, too, taking a walk on the wild side meant exploring the limits of living as a fox (as well as a badger, deer, otter and swift). To connect with his family, he said, required a connection to the animal other. Written up as *Being a Beast* (2016), Foster's antics in crossing the species divide were bizarre, self-deprecating and entertaining. He snacked on crane flies in Bethnal Green Park, crawled about on all fours to see London's streets from a 2-foot-high perspective, wandered the night city for 5 miles at a time and slept rough under a rhododendron. The fox, he said, was the animal he felt closest to becoming, giving him (as it stole a chicken leg) that look of 'reciprocity' he 'longed for.'

And what of the twenty-first-century fox? For Foster, *Vulpes vulpes* is 'a truly cosmopolitan creature' whose evolutionary journey is headed in a positive direction. Smart, athletic and adaptable, it seems far better equipped for the future than the average Brit turning to mush on the sofa. However, for all their sensory powers, these animals (along with most of the contingent of *Beastly Britain*) face a complex and challenging anthropocentric landscape which, as Mary Colwell notes, dictates their 'place in the world'. An estimated 100,000 are killed every year on our roads. Another 70,000–80,000 are taken by gamekeepers and farmers. Added to this are mortalities from dog attacks, poisonings and illegal deaths in England, Wales and Scotland under the cover of trail-hunting or 'flushing to guns' (something which the Scottish Parliament recently sought to address in the Hunting with Dogs [Scotland] Act [2023]). Fox hunting as a sport remains legal in Northern Ireland. This may be an animal listed of 'least concern' in terms of its UK conservation status, but there is still a whiff of precarity here. Life is tricky, even for this most accomplished of animal survivors.

Ecologist Adele Brand marvels at how foxes successfully found a way to live with humans on these isles ('beautiful, heart-breaking, eccentric and implausible' is how she describes the great British public). Perhaps all they need is for us to do the same.

Farmed and Fancy

CHAPTER 3

Sheep

We count sheep to sleep. Visions of them vaulting rhythmically across an old dry-stone wall is said to invite drowsiness. In *Insomnia and its Therapeutics* (1891) Alexander Macfarlane put the success of this method down to a combination of repetition and concentration. One of his patients, he said, never got beyond seventeen woolly jumpers before falling asleep. Perhaps their fluffy coats, contemplative munching of grass and lulling bleats are naturally soporific. Not so to poet William Wordsworth, who remarked that no amount of thinking about the leaps of a docile flock could prevent a sleepless night (he took to a Turkish bath instead).

Nobody knows exactly where this old adage comes from, though it has certainly been around as an idea since medieval times. Petrus Alphonsi, a twelfth-century Jewish physician and writer, made reference to it in his *Disciplina Clericalis*, a selection of thirty-three fables drawn from the Moorish world which he transcribed into Latin. 'The King and the Jester' told of a restless monarch who called for his favourite storyteller to entertain him with tales one night. The jester proceeded with a long tale about a man who went to market and purchased 1,000 sheep. Faced with a river crossing on his way home, he transported the animals one at a time in a small boat. As the storyteller narrated this part of the journey in real time (one by one), he became consumed by tiredness and fell asleep. The king woke him up, so that he could hear the end of the tale, but fell asleep himself. Alphonsi wrote up the (less than riveting) story when he arrived in Britain in the early twelfth century. The first known account of sheep counting as a device for bringing on sleep, this story (along with the rest of the *Disciplina Clericalis*) was translated into Anglo-Norman in the thirteenth century.

Shepherds didn't just count sheep at night. And they certainly didn't count for the purposes of sleep encouragement. Instead, the headcount happened throughout the day and had an important practical function. It began at first light, when herds moved pasture or when anything was done to the animals (lambing, shearing and the like), finishing with a last check at sundown. An integral part of livestock management, the practice was especially important when flocks were moved across communal grazing lands or when 'folding' (a practice where sheep were turned onto fallow fields to enrich the soil with their manure) and individuals could go astray. One could easily imagine, however, that the shepherds slept more soundly after a last count of their flocks before turning in.

Practised up and down the country, sheep counting developed its own regional variations, but was typically arranged vigesimally (in twenties rather than tens). When the shepherd got to twenty, he cut a mark on his crook, raised a finger on his left hand, or put a pebble in his pocket and started over. Writing of such things in her blog 'Keeping Score' (2013), novelist Laurie Graham related how the tumbling count for Wiltshire went something like this:

Hant, Tant, Tothery, Fothery, Fant
Sanny, Danny, Downy, Dominy, Dix
Haindix, Taindix, Totherdix, Fotherdix, Jiggen
Hainjiggen, Tainjiggen, Totherjiggen, Fotherjiggen, Full Score

Musical and amusing in its rhythmic patter; if decimal numbers don't cure your insomnia, why not try a shepherd's chant?

Wandering further into the linguistic pastures of the English language, it is not long before we stumble across sheep references. Mutterings about 'the black sheep of the family' or 'mutton dressed as lamb', 'dyed-in-the-wool' attitudes or 'wolves in sheep's clothing'. We are advised to exercise good judgement by 'separating the sheep from the goats' and to measure time in the 'shakes of a lamb's tail'.

These idioms are familiar, written into our collective memory and universally understood, even though modern society is far removed from the messy intimacies of animal husbandry. They still make sense, though we might not recall exactly why red sky at night or in the morning brought delight or warning to our pastoralist ancestors. Meanwhile, on a basic level, the survival of sheep-isms in our everyday speech highlights a long history of entanglement between *Homo sapiens* and *Ovis aries*. Sheep (and sheepdogs) herded with us in a shared Neolithic past, populated many a story and gave names to many settlements, from Skipton in Yorkshire to Shepton Mallet in Somerset, Shiels in Aberdeenshire to the Isle of Sheppey in Kent. In London you can still wander historical sheep trails from the old heathlands of Shepherd's Bush to the riverside trading post of Woolwich, perhaps making a halfway refreshment stop at the Cat and Mutton, Hackney (the 'cat' speaks to the name for coal barges on nearby Regent's Canal). The town of Wool, Dorset, an obvious candidate for a sheepcentric past, is an unlikely outlier here, named instead after *wiell* or spring in Old English.

With a forgiving climate and an array of vegetation types, the environmental conditions of Beastly Britain provided ideal sheep country, perhaps unmatched anywhere else in the world. In fact, from the time of the Norman Conquest to the Industrial Revolution, sheep rearing was an – if not *the* – agricultural staple on these isles. Their collective hoofprint left a mark in economic, social and political worlds, as sheep bankrolled grand medieval churches, provided the name (and the filling) for the Lord Chancellor's plump crimson seat in the House of Lords (the Woolsack) and rattled the newfangled weaving machines of Yorkshire mills (with carboniferous and water assistance). Sheep leapt through fields and folklore, made pies and pullovers, and inspired great works of art and architecture.

In modern times, too, they made their presence felt at critical ecological and cultural moments, from Dolly, the first living mammal to be cloned (1996), to artist Damien Hirst's *Away from the Flock* (1994), a gambolling lamb in formaldehyde that the *Sun* newspaper labelled as 'Baa-rmy'. Even today, we are not as far away from sheep as many might assume. Outside cities and towns (and even in some of them), the UK supports 31 million of them, 2.5% of the world's population. Our islands boast a remarkable diversity of breeds (ninety-odd), some shaggy, some short-coated; long-, curly-, stubby- or no-horned breeds; mountain, hill and lowland dwellers. If you are looking for variety in your nocturnal counting, there are many to choose from.

Ancient Paths

Short-horned and foot-sure, the Soay sheep has a strikingly ancient look. I stop for a moment every time I walk past a small flock near my home to look at the hooved gang of five staring with eyes of yellow intensity, stomping the ground purposefully when the Terrier dares to appear on their patch (see Fig. 9). Named after the island of Soay in the St Kilda archipelago in the Outer Hebrides, the Soay remains one of the most ancient of Britain's sheep, a small, agile goat-like animal with a brown coat, neat horns, short tail and a moulting fleece, all characteristics of the wild ancestors of today's domestic breeds. Known for their fine wool or *mouflon* (which is typically hand plucked in a process called *rooing*) and renowned for their refusal to be herded, these resilient animals are associated with 'Sheep Island' (the translation of *Seyoøy* in Old Norse) where they arrived with Viking settlers (along with the St Kilda field mouse) sometime in the eighth century. Writing of the flock when he visited in the sixteenth century, Scottish philosopher Hector Boerce described them as 'so wild that they cannot be taken with a snare; their hair is long . . . neither like the wool of a sheep or a goat . . . with horns longer and thicker than those of an ox'.

One of the first animals to be domesticated as livestock, sheep started their co-evolutionary journey with humans more than 10,000 years ago, when pastoralists in the Fertile Crescent decided to cultivate the wild mouflon which roamed the

9. Soay sheep eyeing up the author (and the Terrier) with suspicion.

mountains of Southwest Asia for its meat, milk, skins and (subsequently) wool. A herd animal well adapted to forbidding terrain but relatively unprotected from wild predators, *Ovis aries* is a ruminant, meaning it has no upper teeth, just molars on the lower jaw which are used to pulverise food (short-cropped grass and roughage) using a grinding motion. Brown, horned animals similar to the Soay were brought to these isles by Neolithic farmers somewhere between 5000 and 3000 BC. A good illustration of the conjoined history of human and animal migration, two-legged settlers carried with them a host of other species, some deliberate (livestock, dogs) and others less so (rodents, insects). Archaeological evidence of early British ovids remains scarce. Bones found at Windmill Castle, near Avebury, and Maiden Castle, Dorset, offer a few skeletal fragments of an ovine genealogy: probably the vestiges of sacrifices or rituals designed to bring bountiful harvests, encourage fertility or good health, even perhaps to foretell the future.

By 1900 BC, the British sheep frontier had advanced, probably due to the cutting down of forests and the adoption of a successful pastoral nomadic culture focused on milk production, but with important meat and wool sidelines. When the Romans arrived in AD 43, they brought white-faced Mediterranean sheep akin to today's Merino and plugged the developing domestic industry into a busy market that serviced the empire. The Cotswold Lion, a long-haired sheep, was imported to estates around Corinium (Cirencester) and could be seen nibbling the succulent grass in enclosures (cots) on the gentle hillsides (wolds), garbed with a luxuriant coat befitting classical legend and Jason and the Argonauts' quest for the Golden Fleece. It even gave rise to an intriguing proverb, 'As fierce as the Lion of Cotswold', which runs counter to the usual sheep sayings that focus on stupidity or docility. In fact, we now know sheep can recognise up to fifty faces, successfully traverse mazes and pass knowledge of ancestral tracks onto youngsters in the flock.

Writing in *Natural History*, Pliny the Elder saw much to applaud in this humble grazer. 'Many thanks . . . do we owe to the sheep, both for appeasing the gods, and for giving us the use of its fleece', he proclaimed. The Romans believed wool contained a spirit or an *animus* because it had been grown from a living being and was therefore connected to health, vigour and the deities. In balmy Mediterranean climes, lightweight fabrics were woven and dyed using all manner of pigment sources, including marine snails, which were boiled in vats for days on end to create a vivid imperial purple. The heavy weave of the 'gallic coat' (a wool tunic) became standard issue for legions stationed in chilly northern European garrisons and this was where British crafters came in. Facilitated by a weaving centre at Winchester (c.AD 50), producers on these shores came in for special praise for their lightweight, toasty and waterproof wares. The Edict of Diocletian, a trading inventory of Roman imports and exports compiled in AD 301, identified the British-made *birrus* (a woollen cape with a hood) and *tapetia* (a woollen rug) as premier quality goods, while a surviving mosaic floor at Chedworth Roman Villa, Gloucestershire, depicted a figure representing Winter wearing a toasty *birrus* and holding a branch in one hand and a hare in the other (another Roman import). By the third century, wool cloth manufactured in Britain, it was said, was 'so fine that it was comparable to the spider's web'.

Woven into a Medieval Landscape

With the collapse of the Roman Empire in the late fifth century, the sheepways of Britain became more parochial. For the Jutes, Angles, Saxons and Vikings, the focus returned to the sheep as milk provider for a largely local economy, though they were still written into the fabric of the landscape in drovers' tracks and subsistence habits. Charlemagne wrote to Offa, King of Mercia, in AD 796, lamenting that he could no longer get his hands on a British woollen cloak 'as used to come to us in the old times'.

Things changed drastically over the next few centuries to place *Ovis aries* at the very heart of the British story once more. By the time of the Domesday Book (1086) more sheep were recorded in England and Wales than all other livestock combined. In subsequent years, meanwhile, a combination of a suitable climate and habitat, manorial and monastic land-tenure systems, and lively wool markets on the continent ensured a boom time in sheep fortunes. The flea (more on that later) proved an unwitting aide to this takeover. As successive waves of Black Death from the mid-fourteenth century reduced the country's population by an estimated third, sheep farming – much less labour-intensive than subsistence agriculture – seemed an obvious choice. From the hills of the Pennines and the Lake District to the undulating downlands of the West Country, the green grass of the Welsh Borders to the marshes of Kent, the wool trade exploded. It was said that 'half the wealth of England rides on the back of a sheep' by the 1500s. Joseph Hall, later Bishop of Norwich, wrote in 1612 of three wonders of England 'to be reckoned with': churches, women and wool.

Among the biggest producers of sheep in the Middle Ages were religious groups and monasteries, which capitalised on large landholdings, a ready labour supply of monks and lay workers and their critical placement at the centre of the economic and spiritual life to build wildly prosperous sheep-wrangling enterprises. Ely Abbey boasted a flock some 13,000 strong in the eleventh century, spread across landholdings in six counties. By 1322 the Augustine Priory at Canterbury presided over forty manors, on whose lands grazed 14,000 sheep and contributed to 20% of its annual income. Different religious orders specialised in various types of sheep-craft: the monks of the Cistercian Order, known for their undyed habits and penchant for austerity, specialised in transhumance herding at remote communities such as Strata Florida in the Welsh hills. Medieval historian Eileen Power estimates something in the region of 12 million sheep in England and Wales by the early fourteenth century. Most of this trade was bound for Europe, either Italian merchant traders or the Low Countries, to the extent that one thirteenth-century French poet from Artois made merry with the fancy of 'carrying wool to England'. Coals to Newcastle, sand to the Sahara, and all that.

Medieval landowners, peasant farmers and merchants also bought into the trade, with the result that sheep became not only a common presence in the landscape but were also threaded into the identity and architecture of places. So-called 'wool churches' – built from the donations of wealthy farmers and merchants – towered over the villages of sheep-rich regions such as the Cotswolds and East Anglia. Holy scripture, of course, gave plenty of airtime to sheep (they were the animal most mentioned in the Bible), not least in Psalm 23's invocation of a pious pilgrim safely shepherded to green pastures by a pastoral Christ. Representing innocence and purity, sheep, it was even said, were able to talk for an hour at midnight on Christmas morn to celebrate the birth of Jesus.

Investment in spiritual bricks and mortar for well-off woolers counted various advantages: at once a powerful message of devotion to the Almighty and an equally demonstrative signal to earthly folk of philanthrophic benevolence and regional clout. At St Peter & St Paul, the soaring 'Cathedral of the Cotswolds' that dwarfed the adjacent village of Northleach, the fusion of faith and mammon created a flock of creaturely references, from the stained-glass window depicting principal benefactor John Fortey kneeling among grazing sheep to the memorial brasses commemorating other local merchants (complete with sheep, woolpacks and woolmarks) who lent their financial support to the rebuilding of the church in the fifteenth and early sixteenth centuries (see Fig. 10).

10. The so-called 'wool churches' of the Cotswolds were built on the back of the medieval textile trade. At the Church of St Peter & St Paul, Northleach, Gloucestershire, known as the 'Cathedral of the Cotswolds', a number of wool merchants had their images preserved in brass. This one depicts Thomas and Joan Bushe, their feet placed on woolpacks and sheep. Above each of their heads, an ornate canopy illustrates three sheep sheltering under a bush (a play on the Bushe name).

Secular landscapes were similarly shaped by this medieval sheep-trading bonanza. Stow-on-the-Wold, the highest town in the Cotswolds and a meeting point of various medieval roadways, featured narrow alleyways or 'tures' designed to be a sheep's width. They were built in this way to enable the counting of flocks one by one as they were driven into and out of the central square. Alphonsi's storyteller may well have fallen asleep. Markets began here in 1107, when Henry I granted the town the authority to conduct commerce. Thereafter, generations of sheep jostled its lanes, bleating their way from field to agricultural produce. In one eighteenth-century fair, Daniel Defoe estimated 20,000 individual animals were bought and sold in a single day.

Travelling along the Fosse Way to the southern edge of the Cotswolds, the village of Castle Combe experienced a sheep-fuelled age of prosperity in the mid-1400s that shapes the character of the place to this day. If you wander down the steep wooded lane on a quiet wintry day – without the tourists that frequent the chocolate-box village in summer months – it is easy to imagine walking back in time, one step for a year, tracking the wool story on the way to the valley floor. Atop the ridge, the hamlet of Overcombe housed the agricultural workers who tended the grassy pastures on which sheep munched. Adjacent lies Rack Hill, where the finished cloth was hung out to dry, while nestled at the foot of the hill was Nethercombe, home of the clothworkers who turned raw wool into cloth. Women typically spun the wool into yarn and men or 'websters' used handlooms to weave it into the red and white cloth for which the area was renowned. 'Castlecombe' became a favourite of soldiers in the Hundred Years' War and was highly sought after in London.

Emerging from the holloway of broad-leaved dappled shade, warm-hued stone cottages come into view and the eye is drawn immediately to the Market Cross, centre of the village and the venue for weekly sheep markets after receiving a trading charter from Henry VI in 1440. Beyond, St Andrew's Church, established in the thirteenth century and rebuilt and extended by wealthy wool magnates in 1436, gives further clues as to the sheeply airs of the settlement. Its 80-foot tower features a stone carving of a shuttle and scissors. Beyond the churchyard lies the 'tenterfield' (the place where wool was dried after fulling and which gives us the expression 'tenterhooks') and the grounds of the manor and deer park, where rebellious weavers stole in to take deer.

Rounding the corner, more cottages topple down the lane on either side. Fifty or so were built here for clothworkers in the fifteenth century – complete with strict regulations on the style of buildings and rules for inhabitants (no dice games or football). In the early 1400s, landowner Sir John Fastolf reputedly tried to stop locals owning dogs but, as scribe William Worcester noted, the residents of Castle Combe had more affection for mastiffs, spaniels and turnspits than for the Lord of the Manor, so the edict was abandoned.

Outside each cottage would have been a small bucket, in which villagers left human urine or 'sig' for collection by the fulling millers who mixed it in vats of pig manure and oatmeal to degrease the cloth after it had been woven. Walking further on, a bridge over the Bybrook gives sight of the shallow, fast-flowing stream which provided the all-important power for the fulling mills and dye houses which sprang up along the vale floor. Here, too, lies the huddle of weaver's cottages along Water Lane which have graced many a photograph over the years. Legend has it that it was here, in the end cottage, that two brothers with the surname Blanket created a new style of heavy bedcover ideal for chilly Wiltshire nights. Sitting beside the bridge at twilight, with the bubbling stream and swirling mists that often hang in this secluded valley, you can almost hear the sound of ancient sheep hooves and the clanking looms of those old weavers.

Sheep Sales and Smuggling

There is something enchanting about a sheep fair, an occasion that speaks not only of economic transactions, but also of merrymaking, the marking of time, and meet-ups both convivial and clandestine. While the likes of Stow-on-the-Wold and Castle Combe had their weekly markets, at particular moments in the sheep calendar there were larger gatherings, transient, lively masses of animal and human bodies that took place over several days. There were many such sheep fairs in medieval and early modern Britain, but among the most famous were Priddy, Somerset, which dated to 1348 (when the Wells Fair was relocated there because of the Black Death), and Corby Glen, Lincolnshire, reputedly the oldest of such gatherings, courtesy of its 1238 charter granted by Henry III.

Arguably the largest of these get-togethers was at Weyhill, Hampshire, described by the *Magna Britannia* (1720) as 'the greatest fair in the Kingdom'. The earliest recorded reference to a sheep-meet on this site was 1225 and it was certainly in existence by the time it appeared in the tapestry of English rural life recorded in William Langland's *Piers Plowman* (c.1377). Located at a confluence of major routes, including the Harrow Road from Cornwall to Dover, which transported tin to the continent and pilgrims to Thomas Becket's shrine in Canterbury, and the Gold Road from North Wales to the continent, the Weyhill Fair attracted much passing traffic, as well as the sheep traders who gathered here every July to haggle over the lambs of the season.

En route to the grand sheep gathering, drovers from the West Country and the Welsh Borders stopped at East Woodhay to graze their woolly wares, sometimes fitting them with tiny iron shoes to preserve their hooves on the gravelled road to the fairground and thus secure a fine sale price. Alongside the lamb sales, labourers came to look for work and artisans traded cattle, geese, hops and cheese. A whole range of entertainments was on offer, from cockfighting to mummer plays. One year even a lion and lioness from the Tower of London menagerie were paraded before amazed onlookers. Geoffrey Chaucer, on whose land the fair was located in the fourteenth century, reputedly took inspiration from the melee of human life on display here for his *Canterbury Tales*. By the sixteenth century, the Weyhill Fair had become such a happening that it even sported its own disciplinary structure in the shape of the Court of Pie Powder (a corruption of the French *pieds poudrés*, or dusty feet), which presided over disputes and dust-ups during the seven days of the event.

A place of spirited exchanges, Daniel Defoe estimated that half a million sheep changed hands here. Thomas Hardy immortalised its reputation for commerce and carousing in *The Mayor of Casterbridge* (1886) where a drunk Michael Henchard sold his wife to a sailor for 5 guineas. One longstanding fair custom at Weyhill stands out for its sheeply stylings, the so-called 'Horning the Colts' where newcomers were taken to one of several hostelries and baptised into the festivities with rhyme and ritual. With a silver cup mounted on a ram's horn balanced on their heads, inductees were toasted with a ditty: 'So swiftly runs the hare, so keen runs the fox, Why should not this young calf grow up to be an ox? And get his own living among briars and thorns, And drink like his daddy with a large pair of horns.' After drinking the cup, newly ordained Colts bought a round for all and were welcomed to the fair.

With so much money around sheep, it was perhaps unsurprising that a succession of monarchs and their governments turned their eyes to revenue generation. Looking to bankroll his war with France, Edward I introduced an export tax on wool in 1275 to the tune of a 'half mark' (6s 8d) per sack and, in subsequent years, the wool subsidy ensured considerable cash flow to royal coffers. As much as two-thirds of Crown revenues derived from the wool trade through to the fifteenth century. The rhyme 'Baa, Baa, Black Sheep' paid heed to the punitive terms of what wool merchants of the time called the *maltolt* or 'bad tax' as well as the rare dark wool of a beast (the result of a recessive gene) whose fleece was difficult to dye. First recorded in print in *Tommy Thumb's Pretty Song Book* (c.1744), two of the 'three bags full' went to the King (the master) and the Church (the dame), with the farmer and shepherd picking up the other third of the profits. None, in this original version, went to the boy 'who lives down the lane'.

In the time of Edward III – and very much with an eye to financing military campaigns in Scotland and France – various levies were placed on wool, the most important of which was the Ordinance of the Staple (1353) that controlled domestic sales through fifteen 'Staple' towns in England, Wales and Ireland and the export market by a depot first in Antwerp and then Calais. Some £250 million a year was raised through loans secured from merchants in return for the right to trade abroad, making wool one of the most lucrative sources of finance for the Crown.

One way of avoiding these taxes was to indulge in wool-running to the continent. Illegal sales undoubtably took place as soon as the Crown slapped duty on the commodity, and reached a fever pitch in the seventeenth and eighteenth centuries. Wool exports were banned in 1614 in an attempt to protect the struggling domestic cloth industry and restrictions on the free movement of wool remained in some form until 1825. A signal of the importance of keeping wool at home, smuggling sheep was made a capital offence in 1662 (most likely the source of the 'hang for a sheep as for a lamb' adage). The Kent and Sussex coasts, proximate to France and with good road links to London, became hives of contraband animal movement.

Romney Marsh, especially, emerged as a centre of smuggling activity, with so-called 'owlers' (named after the fact that they operated at night and used a calling system of hoots to communicate with one another) moving creaturely contraband across foggy and remote marshland paths to be loaded onto luggers at Dungeness and Camber Sands for a swift dash across the English Channel. By 1700 an estimated 150,000 woolpacks a year were shepherded across the water and landed on the coast near Calais, where enterprising 'free traders' collected tea, spirits and tobacco for clandestine passage back to Britain. Half the gin coming into England was said to be trafficked illegally into Kent in a government report from 1782. A high-profits and high-stakes business, the smuggling trade was highly armed, well-organised and included hundreds of men who routinely traded in violence, extortion and political agitation. One such band of wool-runners notorious in the 1740s was the Hawkhurst Gang – viewed by some as social criminals and others as murderous desperadoes – who were regularly seen at their favourite drinking hole, the Mermaid Inn in Rye, with pistols and tankards fully loaded.

Productivity and the Pastoral: Revolutions in Agriculture

At the time when the Hawkhurst Gang were dodging excise men on Romney Marsh, the shape of sheep raising and trading in Britain was in the throes of transformation. Changes to landholding systems, animal husbandry practices and new technologies in the eighteenth and nineteenth centuries fundamentally altered the worlds of sheep and the everyday routines of those involved with their care. Enclosure was a critical element here, a term used to describe the privatisation of communal lands with dramatic ramifications for rural tenants. Piecemeal enclosures had occurred since the twelfth century, but the practice accelerated hugely from the Tudor period and was codified by parliamentary statutes in the late 1700s and early 1800s. By 1914 some 6.8 million acres in England and Wales had been enclosed.

In *Utopia* (1516), Thomas More spoke critically of the sheep as an unwitting enabler of this process, with capital-hungry landowners endorsing the wholesale conversion of arable into pasture to increase their stocks of woolly currency. 'Your sheep . . . that commonly are so meek and so little, now, as I hear, they have become so greedy and fierce that they devour men themselves. They devastate and depopulate fields, houses and towns,' he exclaimed. Perhaps it was a coincidence, but it was from the 1570s that the term 'fleece' passed into popular use as a phrase to describe an act of cheating or swindling.

In Scotland, the Highland Clearances (1750–1860) starkly illustrated the colonial aspects of enclosure and the far-reaching social and ecological consequences of measures carried out under the goal of agricultural improvement. Touting mantras of modernisation, productivity and efficiency, owners of landed estates looked to consolidate their holdings and evicted thousands of tenant farmers from traditional lands. The black cattle, which had formerly been raised on small crofts, were replaced by expansive pasturelands on which sheep were grazed. Viewed from the perspective of an evicted highlander, the sheep resembled not an icon of soporific pastoralism but a voracious symbol of Crown dominion. In 1792 matters came to a head when the mass eviction of highlanders during the *Bliadhna nan Caorach* (or 'Year of the Sheep' in Gaelic) saw various scuffles between crofters and farmers, culminating in an anti-sheep riot in Ross-shire in late summer that was punitively crushed by the English Army.

Other so-called improvements included technological developments, new husbandry methods and a special interest in animal yields. The science of sheep keeping took off in a big way as producers delved deeply into matters of stock management and selective breeding to improve old varieties for meat as well as wool production. Thomas Coke tried out new kinds of grass and instituted shearing competitions at his

Holkham estate, Norfolk, in the late 1700s, while contemporary Robert Bakewell trialled new manure and field-flooding schemes, as well as seeking to improve the quality of his stock by an intensive management regime that involved the separation of male and female populations, cross- and in-breeding, and the studding of prize rams. His most famous 'redesign', the Dishley or New Leicester, transformed the old-style Leicester lowland sheep into a quick-growing, much larger animal known colloquially as the 'barrel with short legs'. Bakewell's experiments were hugely influential in establishing new techniques and uniform standards for the British sheep (and cattle) industry, and fuelled the creation of a lively agricultural topography founded on the interbreeding of Dishleys (and Sussex Southdowns; see Fig. 11) with local stock suited to specific environments.

Another evangelist for agricultural innovation, Sir John Sinclair, an English baronet with a 100,000-acre estate in Caithness, introduced a new breed of long-wooled hardy sheep christened Cheviots (after their stomping grounds in the Scottish Borders) as part of a swathe of methods, including crop rotation, drainage and enclosure. A committed advocate for 'the spirit of investigation and experiment', Sinclair campaigned extensively in Parliament for scientific agriculture and was a critical figure in the establishment of the Board (later Department) of Agriculture in 1793. Back in Caithness, his zeal for commercial farming involved assimilating the 'active industry' of crofters by employing them on large farms and moving them to clearance villages such as Badbea, a windswept coastal outpost perched at the edge of the new sheep territory. From the other side of the fence, the experience was brutal and traumatic. It was nigh on impossible to raise crops or graze cattle on the treacherous rocky escarpments, so most families turned to herring fishing (more on that later) and many eventually left for the New World.

The new fancy for science-led farming saw a boom in professional organisations and livestock shows designed to showcase new techniques and technologies. The Royal Lancashire Agricultural Society was founded in 1767, the Bath Society (now the Royal Bath and West of England Society) ten years later. John Sinclair launched the Society for the Improvement of British Wool in January 1791 to advance commercial ends and the genetic quality of British flocks. That July, at the New Inn in Queensferry, a grand Sheep-Shearing Festival promoted the Society and the critters it championed with fleeces from many breeds laid out on the grass, along with drinking, dancing and the firing of guns. Here, and at agricultural shows up and down the country, the spirit of the old sheep fair was given a new twist: old traditions of purchase and play joined by a new performance that celebrated the new agriculturalists and their penchant for statistics, breed standards and scientific methods. At Woburn Abbey, the 5th Duke of Bedford led a flamboyant procession of visitors to his 'New Farm-Yard' as part of a sheep-shearing extravaganza in summer 1800 that was described as a 'truly rational Agricultural Fete'.

This new 'scientific farmyard' was outlined in contemporary literature and offered lengthy instructions on the whys and wherefores of sheep raising. Old folk knowledge of the kind produced in Thomas Tusser's rhyming manual *A Hundreth Good Pointes of Husbandrie* (1557) was replaced by a new narrative that focused on rational approaches. Close observation and research were the order of the day. The first book devoted entirely to sheep in the English language was written by William Ellis, a self-taught farmer and brewer originally from London who farmed in the Chilterns. His catchily titled *A Complete System of Experienced Improvements made of Sheep, Grass-Lambs and House-Lambs* (1749) presented an encyclopaedic dive into all things sheep-related. A comprehensive guide to breeding, fleece management and fattening (especially feeding flocks on turnips), lambing and dog training across three volumes, Ellis focused on what he saw as 'profitable management of these most serviceable creatures'.

Animal health came under the microscope in veterinarian William Youatt's *Sheep: Their Breeds, Management and Disease* (1837). Printed by the wonderfully named Society for the Diffusion of Useful Knowledge, Youatt's manual talked about the long, shared history of humans and sheep and provided an inventory of British breeds. Detailed instructions were given on the treatment of various medical complaints, including tools such as the trocar, a threaded spike used from the early 1800s to alleviate bloat or 'sheep blast', a malady made famous by Gabriel Oak's heroic puncturing of the clover-fuelled, gas-filled bellies of Bathsheba's flock in Thomas Hardy's *Far from the Madding Crowd* (1874).

There was also space in the world of agricultural revolution for the emergence of the sheep as a woolly celebrity. For one thing, the obsession with statistics and breed standards and the theatrical airs of the livestock fete prompted a brisk trade in agricultural paintings depicting 'best in show' specimens. William Henry Davis's celebration of a Southdown ram, captured here in an engraving from H. Beckwith (see Fig. 11), offered an excellent example of the new farm animal genre, with its supersized, mutton-heavy subject painted in dual-aspect profile to emphasise stocky dimensions and fine genetics. Davis contributed more than 160 images of award-winning sheep, cattle and pigs in what became known as the rustic or naive style for inclusion in *The Farmers' Magazine* (1834–80).

Complementing the success of the oblong *Ovis* as a commercial and artistic icon, sheep successfully jumped the fence from being livestock 'units' to enhance the landscape of the English landscape park. Here, in undulating estates crafted by the likes of eighteenth-century designer Capability Brown, roaming flocks provided a perfect foil for sweeping vistas, grazing peaceably in the tree-clumped parkland. Brown reputedly put them to good use firming down the sand-clay mix that lined his newly meandering watercourses with their hooves. However, working countryside merged with pastoral aesthetic only up to a point. In order to create the perfect

11. Etching of a Southdown ram (c.1849) by engraver H. Beckwith. This sturdy variety, first bred in Sussex around 1800, was a 'dual purpose' animal raised for its meat and its wool and an exemplar of the new scientific agriculture. Alongside the New Leicester, it became the breed of choice for sheep farmers seeking to combine the resilience of their local stocks with the new fast-growing and high-producing varieties. This engraving, taken from a painting by animal artist W.H. Davis, celebrates the contemporary fascination for breed lines and stock improvement in its aesthetic focus on body form and stature. A citation underneath details the ownership credentials and prize history of this particular beast.

illusion of the natural, tonnes of earth, roads and even entire villages were dug up to improve the view, while a carefully placed ha-ha (or concealed ditch) prevented hungry sheep from coming up to the house and eating the clipped topiary.

The Modern Sheep: From Dinner Table to the Small Screen

The Industrial Revolution that transformed Britain in the 1750–1850 period is most commonly associated with Lancashire cotton mills. That was not to say the cogs of industry didn't benefit from a sheeply prod. Across the Pennines in Yorkshire, the cottage industry which had operated since medieval times was changed forever as steam power and a string of new gadgets facilitated the mass production of woollens and the gradual movement of production from household to factory. Although less easily mechanised than cotton, new carding machines were used to sort grades of wool from the 1790s, while spinning machines became popular from the 1820s. Production in Yorkshire leapt an astonishing 800% in the eighteenth century, a combination of new technology, successful marketing, the co-option of the regional artisan trade and ready coal reserves that brought prosperity to wool towns such as Leeds, Halifax and Bradford.

Areas which had been stalwarts of the historical wool industry – notably the West Country and East Anglia – could not compete with the cheaper mass-produced Yorkshire worsteds or emerging handwoven Scottish tweeds. Faced with a prolonged agricultural depression, many rural weavers left for the town. Just like traditional regional breeds, such as the Norfolk Horn and the Wiltshire Horn, they had been 'improved' out of existence.

Those adversely affected by the mechanisation of the textile trade did not always go quietly. The most famous of these were the Luddites, machine-breakers from Nottinghamshire, Yorkshire and Lancashire who took their name from the enigmatic Ned Ludd, reputedly a weaver from Anstey, Leicestershire, who was so irked by the replacement of his labour by a mechanical knitting machine that he smashed it up in a fit of rage in 1799. Equally militant were the Wiltshire Shearmen, highly skilled wool-crafters who fought against the installation of gig mills and shearing machines in the 1790s–1810s. Embedded in their local communities and with a strong collective identity, the Shearmen lobbied Parliament, engaged in strike action and indulged in targeted acts of violence (arson and machine-breaking), including attacks on the Staverton Superfine Woollen Manufactory – a six-floor finishing mill that contained state-of-the-art machinery and was opened in 1801 by factory owner John Jones.

For many years criticised as backward-looking ignorants doomed to fail before the march of progress, the rural opponents of the machine age appear rather different when looked through the lens of the Anthropocene, an epoch defined by *Homo sapiens*'s extraordinary capacity to impact Earth's climate and ecosystems and one that is commonly dated to begin with the Industrial Revolution. For the Luddites and their kin, the newfangled devices of mechanisation posed a fundamental threat to the integrity of customary landscapes and lifeways. They saw the connection between technology and politics, of the threads linking economy, ecology and the everyday. While it might be a stretch to see the Wiltshire Shearmen as proto-ecowarriors, their existential anxieties about a new world spun by the machine certainly resonates two hundred years on.

One in ten people in Britain lived in an urban area in 1800. In 1920, for the first time, more people in the UK resided in towns and cities rather than the countryside. The world of urban industrialism prompted a seismic shift in the ways in which people interacted with animals. No longer did most of us get up close to livestock in our daily experiences, instead we typically encountered them first on the meal table. And meat was big business. Fuelled by rapid rises in the urban population, the domestic sheep-raising trade switched from wool to lamb and mutton as its main driver. Also significant was the rise of a global industry in sheep facilitated largely by imperial networks. Captain Arthur Phillip, a champion of agricultural improvement, had arrived in New South Wales in 1788 with a flock of 100 sheep and, a century on, more than 100 million were munching antipodean grass at sheep stations in Australia and New Zealand. Where William Ellis had waxed lyrical as to the sweet-flavoured meat of native breeds fed on British turnips, by the late 1800s most lamb for the table was imported.

The cultural imprint of sheep in the modern age was not only confined to matters of a culinary nature. George Orwell's cautionary fable on communist totalitarianism, *Animal Farm* (1945), featured a pliable flock as early adopters of Napoleon the Berkshire Boar's rousing 'four legs good, two legs bad' chant. Reworked in 1977 by rock band Pink Floyd as a concept album, *Animals* played with Orwellian themes, but this time a cast of beastly caricatures railed against capitalism and the state of 1970s Britain. The cover famously featured an inflatable pig floating over Battersea Power Station, though one of the album tracks ('Sheep') conjured images of an irate flock awakened from their pastoral contentment to revolt against a governing cadre of predatory dogs. Psalm 23 was rewritten from their perspective to include biblical incantations to hang on hooks and be converted to lamb cutlets, though once they formented revolution, the sheep decided to go home.

Elsewhere, *Ovis aries* became something of an unlikely TV personality. Fifty years' of British children have been captivated by a flock of woolly characters oozing farmyard charm – from the puppets of *Toytown* (radio: 1929–31; television: 1956–58, 1972–74) to the clay-cast cartoon antics of *Shaun the Sheep* (2007–20). Appearing for the first time in sparkling colour in an early 1970s reboot, the vagabond charms of *Toytown*'s Larry the Lamb prompted an urgent dilemma for my youthful self as to the morality of consuming a Sunday roast. 'Don't worry,' my mum said as she passed the gravy. 'The lamb died of old age.'

The prize for the greatest televisual sheep-fest, however, has to go to *One Man and His Dog* (1976–2013), a soporific Sunday evening pastoral that brought the competitive sport of sheep herding to the small screen. Ratcheting up the excitement, the *Radio Times* advertised the first show by noting, 'with unpredictable sheep, there is always the element of chance'. Each week, the Black Country tones of Phil Drabble provided voiceover to the trialling skills of teams of shepherds from the four home nations. Wielding crook and whistling their dogs, the two-person, two-dog teams had twelve minutes to herd five sheep across a punishing course involving gates and pens, watched by two eagle-eyed judges. Beloved by the farming community and the public at large, it regularly hit viewing figures of 8 million in the early 1980s: perhaps a signal of the pastoral pasts written into our collective DNA.

Dreams of Dolly:
Science Fiction and Sheeply Futures

Deckard, the taciturn hero of Philip K. Dick's novel *Do Androids Dream of Electric Sheep?* (1968) and its movie adaptation *Blade Runner* (1982), was the owner of a robotic black-faced sheep. Dick's science fiction work, set in a post-apocalyptic future where life was no longer possible on an irradiated Earth, used the old adage of sheep counting to frame his study of cybertechnology and the nature of sentience. Sheep were more suitable than many might assume for a delve into the worlds of digital engineering and artificial life. From the first music ever to be saved on a computer (1951, 'Baa Baa, Black Sheep', for some reason paired with Glenn Miller's 'In the Mood') to Damien Hirst's controversial lamb in formaldehyde *Away from the Flock* – designed to show the inability of biological life forms to cheat death – *Ovis aries* has successively leapt from the romantic pastoral to the dystopian landscapes of science fiction.

Following a futuristic sheep track inevitably winds up at Dolly the Sheep, the world's first cloned mammal to be created from an adult cell. The result of a project designed to find ways to create genetically engineered livestock that carried proteins in their milk, Dolly was grown from three separate female sheep cells in a laboratory at the University of Edinburgh. Born on 5 July 1996, she went on to have six lambs, before being euthanised aged seven due to tumours in her lungs. A landmark in biotechnology, both for those who saw a bright future of genetic modification and those concerned about the moral and scientific implications of humans 'playing God', Dolly was definitely the most famous sheep on the planet. Not since the story of the Vegetable Lamb of Tartary (a fantastical plant from Asia that was widely believed to exist in the Middle Ages and was reputed to bear fruiting sheep) had the idea of a sheep growing from an unusual source captured the imagination. Stuffed for posterity and placed in a glass case, Dolly resides today at the National Museum of Scotland.

What future for Dolly's kin that today graze Britain's fields? From the 2001 foot-and-mouth outbreak, volatile weather due to climate change and the regulatory fallout from Brexit, sheep and those who farm them face challenging times in the twenty-first century. Biologists studying a flock of Soay on St Kilda have recently discovered that the average size of a sheep is shrinking – the result, they think, of milder winters allowing smaller animals to survive. Twenty-seven of Britain's native breeds, including the Soay, are listed as endangered, according to the Rare Breeds Survival Trust.

Panning out beyond the sheepfold lie complicated heritage and conservation questions. The pastoral uplands of North Yorkshire, the Lake District and Dartmoor – spaces defined by a long history of sheeply presence – are among the most represented landscapes in Britain's national parks and areas of outstanding natural beauty. From Capability Brown to *One Man and His Dog*, a rolling countryside of soporific animation has become an important bastion of British identity. For some, however, the environmental imprint of *Ovis aries* has made them intensely problematic: voracious grazers, soil eroders and greenhouse gas emitters who occupy land which could be left to rewilding. Writing in *Feral* (2013), ecologist George Monbiot derided sheep farming as a 'slow-burning ecological disaster, which has done more damage to the living systems of this country than either climate change or industrial pollution'.

Intensive agriculture (the logical outgrowth of the improvement mantra of maximum yield) is certainly no solution. But neither is the abandonment of a working countryside. A sustainable future might lie in finding a solution that is sensitive to both natural and cultural heritage while attending to the urgency of a planetary-wide climate emergency. With thousands of years of shared history on these isles, sheep might now be wandering more decisively into our line of sight. Whether we view them as fluffy icons of pastoral heritage or chomping environmental vandals, they are certainly more than 'white noise in the countryside', to use writer Sally Coulthard's evocative description. A wander through the woolly past of Beastly Britain suggests much to be gained in stopping for a moment by a dry-stone wall and making a sheep count.

CHAPTER 4

Pigeon

How would you feel about a flying dinosaur at the end of your garden? Chances are you have several. The humble pigeon parked on a telegraph cable across the street is one very visible relic of the Jurassic past. All birds, in fact, are 'living dinosaurs'. One giveaway as to the pigeon's Mesozoic origins are its legs and feet – scaly, reptilian appendages that are particularly striking when (as happened to me outside Fishy Evans's in Bath city centre many years ago) a bird lands on your pie and chips and sticks a red foot into the pastry crust. Common fixtures of our urban landscape, these birds are regarded as nuisances by some and overlooked by many. Courtney Humphries, author of *Superdove* (2008), describes them as 'identical gray blobs . . . background scenery'. However, the pigeon is actually a pretty remarkable citizen of Beastly Britain, feathered with an array of fascinating physical traits and a powerful cultural trace.

Picking through their story on these isles, the first thing to note is that there is not one pigeon. Instead, pigeons and doves (which are essentially the same thing) contain 361 varieties, including wood pigeons, homing pigeons (racing homers), utility breeds and fancy types. This chapter sheds light on a few of those, but places centre stage the one with which we are most familiar: the feral, domestic or city/street pigeon. The species can be found on all continents except Antarctica, courtesy of a long history of human domestication, hence its placement in the 'Farmed and Fancy' section of *Beastly Britain*. Second only to the dog in terms of their shared history with us, they are the oldest domesticated bird and carry an ancient presence embedded in British place names, from the 'Culvers' (Saxon for pigeon), including Reculver on the north Kent coast and Culver Cliff on the Isle of Wight, to Colomendy (Welsh for pigeon house) which gives its name to a wood in Monmouthshire and a river in Carmarthenshire.

Our vernacular language is populated by avian idioms. We speak of being pigeon-livered (timid), pigeon-toed, pigeon-holed and of cats among the pigeons (though pidgin English, used to describe a simplified version of the language, derives not from the bird but from the linguistic negotiations of nineteenth-century Anglo-Chinese traders, specifically the Cantonese pronunciation of the word 'business'). Scattered across local dialect, these birds were sometimes used to connote a sense of familiarity, bumbling fatuousness, even cherishment. In Wiltshire, to be described as a *queer quist* (*quist* being an old name for pigeon) was to be gullible or stupid. In Scotland, the word *dhu* or *doo* (a derivation of *dubh* or pigeon in Gaelic) served as a term of endearment, while in Aberdeen the common colloquial greeting *Foos yer doos?* translated directly from Scots Doric as 'How are your pigeons?' Such allusions paid heed to a species which roosted with us over a long span of time. From pigeon holes in the Roman settlement of Isca near Carwent to the brightly coloured lofts of the Niddrie council estate near Edinburgh, the British landscape contains vibrant clues as to an enduring human–pigeon connection. These birds have been our meal tickets and our messengers, decorated war heroes and decorative fancies. Only in the urban jungles of the late twentieth century, in fact, were they toppled off the perch of our affections to become 'flying rats'.

Dinosaurs to the Dodo: The Natural History of the Pigeon

Pigeons are the descendants of *Tyrannosaurus rex*, *Velociraptor* and (most closely) *Archaeopteryx*, a winged dinosaur about the size of a raven with a bony tail, flight feathers and an ability to glide over short distances. The first birds proper emerged some 150 million years ago and pigeons, as we know them, have been around for (at least) the last 23 million. In terms of avian genealogy, all varieties of pigeon and dove share certain traits – round bodies, short legs and small heads – and derive from a common ancestor: the rock pigeon or dove (see Fig. 12), *Columba livia* (which translates from Latin as the leaden-coloured bird that bobs its head). They are also the closest living relative of the dodo, which was essentially a 3-foot-tall ground pigeon, flightless and much heavier-bodied, but with a beak and leg anatomy akin to today's *Columbidae*.

Wood pigeons (*Columba palumbus*) have greyish bodies, pink breasts, white bars on their wings and white neck patches, whereas feral varieties (*Columba livia domestica*) come in many colours, ranging from white and brown through to black, though dark and blue greys are the most frequent pigments. We often think of these birds as dusty. This is due to a special powder made of keratin produced by grooming the feathers that helps keep their plumage in good condition. Their famously radiant neck collar of iridescent greenish-purple is also pretty amazing in design: caused by light hitting threads

12. The wild ancestor of the feral pigeon – a rock dove (*Columba livia*) – etched by C.M. Fessard in 1767.

of latticed filament at different angles. When we change our line of sight, the pigeon's feathers shine and shimmer accordingly to create a mesmerising ocular display. Hummingbirds do much the same thing. Richard Johnson and Marian Janiga, writing in *Feral Pigeons* (1995), describe them as, quite simply, 'one of the masterpieces of nature'.

In terms of size, the average feral pigeon is usually about 30–35 centimetres long, while the wood pigeon is heavier-set and 40–45 centimetres long. Also resident on these isles are the common stock dove (a smaller version of the wood pigeon, but slightly darker) and the rock pigeon (which is rather like the feral variety, but blue-grey in colour). All are communal ground feeders and share the same night-time habit of roosting on ledges (a vestige of their shared cliff-dwelling past) and sleeping on one leg. Eye colour varies from yellow-green (wood pigeon), yellow-brown or orange-red (feral/rock pigeon) to black (stock dove). As with all birds, pigeons have three eyelids – upper, lower and a third, known as the translucent nictitating membrane, which sweeps from the front to the back of the eye and is designed to keep it clean and hydrated (in humans, a vestige of this remains in the form of the skin fold at the corner of the eye). In the UK, all resident species are doing well, except the rock pigeon, which has been pushed out of historic terrain by its boisterous feral cousin and exists only in relict populations on the west coasts of Scotland and Ireland, the Orkneys and Shetlands.

As an animal on the periphery – in countryside or town – many of us know something about the way of the pigeon. We recognise its call, for a start, that resonant coo-coo. This sound is produced in the throat and used to attract a mate, to signal the finding of food, to defend territory and as a device of social chat. Pigeons do this at any time of day, often in the morning (where it can seem especially loud due to the relative absence of other sounds) and sometimes even at night. For some people, it is relaxingly repetitious, for others, a vexatious form of aural torture.

The other thing we notice is the pigeon's distinctive walking style: a stilted gait in which their leg movements are always accompanied by a bobbing of the head. Except that isn't what is happening, it just looks that way. Illuminated by the so-called Treadmill Experiment (1978) – where a group of Canadian biologists studied pigeons on the move using slow-motion photography and a specially built travelator – these birds actually push their heads forward, after which their bodies catch up. It makes for a good comedy turn, but also has an important function of ocular stabilisation. Rather like a kestrel hovering in hunting flight with its head perfectly still, this ingenious panoramic vision allows a pigeon to smoothly view a world in motion and its eyes to process a stable image.

Biologically speaking, the pigeon boasts some pretty incredible attributes nestled among its better-known traits. As Rosemary Mosco, author of *Pigeon Watching* (2021), puts it, 'their lives are both alarmingly alien and charmingly familiar'. For a start, they don't have gall bladders, which classical thinkers took as a signal of their affable disposition. They can also absorb oxygen as they breathe out, thanks to special air sacs connected to their lungs, a trait which makes for an extraordinarily light and efficient respiratory system during flight. These birds are equipped with 340-degree vision (without moving their heads) and can see ultraviolet as well as colours. In sea tests with the US Navy, pigeons spotted targets in the water 90% of the time, whereas human rescue crews maxed out at 40%. Their hearing is also better than ours, with an ability to hear low frequencies and ultrasound waves, even to sense coming storms and earthquakes. Cognitively, their 'bird brain' is actually very intelligent. Possessed with intellectual abilities equivalent to a three-year-old human, they can identify all the letters of the alphabet, recognise their own reflection, distinguish different pieces of visual imagery and music and even detect cancers.

One aspect of the pigeon's profile which has particularly endeared them to us are their romantic relations. Monogamous and attentive couples, artists and writers have long valorised the tender tendencies of the *Columbidae* (see the classical poetry of Anacreon or Jean de la Fontaine's *Les Deux Pigeons*, adapted as a ballet in the nineteenth century). Copulation for the pigeon lasts an average of two seconds, after which the male might well celebrate with a wing clap or two. Eighteen to twenty-one days later, two white eggs appear, delivered two days apart (one from each ovary) and often in the mid-afternoon. With up to six broods a year, this means a healthy pair can parent up to twelve chicks annually.

Successful parenting, however, remains contingent on creating a good habitat for the youngsters (known as squabs), something which these birds are not renowned for. Instead, the erection of haphazard arrangements of stray sticks as a nursery nest makes it quite a surprise that pigeons are so good at reproducing. As does the fact that the adult birds don't recognise their own young until they fledge. There are a few things in the pigeon's favour, luckily. Once the pair have made their nest and the eggs are laid, both take responsibility for babysitting the clutch. Once the hatchlings emerge, their droppings (a combination of uric acid, ammonia and faecal matter) actually stick the nest together quite well. Both parents feed the young by using a type of pigeon milk that is full of fat and antioxidants and is secreted from the lining of the crop, the distinctive oesophagus in the neck which the birds use to store and digest food. Aged twenty-five days, the fledglings are nearly adult-size and self-sufficient.

Lastly, to matters of sustenance. The pigeon's omnivorous tendencies and voracious appetite are key parts of their avian identities. For feral varieties, this means breakfast outside McDonalds, lunch at the local chippy and late-night supper at the kebab van. Wood pigeons instead favour a diet of cereals and field crops (one of the reasons they are larger in size), which can prove maddening for vegetable growers of brassicas, one of their absolute favourites. For this very reason, the Terrier leaps into action at the command 'stop the pigeon' – which means racing down the garden and barking wildly in Muttley style.

In contrast to their generalist eating style, the pigeon has developed a rather more particular – and highly unusual – way of drinking. Take a look at birds gathered on a lake or a riverbank, and you'll notice the majority fill their beaks with water and tilt their heads to swallow. Not pigeons. Instead, they have developed a unique and canny superpower ability that involves sucking water into their throats, thereby allowing them to drink efficiently and stay alert to predators at the same time. This seems particularly useful when you're supping at a bird bath and a small barking dog is running towards you at top speed.

Of Feasts and Feathers: Food, Pharmaceuticals and Pigeon Fanciers

Humans domesticated the rock pigeon somewhere in the region of 10,000 years ago, the time when Neolithic communities in the Tigris and Euphrates valleys began to grow cereals and raise sheep, goats, pigs and cattle. Their image features on ancient Mesopotamian tablets, Sumerian temples and Egyptian hieroglyphs. Easily captured and easy to raise, these birds were a popular husbandry choice and, from the Fertile Crescent, spread with human communities across Asia, Africa and Europe. Domestic pigeons reached Britain with the Romans, who bred them for food and wrote about them in agricultural and medicinal manuals. In *On Farming* (AD 36), Varro created an evocative picture of a tended Mediterranean landscape where birds roosted in the walls of farmhouses and high turrets, from which they swooped down to feast on nearby fields.

The Norman Conquest brought a major influx of *Colombidae* to Britain, as lords of the manor purposely cultivated pigeons for the table. Commoners were not allowed to own them (on penalty of fines and prison sentences) and, accordingly, they grew to hold a certain decorative prestige. Tudor physician Andrew Boorde remarked: 'The country gentleman's residence is not complete without dovecote, a payre of buttes for archery and a bowling alley.' This also made them highly contentious animals, especially for peasant farmers whose strip plantings of barley, oats and legumes were routinely consumed by hungry flocks. A flock, incidentally, is the collective noun for a group of pigeons on the ground. On the wing they are known as a loft, litter or kit. Many dovecots were smashed up by parliamentarians in the English Civil War as symbols of lordly oppression. As one soldier put it: 'Pigeons were fowls of the air given to the sons of men, and all men had a common right in them that could get them and they were as much theirs as the barons.'

Medieval pigeon husbandry was pretty straightforward: they needed little looking after and cost nothing to feed. The key ingredient to a successful avian economy rested on the provision of an attractive and safe house where birds could return at the end of a day's feeding, sleep and raise young without fear of attack from predators (birds of prey, weasels, foxes and, at that time, the odd wolf) and which could be accessed easily by humans to gather them for slaughter. Roosting holes were built into the gable ends of houses and churches, while free-standing circular towers made of stone provided lofty perches for 200–500 pairs. The oldest surviving dovecot in the UK is still standing today. Located at Garway, Herefordshire, it was built in 1326 by the Knights Templar and once housed more than 600 pigeon pairs.

Feudal lords, monastic communities and church authorities eagerly built their own columbariums, from which they generated significant nutritional capital. A de facto poultry farm, the prodigious capacity of pigeons to reproduce meant a regular supply of squabs, which were killed at three to four weeks old and prized for their tender meat (which was cooked on a spit and baked into pies) from late March through to the end of November. These utility animals were also useful in producing feathers (for stuffing mattresses) and guano, which was used as fertiliser and as a key ingredient in gunpowder (saltpetre or potassium nitrate) from the 1500s.

The medieval trade had a powerful linguistic legacy – one which split the ancestors of the rock pigeon into two avian camps based on their status as edibles. Pigeons were definitely for the table, their name heralding from the French *pipiare* (chirp), whereas the non-edible and smaller varieties (doves) were named after the old English or Germanic for dip or dive. To add a confusing twist to the nomenclatural trail, however, pigeon houses were still called dovecotes regardless of which species roosted in them, the British contingent of which grew to encompass some 26,000 by the early modern period, including timber-framed buildings, rectangular structures and octagonal houses. Each was typically built from local materials and in the local architectural style, meaning that not one was quite the same.

Allied to the nutritional was another use: as all-purpose medicine. Building on the classical tradition of the four humours, so-called 'hot' bird species were used for phlegmatic and melancholic conditions. Blood from under the wing of a pigeon could be applied directly into the human eye to alleviate a bloodshot sclera, while a diet of their meat was seen as a healthy prescription for keeping fever at bay. Those suffering from plague were advised to place a live pigeon on the soles of their feet, a treatment favoured by Queen Catherine, wife of Charles II, and described by Samuel Pepys in his diary. According to *The London Pharmacopoeia* (1618), the very best results were to be obtained by plucking out a few feathers, keeping the beak closed and pressing the exposed skin onto a lesion to extract the 'plague venom'. For conditions including gout, vertigo, colic, joint pain, swellings and angina, faeces could be dried, ground up and taken as powder or made into an ointment, while William Salmon's *Pharmacopoeia Londonensis* (1716) heartily recommended cutting a pigeon in half and placing the dead bird on the head of a patient to relieve 'Headaches, Frenzy, Melancholy and Madness'.

The early 1700s brought big changes for Britain's *Columbidae*. Attention to the laws on domestic pigeon possession had become more relaxed by the turn of the century (though statutes formally stayed in place for another two centuries) and some small farms added utility breeds to their husbandry portfolios. In general, however, medieval meat economies (dovecots, warrens and fishponds) were on the decline, in favour of a shiny new system founded on improvement, enclosure and higher returns. This agricultural revolution brought new technology in the form of seed drills and ploughs, as well as resilient root crops such as turnips. With huge increases in the land under cultivation, wild wood pigeons (traditionally seen as forest dwellers) found themselves with a surfeit of food and a burgeoning reputation as 'voracious and insatiable vermin'. Meanwhile, as affluent landowners turned to remodel their country estates into ornamental landscapes, domestic breeds successfully leapt the fence to become objects of fancy.

Breeding and bloodlines became the talk of the hour. *Columbarium*, John Moore's famous book on breed standards and aesthetics, was published in 1735 while, across the country, a frenzy of decorative dovecot construction took place. Lord Atherton (colloquially known as 'Mad Richard'), owner of Atherton Hall, Lancashire, built four turrets on top of his new stately home (1723–42), where birds were grouped by breed and heredity. Forcett Hall, Yorkshire, renovated in the Palladian style in the mid-eighteenth century, included an octagonal dovecote in its parkland which incorporated a cattle byre on its ground floor and was designed after the fashion of a bandstand from the Vauxhall Pleasure Gardens. Another particularly dramatic rendition, the 'doo-house' of Mounthooly, Aberdeenshire, built in 1800 by a local landowner on the top of a hill, presented a mock-Gothic mash of functional avian space and castellated folly. Many of these grand pigeon houses have long since fallen into disrepair, though the 1,500 or so that survive today pay heed to a time when the design of your poultry house provided an opportunity for architectural flourish and bragging rights over your neighbours.

Neither did the world of nineteenth-century industrialism extinguish the fire of pigeon fancy. Instead, a fresh round of avian obsession drew from period interests in scientific agriculture, natural history, pet keeping, animal breeding and aesthetics. In this Victorian explosion of 'fowl mania', the elite flocks of the Columbarium Society (1750) were joined by an urban audience that included people (well, men: even in 1931 only 1% of pigeon enthusiasts were women) from all walks of life. London's Spitalfields emerged as an early hub, located near the famous animal markets of Club Row and home to Huguenot silk weavers from France whose wooden houses contained weaving workshops atop which were ad hoc pigeon lofts. Before long, the fancy had spread across the country, to small towns and villages and especially the industrial towns of the Midlands, northern England and South Wales.

Joining together in local societies and sharing expertise across specialist print media – including *Fancier's Gazette* (1874) and *The Feathered World* (1889), the latter of which had a circulation of 34,000 in 1896 – avian aficionados from a broad social spectrum jostled to create the perfect specimen, based on what George Ure, author of *Our Fancy Pigeons and Rambling Notes of a Naturalist* (1886), described as a union between 'the forces of nature . . . and the control of human will'. According to Charles Arthur House, writing in *Pigeons and All About Them* (1920), those who took up the hobby did so for various reasons: income, pleasure, relaxation and to add 'zest' to their lives. The scene was a great leveller, he noted; anyone might cultivate the most prized bird, based on what Joseph Lucas, author of *The Pleasures of a Pigeon Fancier* (1886), called 'the art of propagating life'. English carriers, fantails and ornamental varieties inspired particularly devoted attention, and specific geographies (and climates) came to specialise in different types, hence the creation of subcultures around the London Beard, the Norwich Cropper and the Birmingham Roller, to name but a few.

The principal venues for the fancy were the local club – of which most towns had at least one by 1900 – and the public show, the first of which was hosted in London in 1848 and went on to grace municipal halls and county shows the length and breadth of Britain. One particularly striking event in the pigeon-fancy calendar was London's Crystal Palace Show, established in 1869 and featuring row upon row of remarkable specimens, strutting their stuff in special cages, parading excellence in size, colour, frills and feathers, acrobatic or behavioural traits. Kate Whiston, expert in 'pigeon geographies', counted some 200 shows with pigeon classes in November 1895 alone.

With up to 1 million birds bred annually and some 100,000 fanciers, some choreography was needed, and this was provided by the Pigeon Society (1885) which was formed to promote the fowl fancy and to crack down on foul play. According to Reverend William Lumley, who raged in the pages of *The Feathered World*, the hobby was rife with 'pot hunters' who flew from regional show to regional show and stole all the prizes.

The pigeon fancy, of course, counted many upstanding devotees, not least Charles Darwin, who was an enthusiastic bird-keeper and became 'immersed' (by his own admission) in the mechanisms by which centuries of human breeding had created a multitude of ideal types. Observations of pigeon behaviour critically influenced his emerging thinking of natural selection and adaptation (Darwin famously became so attached to his loft that he was unable to kill any of its residents). *On the Origin of Species* thus owed as much to the domestic pigeon as the Galapagos finches. Not that everyone saw the merit in Darwin's approach. Many fanciers pooh-poohed his contention that all *Columbidae* had one common ancestor in the form of the rock dove, while an early reviewer of the manuscript, clergyman Whitwell Elwin, had advised him to ditch the 'wild and foolish imagination' of evolutionary theory and write a much shorter book focused entirely on the birds he studied. After all, he argued, 'every body is interested in pigeons'.

Magnetism and Messages:
From Racing Pigeons to War Heroes

The hollow bones and well-developed wing and chest muscles of the pigeon make them experts in long-distance flight. They can fly for 600 miles without a stop (though they don't fly at night and tend to avoid trips in heavy rain) and can reach speeds of up to 60 miles per hour. When engaged in flight, the bird's heart rate jumps from 100 to 700 beats per minute, a level it can sustain for several hours. Their homing ability is utterly remarkable and still not entirely understood. Various scientific studies have puzzled over this most powerful of instincts, deducing that pigeons choreograph their flight paths by the placement of the sun; follow a cognitive map of the landscape and its landmarks; deploy a skill called magneto-reflection, which involves reading the Earth's magnetic field using special iron elements in their beaks; or perhaps utilise infrasound (sonic frequencies) and even chemical traces in the atmosphere to find their way home.

Aeronautical athletics, combined with an easily domesticated habit, made the pigeon a formidable aide in conveying messages. They were used by Egyptians, Romans, Persians and Greeks (including delivering the news of the first Olympic Games in 776 BC), Etruscans, Mongols and Mughals. The first pigeon post was deployed by the Sultan of Baghdad in c.1150, when the so-called 'King's Angels' carried important despatches to and from the palace. In more recent times, governments, financiers and commercial interests have utilised the services of avian airmail, most famously Paul Julius Reuter, who used the birds to plug a 76-mile gap in the telegraph line between Aachen and Brussels in 1846 to deliver news of stock market prices. Perhaps most famously of all, details of Napoleon's defeat at Waterloo (1815) reached London courtesy of a winged messenger owned by the Rothschild family. The service was pretty speedy, too. In 1874 *Scientific American* reported on a flight from Paris to London, where the intrepid 'post-geon' covered the distance from the French capital to a 'wild and rocky part of Kent' in an hour and a half: faster than today's Eurostar.

This bird's flight services have been used particularly in two fields: sport and war. Pigeon racing as a modern phenomenon started in Belgium, where the first long-distance race, the Cannonball Run, took place in 1818, drawing inspiration from the fancy circuit to develop a dedicated breed with endurance flying and keen homing instincts in mind: the racing homer or homing pigeon. The sport leapt the English Channel and spread out from London, buoyed by the Belgian breeders who used the capital as a starting point for their races and, especially, by the extension of telegraph communications in the 1830s and 1840s which signalled the obsolescence of the pigeon post and the selling-off of redundant messengers to hobbyists at knock-down prices. According to historian Martin Johnes, from early roots in London the short-haul racing circuit spread northwards, to Derbyshire by the 1860s and Northumberland by the late 1870s.

Early racers came from predominantly working-class circles, the birds raised in brightly coloured lofts (to attract the animals back) which were built in yards, allotments and even on window boxes in tenements. Animals were trained to return to the roost from local drops and then, come race day, were taken to a release site (typically up to 10 miles away) where they were marked with ink and cast into the air. Excited racers dashed home to wait for their birds to land, then made haste to the local pub, commonly used as race headquarters, to see which had the fastest time, toast the occasion and collect gambling dues.

As the sport evolved, the distances became longer and the technology more complex. Special trains were laid on to transport pigeons and their owners between home and release sites, birds were ringed for identification purposes and specially designed clocks placed in home lofts to accurately determine the flight times of each individual racer. A testament to the growth of the sport, the National Homing Union was founded in Leeds in 1896 and the journal *The Racing Pigeon* two years later. Long-distance racing also took off in the late 1800s, marked by the first National Race from La Rochelle (halfway between Nantes and Bordeaux) back to the UK in 1894 and patronised by some 384 owners (including royalty) and 610 birds.

From the late 1800s to the mid-twentieth century, pigeon racing represented an integral part of the working-class masculine leisure economy, especially in the industrial areas of South Wales, northern England and central Scotland. Some 500,000 people counted themselves as pigeon fanciers

13. A miner releasing pigeons from their transport basket, with the houses of the Unicorn Head Colliery in the background (1954). The image was snapped by Harold White, a photographer commissioned by the National Coal Board to capture Britain's mining landscape and its vibrant communities.

in the heyday of the sport, the 1950s. Each street was home to several pigeon lofts and local life stopped on a Saturday to enjoy the flurry of feathers and promise of avian fame as up to 1 million birds with suitable aspirational names – perhaps the most famous being the King of Rome, who survived blizzards over the Alps and a bullet in France to win the Rome Cup endurance race in June 1913 – were released into the air.

Though dubbed 'the poor man's racehorse', pigeon racing was not inexpensive as a hobby. Social historian Alexander Lee estimates that birds cost £5 to £20 in the 1880s. Then there was the cost of feed, housing, baskets for transit, club membership dues, entry fees and train fares. In the way of most hobbies, one could spend a fortune if you were minded to. That said, the prospects of pigeon racing were literally sky-high: excitement and the thrill of the race; community camaraderie with like-minded people; an energising connection with nature and the chance to soar vicariously above the factory and the workday routine; immersion in a vast knowledge economy of tactical preparation and training where agency mattered; and the opportunity to spend time set apart from the domestic realm, as Johnes notes, a 'masculine enclave' where it was normal to express tenderness to your animals. According to Welsh poet D. Gwenallt Jones, the sport made 'the worker into a living person'. It could also be a cold-hearted enterprise. Breeding techniques such as 'widowhood' deprived male birds of contact with females before race day in order to foster a compulsion to speed home. Any that were not fast enough or prone to getting lost – into a pie with them.

Pigeons were also used for centuries as military message bearers: from the advances of the Roman Empire and the Crusades to the Siege of Paris and the Franco-Prussian War. In the UK, the armed forces began to look at the possibilities of avian accomplices in the late 1800s, a time when Royal Navy commanders experimented with releases at sea and raised birds for the task at Sheerness, Portsmouth and Devonport. The first official loft was constructed at Gosport in 1897, with a contract for bird acquisition awarded to the wonderfully named Mr Coop. The Royal Navy Pigeon Service was established in 1914 and the First World War saw pigeon deployment across all the services. The RAF installed them as pairs in seaplanes, from whence they were hurled in emergencies, while the Army added them to land forces in 1916 under the auspices of the Carrier Pigeon Service.

Under the guidance of Major Alec Whaley and administered by the Royal Engineers' Signals Section, sixty birds were initially sent to France as message bearers. By the end of the war, 22,000 had seen service in the British Army. These were raised at battalion headquarters and, once old enough, brought to mobile lofts (which numbered in the region of 150) nearer the front to become orientated to gunfire. Snapped by a correspondent from the *Illustrated London News*, wartime photographs depict various horse-drawn and motor vehicles assigned to this cause, with even a London bus converted into 'the Pigeon Express'. Four hundred handlers looked after their welfare, many of whom were drawn from the Midlands and the north of England and had prior experience as racing enthusiasts.

Writing in *Memoirs of a Camp-Follower: A Naturalist Goes to War* (1950), Lieutenant Philip Gosse of the 10th Northumberland Fusiliers remembered an officer calling for men with bird-keeping knowledge to come forward to supervise the mobile lofts, a request that inspired 'much excitement' in the ranks as it spoke to 'peacetime callings' and meant time away from the trenches. When the order 'Advance' was sounded, the entire battalion, some 400 men, took two steps forward to volunteer their services.

When it came time for active service, four pigeons were put into crates and taken to the front, where they were split into pairs and assigned to specific units. Laid out in the British Army pamphlet *Carrier Pigeons in War* (1918), the messaging process was as follows: take one pigeon out of its crate, scribble down a message on special wafer-thin paper, place the slip inside a small aluminium tube fitted to the animal's leg and commit it to the air. For infantry units, this was pretty simple: propel the bird skywards. When despatching from a tank (which had special portholes cut in the side for this purpose), men learned to throw the birds downwards to allow them time to spread their wings. Some advised keeping them thirsty so they were eager to take flight. Once in the air, the idea was that pigeons raced fervently back to their lofts at battalion HQ. When they landed, an electric bell alerted those on duty to the arrival of a new message.

There were a few downsides to the use of pigeons as combatants. It took about six weeks to train them and then they were limited in the sense that they would only fly back to one location: their home loft. They wouldn't fly at night, sometimes got spooked by inclement weather or explosions and were highly affected by gas (birds in the trenches were thus deployed with specially made flannelette masks and treated with chemicals if afflicted). Lieutenant Alan Goring of the 6th Yorkshires related one stormy day when a small group from his regiment was trapped by enemy fire in no man's land. They released their SOS pigeon, only for the bedraggled bird to flap about, land in the mud and wander off towards the German line. Desperate to avoid being detected, the men reluctantly shot it. Attention then turned to the other bird, which needed to be dry enough to fly. The men discussed how to do this, ruled out putting it over a flame and decided to huddle around the bird, blowing on its feathers. It worked. The pigeon flew off in the direction of friendly forces and the men were eventually rescued.

In the First World War, 95% of British pigeon messengers got through, making them highly effective wartime correspondents. Their use was particularly helpful when communicating information across challenging terrain where travel by human or dog was impossibly slow and – which happened frequently – radio equipment and wires were destroyed. A signal of their value, the Germans assigned hawks and handlers in the trenches to intercept British birds (as well as using them as messengers themselves). Pigeons also performed an important emotional role as companion animals. Gosse confessed that 'without the birds I dare not think how I should have got through the war at all'. Back home, newspapers waxed lyrical about the heroic deeds of the plucky messengers, while the Defence of the Realm Act (1916) required all fanciers to hold a licence for their animals. If any flew off in the direction of Europe, the owner received a visit from the police to check their patriotic credentials. As MP Sir Frederick Booth put it, 'an alien enemy with a racing pigeon is far more dangerous than one with a bomb'. Sportsmen were also prohibited from shooting homing pigeons, with financial penalties imposed for lawbreaking, such was the value of these birds to the war effort.

In 1938 Major W.H. Osman founded the National Pigeon Service, a volunteer organisation expressly set up to provide pigeons to the British forces. The timing was prescient. When the Second World War broke out in September 1939, measures proceeded apace to put the war birds, evocatively described as 'feathered battalions' by journalist Victor Newton, into active service. Some 200,000 of them were housed with air, sea and land units, as well as working with the intelligence services. Under orders from MI5 and orchestrated by the Army Pigeon Service Special Section, birds were dropped into occupied France, armed with a small package. This included sheets of paper, a pencil and guidance notes in French and Dutch that instructed the finder to write down useful intelligence, feed the bird up and send it back across the Channel. A London newspaper was put in the container to prove the British origins of the messenger.

On their flight home, pigeons ran the risk of peregrine falcon attack – their main predator – 50% of which were killed by the British military along England's southern coastline to aid the return of the winged messengers. The scheme also ran the gauntlet of German counter-intelligence, which put into French circulation an alternative pigeon packet, authenticated not with a newspaper but English cigarettes and containing a bird who'd fly east towards Berlin. The Resistance were duly advised to intercept these imposters, smoke the fags and eat the birds. Fearful of Axis intelligence operating a similar programme on home turf, MI5 established a falconry unit, based first in the Scilly Isles and then Swanage in Dorset, tasked with hunting down German pigeons who might have infiltrated the UK. Fifteen birds were captured. None turned out to be active agents, but two were marked as possible German trainees (official files stated 'they are now POW').

14. An inspection of RAF pigeons at a Scottish Coastal Command station (c.1939–45). Flying Officer Joyce Warmer writes up notes on the flying recruits in a dossier marked 'Secret', as Sergeant T.L. McLean, a renowned pigeon fancier in Scotland, comments on the condition of the birds.

The adventures of the Pigeon Service Special Section sound like something from *'Allo 'Allo!* or *Blackadder Goes Forth* (both of which featured pigeon-themed episodes where, respectively, Edith thwarted René's plans to secure new uniforms for the British airmen by baking a London-bound messenger in a pie and Lord Melchett fretted over the deployment of his pet, Speckled Jim, to the trenches). In all seriousness, however, these animals performed extraordinary wartime feats. Some 16,500 saw active service in the Second World War, including Dark Chequer, a hen that was floated into France in 1940, spent eleven days on the ground and flew back 300 miles to Blighty to deliver her message. A mark of their importance, the Dickin Medal, created in 1943 and popularly known as the animals' Victoria Cross, was awarded to thirty-two birds for heroic service (the highest of any species, dogs coming second with eighteen medals). The honour roll included Paddy, a bird trained at RAF Hurn in Hampshire who flew from Normandy to England on 12 June 1944, covering 230 miles in a record time of four hours and providing essential intelligence for the D-Day landings; Mary of Exeter, who received honours for her many flights from occupied France, despite having serious shrapnel injuries; and Winkie, commemorated for alerting British services to a downed RAF bomber stranded in the North Sea in February 1943, allowing all crew to be rescued.

Re-homing the Pigeon: Winged Rats and Feral Fantasies

Fast-forward to the late twentieth century and the cult of the pigeon counted some big names. Imagine, for a moment, a fantasy dinner table where, hotly debating the merits of racers versus rollers over their prawn cocktail, were Queen Elizabeth II, Yul Brynner, Pablo Picasso, Elvis Presley and Mike Tyson. Tyson famously became devoted to the fancy aged nine, an overweight kid in Brooklyn who found solace from the local bullies in a pigeon loft and threw his very first punch at a neighbourhood thug who snapped the neck of one of his precious birds. After a career in the ring, the boxer built a lavish pad for his 350 birds at home in Vegas and voiced a cartoon series (somewhere between *Scooby-Doo* and *South Park*) called *The Mike Tyson Mysteries* (2014) that featured the ghost of the Marquess of Queensberry and an alcoholic talking pigeon.

Putting aside these celebrity endorsements, however, Britain's affection for all things *Columbidae* had taken a definite downward dive. New leisure economies pecked away at their allure as objects of racing and breed attraction, while industrial decline, an aging population of devotees and the rising cost of living saw the sporting community shrink considerably from the 1980s. Stalwarts complained of rising populations of predatory birds and raised concerns about a range of debilitating factors from UPVC windows (which prevented council tenants fitting nesting boxes on windowsills) to hypersensitivity pneumonitis, an immunological condition contracted by inhaling dust, fungus or mould (colloquially known as pigeon fancier's lung). Elsewhere, changing culinary tastes and military technologies saw the birds taken off the menu and the army service roll. At best, they had become obsolete and irrelevant and, at worst, a health hazard.

On this last point, a fire of civic vitriol was increasingly directed at feral pigeons. Lambasted in radio phone-ins, government despatches and medico-environmental reports, they took on a new identity as *avis non grata*. In town centres across the country, aversive conditioning and programmes of population reduction became the norm. Hawks (real and animatronic) were brought in to hunt them. Spikes, netting and plastic owls were placed on buildings to dissuade their presence and contraceptive-laced seed was tossed around feed sites. To throw these birds a few crumbs became an antisocial act, even a criminal one.

What happened? For thousands of years, we lived happily with pigeons. Fed them, bred them, were entertained by them. They have been a fixture of London's streets since at least the second half of the fourteenth century, when avians of utility escaped their rural dovecots to set up home in the city.

From a bird's-eye perspective, the city presented fabulous sleeping and sustenance options, and none more so than in modern times, when Victorian civic architecture (think Gothic crevassed museums and perchable railway station roofs) and twentieth-century brutalist town planning (tower blocks and concrete-poured underpasses) offered a veritable pigeon utopia. Feral birds took readily to tall, cliff-like structures for roosting sites and foraged eagerly in open squares to become 'naturalised urban citizens', as author Colin Jerolmack calls them. Sure, there were pitfalls – foxes, automobiles and, especially, the gamut of rubbish that regularly snared Jurassic legs (the Fishy Evans's pigeon, I recall, had a particularly gruesome foot injury, which added to the horror of the pie incident) – but, in the main, the city presented a pretty cushy pad.

The 'pigeon problem' that emerged in the second half of the twentieth century boiled down to two things. Firstly, the success of these birds at colonising urban space: London counts a population in the region of 3 million. And, secondly, critiques of the inner city as a site of post-industrial decay, criminality and pollution. A poster animal for this derelict urban jungle, the pigeon seemed to embody all that had gone wrong with the dream of metropolitan modernity. One of the leading drivers was public health, as feral birds (and especially their poo) were blamed for dirtying up the city (an adult pigeon in one year produces 25 pounds of faeces) and operating as active agents of zoonotic disease transmission. Yes, they are carriers of various nasties (including cryptococcal meningitis, encephalitis, toxoplasmosis and Lyme disease) and most of us at least once have been defecated on from on high, but evidence of disease transfer from pigeon to human is actually very rare.

Trafalgar Square emerged as a particularly contentious site in this gathering storm of pigeon pariahdom. One of the capital's iconic landmarks, tourists had come here for decades to feed the flock (up to 5,000 strong) 'tuppence a bag' from the traders who made a living from selling bird seed (see Fig. 15). To be milled around by hundreds of hungry, bobbing birds was amusing, entertaining, part of the romance and life experience of this very public space. Like Nelson's Column and the stone lions, pigeons were fixtures of the place. The *Daily Mirror* peered at them through the gloom in December 1952, when the Great London Smog meant 'even the pigeon was grounded and had to WALK home'.

Then things changed. As the new millennium approached, city authorities inaugurated plans to remodel Trafalgar Square into a refreshed cultural space marked by cosmopolitan café culture rather than what they described as a glorified traffic interchange marked by disease-carrying pigeons and their unsightly, corrosive poo. Ken Livingstone, who

15. Families feeding the birds in Trafalgar Square, London, in the 1920s. This famous site has a long history of association with feral pigeons, although in recent years they have been rebadged as public nuisances by city authorities.

became Mayor of London in 2000, emerged as a leading advocate of the redevelopment and, that year, signs were duly placed on site warning passers-by not to feed the birds which 'cause nuisance and damage the square'. Bernie Rayner, a seed seller whose family had worked here since 1956, had his licence revoked. Loud alarms and vacuum equipment were installed to shoo away the birds and anyone tempted to feed them faced a £50 fine.

Others, though, had different ideas. A crop of defenders swooped in to argue the pigeon's right to the city, including the Pigeon Alliance, the Save the Trafalgar Square Pigeons and the Pigeon Action Group. Legal redress was sought by PETA on the grounds of cruelty. Without feeding, they argued, this effectively dependent species would starve. Guerrilla feeders used the cover of darkness and a legal loophole which meant seed could still be placed on the steps of the National Gallery (technically in the City of Westminster) to deliver food parcels.

To no avail. Compensation was paid to Rayner, a phased withdrawal scheme put in place and the Greater London Authority and Westminster Council successfully imposed feeding bans in 2007. New cafés were established, traffic routes adjusted and would-be pigeon trespassers ran the gauntlet of Avian Solutions, a company run by Dave Bishop, who flew a Harris's hawk in the square as a form of aversive therapy. This service cost in the region of £250,000 a year (or £86 per bird) and, while it stopped pigeon presence at the time of the hawk's flights, the flock learned the schedule and simply showed up before and after (though in fewer numbers).

One might say the feral pigeon today has a homing problem. What happened in Trafalgar Square is reprised across many British cities and towns. There is seemingly no place for this bird in a sanitised modern metropolis where nature has to be organised and neat. Neither has it much of a space in visions of a rewilded urban jungle. In George Monbiot's *Feral*, the pigeon does not appear once. Floriferous verges and hedgehog highways we gladly embrace, but a shower of poo seems just *too* disorderly. Could we reimagine civic space to give this bird a place to land? The Pigeon Control Advisory Service, based in Hampshire, has pioneered a pilot scheme that helps local councils establish new lofts and feeding stations away from town-centre tension points. New tales of the twenty-first-century city, meanwhile, plot out ways in which we might revel in this animal's quirky charms. For Damon Albarn, lead singer of Britpop band Blur, pigeons were the prize carriers of the vignettes of *Parklife*; for Esther Woolfson, author of *Field Notes from a Hidden City* (2013), a comforting slice of the 'wild ordinary'. If we think in less rigid terms about the wild and the tame, the pristine and the polluted, perhaps pigeons and people can find some common ground. For author Barbara Allen, they are the avian emblems of our 'denial and dreams'; for wildlife writer Steve Harris, resilient and adaptable 'urban heroes'. Successful, yes. Messy, sure. But no more than we are. It may be, even, that the feral pigeon is about to find itself a new niche, rising phoenix-like to the rooftops to reinterpret its traditional role as winged messenger. In an article in the *Journal of Urban Ecology* (2018), social scientists from the University of Montana champion it as a 'gateway species', able to spark human–nature connections in the built environment, and an 'urban keystone species' through which the ecological health of our cities can be tracked. Easy to capture, monitor and compare, these ubiquitous animals might just serve as the 'canaries in the mine' when it comes to ascertaining the impact of climate change, pollution and zoonotic disease on the cities of the future – places that we, as a species, and in increasing numbers, call home.

Take a closer look at that 'winged rat' when you next see one. Listen with fresh ears to its coo-coo. Delight at its dinosaur feet. Maybe, even, greet it with a smile when it swoops down to steal a chip.

From Stream to Sea

CHAPTER 5

Newt

Terrestrial animals ourselves, we are more likely to notice beasts on land. We are also programmed, instinctively, to find affinity with fellow mammals. Creatures of the air and (especially) the aquatic reaches of stream and sea often escape our attention. Newts are interesting customers in this regard – amphibious beasts who mostly slither beneath our radar. When they do appear, however, they seem to create something of a frenzy.

The newt has something of a dual identity in British life. In the first, it animates recollections of bygone times: of long, lazy summers and streamside safaris. 'Nature Notes' in the Cheltenham *Chronicle* (May 1914) paints the scene admirably, an 'opening pageant of summer' in a meadow idyll of daisies, orchids and milkwort, with a pond buzzed over by caddis and dragonflies. Below the surface, the great crested newt, 'gorgeously arrayed in orange and black waistcoat, and splendid in crest and tail, goes about his courting business'. This wriggling panorama of aquatic life was not only confined to the countryside. Plenty of Britons – myself included – found aquatic wonder in the scrubby commons and remnant pools of the urban edgelands. Whether concrete culvert or chalk stream, we waded in: filling our wellingtons with sticklebacks and grasping curious, alien bodies in our hands.

Youthful expeditions often had ideas of capture in mind – armed with a jam jar and a dogged determination to collect a tiny dragon and rehome it in the great indoors. In *Cold Blood* (2014), Richard Kerridge describes a powerful connection with the amphibian world that allowed him to bridge the gap between consuming nature on TV – exotic African megafauna – and getting up close with the small and charismatic critters of the British locality. On one childhood holiday to Dartmoor, he bagged two newts from a bog, transported them home to London and installed them in a snazzy new 'underwater zoo'. Grand plans for nature study, however, went out of the window when the animals escaped from the tank overnight to disappear without trace. Sometime later, they were found shrivelled up on the floor behind the curtains.

Before legislation on the keeping of exotic and endangered species was passed in the 1970s and early 1980s, there must have been thousands of bedroom simulations of the local (and not so local) life aquatic. In 'Bobby Keeps a Backdoor Zoo', a piece in the Dundee *Courier* (1949), one young naturalist presided over a menagerie that included a pair of great crested and palmate newts, lizards, frogs, snails, slow worms, minnows, tadpoles, eel, four goldfish and a bronze carp, alongside the more typical fare of rabbits, guinea pigs and hamsters. 'With such a hobby,' the paper noted, 'Bobby has little spare time.'

Ken Livingstone, antagonist of Trafalgar Square pigeons, was another high-profile amphibian-o-phile, an obsession which started in the late 1950s when he captured a smooth newt on Streatham Common, South London, during an afternoon skiving off school. He took it home in a jar, introduced it to its new fish tank home and, armed with a new natural history guidebook, eagerly fed it a live worm supper. As Livingstone related, over the next few years, his bedroom menagerie grew to include snakes, salamanders, lizards, even an alligator, becoming a 'sub-tropical environment, with rich smells wafting through the house'.

Set against these bucolic (and often pungent) visions of childhood fancy is a very different newt. Here, it swaggers forth as cold-blooded ecoterrorist, only a few inches long but a devastator of development projects and arch-enemy of the housing tycoon.

Empowered by a protective armour of UK and European legislation enacted in the late 1970s and 1980s, these titans of the freshwater were said to block bypasses and housing estates with abandon, prompting accusations of conservation regulations gone mad, the bullying spectre of big government (from Westminster or Brussels) and the desecration of the rights of the two-leggeds to climb the property ladder. 'Newts hold us hostage in caravan', 'Newts block hospital', 'Newts obstruct badly needed housing', 'Mum can't fill in her pond to protect her children', 'No newts is good newts' – these are just a few of the sensationalist headlines that featured in the British press over the years.

In 2020 Prime Minister Boris Johnson railed at the 'newt-counting delays' which (he said) were a 'massive drag on prosperity' and negatively impacted Tory plans for a major UK-wide house-building bonanza. His comments spurred widespread criticism from various conservation groups, including the Wildlife Trusts and the RSPB, who labelled his remarks as unhelpful, inaccurate and 'sinister' examples of an anti-amphibian rhetoric routinely hurled about in anti-environmental and pro-development circles. Fast-forward two years and the spat between Johnson and the Great Crested was back in the news, this time with a 'Revenge of the Newts' B-movie strapline, when Johnson's plans for an outdoor swimming pool at his home in rural Oxfordshire were (temporarily) sabotaged by this small amphibian.

Framed by these two imprints – the delightful and the devilish – the tale of newts on these isles takes in legends and legislation, natural history and nostalgia, a world of deep ponds and deep pasts, hellfire and fertiliser, regenerating limbs and rewilding. Discussing one of the many newt-vs-developer stand-offs in recent years, the *Sunday Express* wondered just how it was these creatures ended up as 'protected pond life'. This seems like a useful platform from which to dive into the story of one of Beastly Britain's most spellbinding species.

Of Genealogy and Geography

The newt's genealogical trace on these isles is a still unfolding story. As recently as summer 2022, fossilised remains found on the Isle of Skye and dating to 166 million years ago signalled the ancient presence of a stem species which shares attributes with modern newts. This new variant of the *Marmorerpeton* genus, christened *wakei* (after leading herpetologist David Wake), was different to its descendants in that it sported a head more froglike in shape and had bony spurs on its forehead rather like a crocodile. At 20 centimetres long, with powerful rear limbs and a wide-set jaw, it packed a powerful predatory punch not dissimilar to today's hellbenders of the eastern United States, giant stream-dwelling salamanders. An incredibly important find, the Scottish denizen of the mid-Jurassic was the oldest of its kind in Europe.

Newts are members of the order *Salamandridae*, which includes more than 740 species, such as hellbenders, conger eels and axolotls, all of which have tails by the time they reach maturity and four legs (except the eel-like sirens, which have two forearms and are native to North America).

Some are land-based – tiger and fire salamanders, found in Europe – and a few are entirely aquatic, the largest of the species, at 1.8 metres long, being the Chinese giant salamander, for instance. Newts, of which there are more than 100 species globally, fall into the semi-aquatic category and are thought to have colonised these shores at the end of the last Ice Age, some 10,000 years ago, when they wandered across the Doggerland to East Anglia and took advantage of the warming climate and presence of fish-free ponds to make a new home.

Their name derives from the Old English word *efte* or *ewte*, meaning small lizard-like animal, and the 'n' was added by the time Middle English came along. They are the only British amphibians with a tail and possess a number of remarkable attributes, including the ability to breathe with gills (as larvae), with lungs (as adults on land) and through their skins (as adults in the water). They can also regenerate parts of their bodies, including limbs, tail, spinal cord, jaws and even some parts of the eye, intestines and heart. A cold-blooded species, newts claim an ectothermic benefit in that they don't need to expend lots of energy fuelling their internal heating system. Unlike mammals, they don't have to use a lot of energy raising young or keeping eggs warm. They never need to drink water, either.

We have three different types in Britain. The smooth newt, *Lissotriton vulgaris*, is the species most of us have probably seen. They are common to lowland areas across England, Wales, Northern Ireland and mainland Scotland, though they are absent from the Isle of Man and the Scottish Islands. Brown in colour, with spotty stomachs and black markings on the throat, they grow up to 10 centimetres long. In the breeding season, males develop a wavy crest along their backs, which stretches all the way along to the end of the tail and is absorbed back into the skin for the rest of the year. John Morton, in *The Natural History of Northamptonshire* (1712), described them as 'not uncommon in Pools and

16. An undated illustration, probably nineteenth-century in origin, entitled 'The Waves – Their Inmates', which features two newts, aquatic plants and sea anemones.

Ditches' and noted they could be found 'under old Logs of Wood, and in the Clefts at the Bottoms of Stone Walls'.

The palmate newt, *Lissotriton helveticus*, appears rather similar, with smooth skin but without spots on its throat. It is named after its webbed feet – which develop during the breeding season on males – and is a little smaller than *vulgaris* (6–10 centimetres long), brown in colour and sports a smaller crest. It shares the same habitat but prefers acid-rich soil such as that found on heath and moorland.

Last but not least is the largest and most famous of Britain's native newts, the great crested, *Triturus cristatus*, identified by Morton as the 'greater verrucose or warty water-newt'. Much less common, this species has a similar range to the other natives, but today is mostly confined to lowland regions of England, especially Cheshire, Lancashire, Norfolk, Suffolk, Kent, Sussex, Surrey, Hereford and Worcestershire, in areas of woodland and grassland where there are remnant pond habitats. Population numbers are hard to estimate, but herpetologist Robert Jehle, writing in *The Crested Newt: A Dwindling Pond-Dweller* (2011), suggests the UK perhaps supports between 50,000 and 100,000 individuals.

Double the size of the other British varieties (growing to 18–20 centimetres long), great cresteds are black or brown, with bumpy skin (hence their colloquial label, the warty newt), orange stomachs and yellow or white spots on their flanks. As with the other varieties, the males produce an impressive crest for the breeding season, but – as their name suggests – this species has the most striking of the bunch, sporting a toothed comb along its back and another along the run of its tail.

A Year in the Life of the Newt

Newts have a surprising longevity, being able to live for up to twenty years. In the wild, however, their typical lifespan is more like seven or eight. This time is spent in two worlds, a life on land and a life submerged, making them perfect illustrations of an amphibian existence (which literally translates as 'living in two places'). This ability to move between terrestrial and underwater realms is remarkable – and perhaps explains why we find these species so fascinating – and is made possible by an adaptable biology which involves dramatic bodily changes across life stages and the yearly cycle.

Newts start their lives in the water as eggs, which have been attached carefully by their mothers to pond plants and wrapped neatly in leaves to stop them floating off as well as to protect the developing young from UV rays. Between fifteen and forty days later, the eggs hatch out to become aquatic larvae, 1-centimetre-long ungainly blobs with tails, heads, stubby forearms and prehensile balancers around their mouths that help attach them to vegetation. For the first few days they feed from a yolk sac, before adopting a sedentary feeding style that effectively sucks in plankton and other small insect larvae. At this stage of life, they have gills to breathe underwater. Around ten days after hatching, they start to move around more, sprout front legs (unlike frogs, which grow rear legs first) and become more active predators. Rear legs are grown next, the limbs grow stronger, gills disappear and eyelids emerge – all of which equip them for a metamorphosis in late summer when the juveniles emerge from their freshwater nurseries and journey above the waterline for the first time. For the next few years, these 'efts' remain landlubbers, until returning to their ponds to breed, aged between two and four years.

Both adults and juveniles spend autumn and early winter on the edges of the ponds, sheltering in grasses, stone piles, tree stumps and log piles, before emerging at dusk to feast on invertebrates such as slugs, snails, worms and even other newts. They are eaten by hedgehogs, badgers, herons and birds of prey and, as relatively slow-moving terrestrial animals, have limited defences against predators. When under attack, great crested perform an elaborate defensive display, arching their supple bodies in such a way that their noses touch their cloaca and show off the 'danger' of their orange bellies to would-be foes. This is not just bravado. Newts have a gland in their skin which produces a toxic secretion (tetrodotoxin) and is designed to dissuade an assailant from biting them. More than 100 different animals have this special ability – including toadfish, moon snails, blue-ringed octopus, newts and salamanders. The American rough-skinned newt packs a very toxic punch, with enough mucosal compound in its skin to kill 25,000 mice. European newts are among the least toxic varieties. Still, it is always a good idea to wash your hands after handling one and not to get the compound anywhere near broken skin, the eyes or the mouth. Eating one is *definitely* not advised – unless you are a puffer fish or a garter snake, the only animals resistant to tetrodotoxin.

As soon as the temperature falls below 5°C, newts start to get sluggish and seek out places to hibernate for the winter, typically in crevasses of cellars and sheds, the cracks of stone walls and under fallen logs. Juveniles are said to follow an olfactory trail laid by adults to these refuge spaces. Often, they bunk together in groups and, in the UK, most are normally in an extended slumber by mid-November.

Spring brings a new phase to the newt's life cycle, a wake-up call inspired by rising temperatures and an urge to breed. From March onwards, adults emerge from hibernation and make their way back to their ponds. Great crested juveniles (but not of the other species) also undertake the journey, even though they are not sexually mature enough to breed – perhaps, scientists think, to take advantage of the abundant aquatic life to be found in a submerged larder: water fleas, tadpoles, snails and shrimps. The migration typically takes place on warm rainy nights after midnight, when the temperature is high enough to charge their metabolism and the habitat wet enough to stop them drying out en route. Some of these journeys are veritable endurance events, with recorded instances of newts traversing up to a kilometre across several nights, but most tend to cover about 200–300 metres, with nightly yomps of 10–50 metres, or 4 miles an hour, terrain and tree cover permitting.

How do they know where to go? Newt navigation is a multifaceted skillset taking in sight, sound, astronomical landmarks and the Earth's magnetic field. They tend to walk/slither downhill, based on a sensible calculation that water flows in that direction, as well as listening to the sounds of other amphibians (croaking frogs and toads) and possibly even birds. Often the springtime migration is to the pond where they came from as juveniles though if other choice pools are also around newts will switch sites.

Writing in *Wonderland* (2018), Brett Westwood and Stephen Moss describe the breeding habits of the newt as a magical melodrama in which they morph into duelling 'tiny dragons'. By the time these animals descend into the pond, male crests are fully developed and colours strikingly defined. This most mesmerising of aquatic galas starts with males emerging from the deeper parts of the pond to congregate at dusk, engaging in competitive displays of dominance with one another. Several animals cluster together, but rarely engage in direct physical contact, arching their bodies, doing little handstands and wagging their tails in a manoeuvre known as the 'cat buckle stance'. The gap between groups is typically about 2 metres. This behaviour – known as lekking – is an unusual mating strategy but is common to a few, quite different, species, including black grouse, bustards, Atlantic cod and bats. Scientists articulate various reasons as to why this breeding method is favoured. The 'hotshot' hypothesis speculates that males congregate around their most impressive peer; others think these animals gather in kinship groups, or perhaps mingle together as a protection against predation or even to conserve energy.

A similar range of dance moves is used to attract females, who arrive at the lek to check out displaying males. Males instigate the 'cat buckle' when one approaches and, if she continues to be interested, follow up with an added handstand and lean in towards her. The male whips, fans and beats ('rocks') his tail fiercely to show bodily vigour and to release enticing pheromones into the water. The performance can take a long time and is limited mostly by individual energy reserves and oxygen levels in the pond. Female newts are notoriously hard to please and pay close attention to the moves of their would-be paramours, the potency of their wafted newt-cologne, the height of their crests and bodily attributes. In fact, mating only takes place after 10% of courtships.

In successful couplings, the male moves away slightly, inviting the female to do the same. She follows, before signalling her attraction with a quick nudge of the male's tail with her nose. At this point, the males often emit an air bubble from the mouth (known as 'guffing'), which does two things. Something of a masculine swagger, it shows the female he has plenty of puff left and so is an excellent genetic choice for a mate. It also reduces ballast, making it easier to stay on the bottom of the pond, a process necessary for their next stage of the mating ritual, the deposit of the spermatophore (a packet of sperm), which he leaves on the substrate for the female to collect and insert into her own reproductive tract. After mating – what Westwood and Moss call a 'sexually charged game of pass-the-parcel' – two or three weeks pass before the female is ready to lay her eggs, which are deposited individually (unlike the strings of frog spawn) and include between ten and forty at a time. Over the course of a breeding season, a female newt produces between 150 and 300 eggs, about six of which successfully make it to adulthood.

The Storied Salamander

Blessed with an ability to move between the firmaments of water and land, newts have enlivened our folklore with visions of metamorphosis and transformation. In *Cold Blood*, Kerridge plotted a personal journey through capture, captivation and comprehension to think about an amphibian way of encountering the world. 'What might it be like', he asked, 'to be cold blooded, to sleep through the winter, to shed your skin and taste wafting chemicals on your tongue?' Otherworldly forms, anatomically and metabolically very different to us, newts intrigue by their strangeness. Able to adapt to radically different spaces and with a life cycle founded on the ability to change shape and regenerate their bodies, they exude an alien and mystical quality. Yet they are also familiar: proverbial, tactile, humanesque, even. In Scotland, their colloquial name is man-creeper, an evocative term which derives from the way they move as well as their anthropomorphic limbs. It brings to mind a creation story told by the indigenous Chumash of California in which Lizard muscled in on Coyote's designs for the human body to leave its mark on the shape of the hand.

Biologist Kay Etheridge identifies reptiles and amphibians as the animals which boast the most powerful of all mythological associations. Snakes, lizards, wyverns, basilisks, they move between the portals of nature and supernature and have been historically linked to all manner of miraculous forces, sometimes benevolent, often less so. Salamanders hold a long-standing association with fire, something which probably related to the fact that they hibernate in logs, hidden from view, and were often only seen during an outbreak of wildfire, whereupon they scuttled away to safety.

From this observation were conjured ideas of their ability to create and extinguish incendiary matter. Saint Augustine in *The City of God* (c.410) looked to them to validate his theory of an eternal Purgatory. If salamanders could walk in fire without being extinguished, so too could sinful humans. The *Liber Monstrorum* (c.650–750) took a similar line, labelling the salamander as a fearsome beast which frolicked in the flames. Several centuries later, Leonardo da Vinci described the species as having 'no digestive organs', instead gaining its sustenance from fire, which 'constantly renews its scaly skin'.

An association with conflagration left the salamander with a particular cultural imprint. Asbestos was commonly known as 'salamander wool' due to its heat-tolerating quality, while a cast-iron 'salamander' (basically a frying plate balanced on two legs, with a long handle) was the name given to a popular eighteenth-century kitchen device. The 'head' was heated in a fire until it was red-hot, pulled out by the 'tail' and then held over food to toast or brown it (especially Welsh rarebit). Equally, these animals appeared on heraldic crests as symbols of burning bravery, for instance the Douglas clan coat of arms, as well as on the livery of firefighting companies, blacksmiths and insurers: outfits seeking to illuminate their command over the world of combustion via a canny animal endorsement. Dudley, West Midlands, a place famed for its metalworking trades, pictured the animal on a bed of flames as part of the metropolitan coat of arms (along with two lions) to channel similar qualities. Today, a giant metal salamander greets visitors to the town centre from its lair on the Flood Island roundabout.

Alongside its fiery connections, the salamander also had a venomous one. Pliny the Elder in his *Natural History* approached the species with a dose of brimstone and poisonous portent: 'It is so chilly that it puts out fire by its contact, in the same way as ice does. It vomits from its mouth a milky slaver, one touch of which on any part of the human body causes all the hair to drop off.' Similar themes infused the early British folkloric record courtesy of the Aberdeen Bestiary (c.1200), which depicted salamanders surviving in fire and poisoning water with their toxic secretions (see Fig. 17). An eye-catching image showed this in action: a tree writhing with salamanders (which looked more like snakes) and a man lying dead underneath. On one side, a single animal slithered from a well and, on the other, a group cavorted happily in a burning conflagration.

For medieval and early modern scholars of animal life, fantasy and field observation were perfectly companionable bedfellows. As Etheridge notes, bestiaries were typically used as the origin texts for later studies, the result being that all kinds of weird and wonderful animal traits translated down the centuries without question. And when Renaissance

17. A striking image from the medieval illuminated manuscript, the Aberdeen Bestiary (c.1200), in which salamanders (which here look rather more like snakes) poison a well with their toxic secretions, writhe in the canopy of a tree, under which a man lies dead, and emerge unscathed from a fire.

proclivities favoured a look at the non-human world as it appeared 'in life', reptiles and amphibians were often the last to be reappraised. As such, the cultural salamander remained a mash-up of the mythological and the material even into the nineteenth century.

Conrad Gessner's *Historiae Animalium* (1551–58) was a groundbreaking, delightful sixteenth-century encyclopaedia that pioneered a zoological presentation of animal habits and gave particular airtime to the amphibians. When it came to the salamander, Gessner offered two versions of the animal for his enthralled audience (see Fig. 18). A detailed naturalistic drawing of a small amphibian sat alongside a bedazzling image of the fabular animal, a furry lizard with a human head and birdlike talons. Widely read and hugely influential, *Historiae Animalium* (along with its abbreviated version, *Icones Animalium* [1560]) tried to draw a line of beastly genealogy between the animals of ancient times and the present, inviting readers to explore the difference between classical and contemporary presentations. It built on the natural histories of Pliny and Aristotle, while leaning towards a new way of looking at the non-human.

A mash-up of the mythological and the material was equally to be found in Edward Topsell's *Historie of Serpents* (1608), one of the first natural histories to be published in English, which drew heavily on Gessner for inspiration. Here, countryside critters rubbed shoulders with dragons and a manticore (which had a man's head and lion's body). The salamander was described as 'audacious and bold', able to stand on its hind legs and in possession of a deadly venomous bite. Born from the fire, it was able, Topsell said, to live in an inferno without being consumed. Drawing together a collection of folk knowledge from various quarters, he quoted a French ditty which translated (somewhat clunkily) as 'if a salamander bite you, then betake you to the coffin' and traded in the popular idea that salamanders could contaminate apple trees simply by creeping upon them.

18. The two salamanders (bottom two beasts) from Conrad Gessner's *Icones Animalium* (1560). The first shows the biological animal, 'drawn from life', and the second depicts the mythical hairy amphibian of legend and lore.

Swine, he noted, were immune to the 'septick power', but not so dogs or humans. The animals were also known to leap onto cows' udders to suck milk from their teats. The fabled dairy-scrumping hedgehog, it seemed, had competition.

Significantly, Topsell's study directly engaged with the newt, which he presented as a sort of parochial mini-monster. It had, he said, the ability to poison like a viper courtesy of a 'white mattery liquid' and could breathe air like a frog. It typically lived 'in standing waters or pools, as in ditches of Towns and Hedges' and was said to breed in water and in soil though it preferred 'white muddy waters'.

Described as black or sometimes a dull earthy colour, with a white belly and spots on the sides, this sounded most like the great crested variety. When captured, he asserted, the animal always shut its mouth tightly, but rarely was aggressive enough to bite. If provoked to anger, however, this little beast stood on hind legs like a salamander and 'looketh directly in the face of him that stirred it', and secreted a white substance from its skin in order to 'harm (if it were possible) the person that did provoke it'. Some of these observations stand up to biological scrutiny, though with a few caveats. Topsell thought this 'water-creeping creature' to be entirely aquatic.

The poisonous qualities of the *Salamandridae* did confer on them a value in certain circles. Medieval and early modern tales alleged that witches collected the venom to make demon-summoning concoctions, while apothecaries advised the sick to put a newt under their bed and to use it as a cure for burns. Celtic tales told how the man-keeper or *ollp-lúchar* might be usefully applied to burned skin, while Topsell reported how salamander secretions could be used to treat corns or remove hair, though he firmly rejected the idea they were able to stop a woman's periods by being strapped to her thigh. Perhaps the most famous manifestation of amphibian medicine was to be found in Shakespeare's *Macbeth*, where the three witches famously cooked up a cauldron brew containing eye of newt, toe of frog, wool of bat and tongue of dog. In this case, the list of animal ingredients was a red herring, all of these being informal names for herbs, specifically mustard seed, buttercup, holly leaves and hound's tongue.

Mostly, however, salamanders (and newts) came in for a bad rap. In Europe, communities were rewarded with gold for killing them, while Irish folklore told how newts were said to crawl into the open mouths of sleeping humans and live as symbionts until the host died. Edmund Spenser, writing in *The Faerie Queene* (1590), railed against the 'marshes and myrie bogs, In which the fearfull ewftes do build their bowres'. These so-called 'devil's beasts' were routinely persecuted and, in fact, the tall tales that swirled around them continued to hold currency through the nineteenth century. Reverend J.G. Wood's *Common Objects of the Country* (1858), which sold 100,000 copies in its first week of publication, for example, accused them of being a danger to cattle and children, including one instance, he said, when a newt shot fire from its mouth and wounded a young girl, whose arm swelled to such an extent 'the doctor was obliged to cut it off'.

A brief scamper through the twentieth century finds a few newts hiding under storied stones. Owen Johnson's 1914 novel *The Salamander* used the name of the ancient fire-conjurer to describe the modern flapper, 'a girl of the present day in revolt – adventurous, eager, and unafraid', while Karel Čapek's surrealist science fiction novel *War with the Newts* (1936) told of the discovery of a community of 3-foot-high amphibians living off an island in the Pacific, their enslavement by a shady elite called the Salamander Syndicate, and eventual rebellion against humanity in a world of rising sea levels. Revolutionary ferment was not immediately evident in P.G. Wodehouse's Jeeves and Wooster series, where Bertie's long-standing associate, Gussie Fink-Nottle, was characterised as a man with a 'strong newt complex'. In *Right Ho, Jeeves* (1934), Bertie described the object of his friend's obsession as 'those little sort of lizard things that charge about in ponds'. Jeeves, naturally, was able to recite their full taxonomical profile off pat. Much of the novel revolved around Gussie's floundering about in the world of society dating. If only life was as simple as in the pond. For the male newt, he noted, things were very straightforward: use bright colours to show off, stand in front of the female, vibrate your tail and bend your body wildly. 'I could do that on my head,' Gussie lamented. 'No, you wouldn't find me grousing if I were a male newt.'

Surprisingly, the animal's famed association with inebriation ('to be pissed as a . . .') only made its way into the *Oxford English Dictionary* in 1957. The phrase was probably in usage earlier, possibly originating from the nineteenth-century recruits – known as 'newts' – to the Royal Navy who couldn't hold their rum. Elsewhere, the animal kept pace with the usual magical allusions. In *Monty Python and the Holy Grail*, one of the peasant mob claimed he was turned into a newt by a witch's spell ('I got better,' he tells Sir Bedevere); *Harry Potter*'s Newt Scamander was known as a wizard and wrangler of fantastic beasts; and one appeared in Roald Dahl's *Matilda* as a prank device to scare Miss Trunchbull (who thought the animal was a crocodile).

Protected Pond Life

The real-life newts of Beastly Britain acquired a powerful defender in the shape of a raft of UK and EU legislation. Central to this was the Wildlife and Countryside Act (1981), which provided protection to native species, enhanced regulations concerning the release of non-natives into the wild, extended provisions for habitat preservation and codified rights of way. Designed to update earlier acts on the protection of wild birds (1902, 1954), wild animals (1975) and national parks (1949), it also satisfied the terms of the Convention on the Conservation of European Wildlife and Natural Habitats, also known as the Bern Convention (1979), a binding European Community directive on the conservation of wildlife and habitats that required member states to engage in the protection of vulnerable species.

Under the terms of the Wildlife and Countryside Act, it became illegal to kill, injure, capture or trade great crested newts or to disturb their sheltering or pond sites (smooth and palmate newts were also protected from collection and sale). One of twenty-eight endangered native species identified in the original legislation (including mammals, reptiles, fish and invertebrates – more have been added since), this Act made the great crested one of the most highly protected animals in the UK. It also provided guidance for the protection of Sites of Special Scientific Interest, areas which had been created as part of national parks legislation in the 1940s but had mostly operated on the idea that landowners would practise 'inherent stewardship'. The new legislation – though criticised by conservationists as not being strident enough – focused well-needed attention on the troubled fortunes of many of Britain's iconic species.

Further assistance came in the early 1990s in the shape of European Directive 92/43/EEC, popularly known as the Habitats Directive, which required member countries to establish Special Areas of Conservation (SACs) for endangered animals. The great crested was listed as a species under threat in Annex II and so required a range of protective measures. Implemented in the UK as the Conservation (Natural Habitats, Etc.) Regulations (1994), the language of the 1981 Act was beefed up to include damage and destruction of breeding and resting sites and more specific guidelines were published as to how the SACs could be created and preserved.

What had happened to the great crested to require these interventions? Long-term and short-term changes to British farming practices, essentially. Many of the natural ponds used by newts in ancient times were long gone, lost to land drainage and new farming systems over several hundred years. Historically, they prospered particularly well in beaver habitat, and the extirpation of these from their range in the 1500s (killed as vermin, for their pelts, medicinal value and meat) removed critical newt breeding ponds. That said, it was still a good time to be a newt on these shores from a few hundred until about a hundred years ago, when they were able to utilise field ponds created to serve as cattle and sheep watering holes as well as the many marginal pools that filled up in sites associated with mineral extraction, quarrying and the like. Here, the great crested found good habitat – large ponds with an open aspect, minimal tree shade and the absence of fish stocks. What was interesting about these spaces is that they were, to all intents and purposes, the artificial by-products of agricultural and industrial activity.

In the twentieth century, however, and especially after the Second World War, things got pretty tricky – for amphibians particularly, due to their relatively sedentary habits. The rise of agribusiness, intensive arable farming and the mechanisation of production, the consolidation of marginal and messy areas, ponds and hedgerows into huge field systems, the use of piped water for livestock and concomitant neglect of pasture-side ponds, stubble burning and crop spraying: all these created a challenging environment for Britain's countryside critters.

Newts, a lowland species, required a terrestrial habitat of woodlands and scrubby grasslands, shady and damp migration routes and a network of suitable ponds. Things were particularly tough for the great crested due to their spatial requirements (50-square-metre ponds and good terrestrial connectivity of up to 500 metres). Added to their sensitivity to changing agricultural practices were the pressures of infectious diseases (ranaviral disease and chytridiomycosis), fish-stocking projects as well as human demographics, industrialisation and the expansion of commercial and residential developments that paved over freshwater pools, terrestrial habitat and travel corridors. Herpetologists estimated a decline in the country's ponds from 1.2 million in the late 1800s to fewer than 500,000 in 2007 and a 50% population decline of great cresteds from 1960 to 1975.

Given these statistics, the enactment of UK and EU protective legislation came at a vital time. It successfully halted (or, more typically, delayed) development projects and helped to preserve critical locations where great crested were found. Conservationists felt the fines were relatively meagre compared to the economic boons of development and many amphibian communities were lost because of a lack of understanding of the biodiversity record of threatened sites. On the positive side, legislation was refined in the noughties to improve the recording of potential and actual presence and to impose custodial sentences for offenders. As were more comprehensive strategies for habitat management.

Although sometimes risky (due to newts favouring historical sites), translocation and other mitigation measures have pioneered ways for agricultural and development schemes to prosper alongside newts. Populations have been moved to new ponds nearby (rather than long-distance relocations), travel corridors have been constructed with ditches, special fences and underpasses to allow for amphibian migrations, and sites are being closely monitored, with health, shade cover and fish predation in mind. One of these is Hampton Nature Reserve – also known as Orton Pit – near Peterborough, a 145-hectare Site of Special Scientific Interest managed by the charity Froglife, which occupies an old clay mine (including 300 pools laid out in long rows) that closed in the 1990s. The subject of an extensive habitat restoration project, 24,000 great crested adults and 9,000 smooth newts arrived here in the early 2000s as part of a scheme to mitigate the environmental impact of a housing development. Today, it provides a home for the largest concentration of newts in Britain, possibly Europe.

Hadspen House, Somerset, is another hotspot on Britain's herpetological map, a country estate dating from the late 1600s and restyled in Georgian times. During a rumoured £50 million development of the house and gardens in the 2010s, a population of great crested was discovered. The project was delayed – the *Daily Mail* exclaimed the amphibians 'almost sank' the garden – but owners Koos Bekker and Karen Roos not only made room for the residents but placed them at the centre of their landscape vision. Today, the remodelled estate boasts extensive ponds, home to 2,000 great crested, smooth and palmate varieties. In a wooded copse above the lake, a bouldered grotto provides a home lair for a huge ornamented wyvern, tucked between glittering rocks – a homage to the legendary trace of the salamander. In the formal gardens, an amphibian body cast in bronze emerges from a wall to spout water from its mouth into a pool below. These most evocative of British amphibians even give the place its name: The Newt in Somerset.

Building Back Newtopia: From Politics to Ponds

Britain's newts face a challenging time with habitat loss and anthropogenic climate change. Our three native species retain slippery footholds in England, Wales and Scotland, but as weather systems change, these lowland dwellers of undisturbed ponds and damp scrubland might well face the prospect of ever-diminishing room to roam. Great crested populations have continued to decline – to the tune of 40–60% – in the last twenty years. The landscape of species protection also looks rather uncertain, legislatively speaking. The National Planning Policy Framework (2012), enacted by the Conservatives and supported by the Home Builders Federation, set the stage for a house-building boom with the relaxing of planning regulations. Post-Brexit, the great crested retains its protective cloak and the Habitats Directive remains in force, but that could change. As the newt (and other species) get caught up in the 'culture wars' and conversations about 'taking back control', let's hope that the ethos of sharing space with nature finds safe ground in the future political landscape of Beastly Britain.

Actually, all of us can make a difference. Keep an eye on local development plans, plug into the chatter on UK wildlife and agricultural policy. And, build a pond! The bigger the better. A few metres by a few metres *might* be enough for a great crested or two and will certainly support smooth and palmate species. It needs to be at least 50 centimetres deep, with shelves to allow them (and others) to climb out. Don't add fish and place it in a sunny spot unshaded by trees, adding marginal and pond plants to the water. Make sure there is some rough vegetation around the edges, with a few stumps, logs or rocks around the perimeter. Once a year, in the autumn, clear the pond of weed, make a hole in the ice if it freezes in winter. Don't use slug pellets, leave some grass unmown and perhaps add a pile of leaves and twigs as a 'dead hedge'. Sit back and watch Beastly Britain do its thing. By next summer, you will be rewarded with an aquatic spectacular to rival the most exotic Attenborough documentary – tiny dragons twisting their trademark dance of love and war – right on your doorstep.

CHAPTER 6

Herring

The *Irish Penny Journal*, a popular nineteenth-century magazine, reflected on the fad for all things nature in an 1841 article on Britain's fish. Other branches of natural history, it pointed out, demanded labour, travel and risk, but ichthyology surely took the biscuit. Those who wanted to discern the secrets of the deep had to venture into a 'fatal realm' which could only be explored with breathing apparatus. Over the last century and a half or so, this aquatic frontier has been investigated by explorers, oceanographers and marine biologists. Think Jacques Cousteau, Sylvia Earle, Rachel Carson, Robert Ballard. Often, the greatest pull has been from the deep – the Mariana Trench, nearly 11,000 metres below the surface of the Pacific; distant and exotic realms – the Arctic, the Great Barrier Reef; and the shipwreck sites of lost and iconic vessels, from the *Titanic* to *Endurance*. There are lots of gaps, even today. Only 5% of the world's oceans have been explored and fewer than 10%

mapped by sonar technology. The four seas around these isles (English Channel, North Sea, Irish Sea and Atlantic Ocean) are no exception. These waters contain more than their fair share of spectacular seascapes and wonderful creatures, about which relatively little is still known. In this chapter, *Beastly Britain* dips its toe into our coastal waters to take a wild swim.

Of the 330 types of fish that reside around these shores (the largest of which is the basking shark), one of the most common is the herring. Described by the *Irish Penny Journal* as 'one of the most universally known, most generally useful' of our native fish, they swim through the history of Beastly Britain in their billions. For John Mitchell, author of *The Herring: Its Natural History and National Importance* (1864), these 'silver darlings' were the most important of all subjects of natural history because of their connection to maritime wealth and power. A closer look at the story of this marine animal offers a bounteous catch: nets filled with fortune, fascinating seafaring migrations, vibrant coastal cultures, gastronomic delights and a fair share of military wrangles. The herring may have fallen out of favour when it comes to our dinner tables, but it once had remarkable clout.

A Flatulent Natural History

The Atlantic herring (*Clupea harengus*) is part of the *Clupeidae* family, which also incorporates some 200-odd species, including sardines, shads and menhadens, as well as its closest relatives, the Pacific herring, which resides in the North Pacific, and the Araucanian herring, which is found off the coasts of Chile. All of these small fish share similar characteristics of silver bodies, a soft dorsal fin and protruding lower jaw. They live in large shoals or schools, a reflection of which can be seen in their collective noun, 'army'. The Atlantic herring is the most common variety of herring and also the largest. Adults grow to 38 centimetres in length and

19. A lithograph picturing a fishy feast of the deep: herring, whitebait, sprat, ling, sole and flounder.

up to 1 kilogram in weight. They are surprisingly long-lived, with a lifespan of twenty to twenty-two years. Their exact age can be discerned from the circulus marks in their scales which grow annually, rather like tree rings.

Historically abundant in the temperate waters of the North Atlantic, these pelagic dwellers feature gills and swim bladders typical to most bony fish species, and also have some distinctive biological features. Making up for their poor eyesight, herring have a well-developed sense of smell.

Two nostrils allow them to sniff out prey species through odour traces left in the water. They also possess a keen sense of hearing, furnished not in the conventional way of land dwellers by outer ears, but by air-filled tubes that connect to the otolith organ via the swim bladder. Evidence suggests they can hear whale and dolphin sounds.

Perhaps the most curious of all the herring's abilities, however, relates to its voiceless vocal capacity – something that was described in the yarns of fisherfolk but remained a biological mystery until relatively recently. Francis Day, writing in *The Fishes of Great Britain and Ireland* (1880–84), reported that 'the noise made by herrings when captured is peculiar, and has been likened to various things – to the cry of a mouse, to the word "cheese", a sneeze, or a squeak.' In *The Herring: Its Effect on the History of Britain* (1919), A.M. Samuel explained how 'this sound is caused by an escape of air from the air bladder, or a movement of the gills. Fishermen, indeed, frequently state that the herrings "sneeze".'

Diving deeper into this phenomenon, a team of Scottish-Canadian researchers in the early noughties began investigating the world of herring soundscapes, with delightfully effervescent results. Findings published in a 2003 paper by Ben Wilson, Lawrence Dill and Robert Batty described the noises made by herring shoals as Fast Repetitive Ticks, pulses or bursts of sound which the fish used to ward off predators and to communicate with each other. These so-called FRTs or 'farts' were, in fact, exactly that, 'high-pitched raspberries' produced by gaseous releases from the swim bladder that allowed them to 'speak' by blowing air bubbles out of their anuses. This activity was a social one and seemed particularly prevalent at night, when the herring moved from the sea bottom to congregate and feed in shallower waters. It was also used – the scientists surmised – to coordinate the movements of the shoal when sight range was limited. Initially, it was thought that only herring could hear their own FRTs, until scientists discovered that cetaceans did, too. Humpback whales, apparently, are particularly adept at using the high-frequency pulses to locate their lunch.

Farting herring even made themselves heard in the geopolitical circles of the Cold War. This story starts in Sweden, where, in the early 1980s, naval intelligence picked up a mysterious sound on sonar surveillance and assumed it to be that of a potentially hostile Soviet submarine moving clandestinely in Swedish waters. Hydrophone monitoring over successive years continued to show up incidences of this bizarre noise – a hissing which analysts likened to the typical sonic trace made by a submarine propeller. In 1994 Prime Minister Carl Bildt even wrote a stern letter to Boris Yeltsin complaining about the aggressive actions of his military forces – which the Russian premier denied all knowledge of. Two years later, Bildt brought in a scientific team led by Magnus Wahlberg and Håkan Westerberg to get to the bottom of a persistent deep-sea mystery which, by then, had outlasted the Cold War.

The team of biologists pored over military data, conducted interviews with Baltic trawlermen and set up a low-pressure fish tank to test their emerging hypothesis – that these sounds of Soviet incursion were actually 'bubble releases' from shoals of herring. Wahlberg and Westerberg published their findings on the 'pulsed chirps' in 2003 and were awarded an Ig Nobel Prize for Biology (2004), which they shared with the Scottish-Canadian team who had discovered the herring FRTs. It was a big year for flatulent fisheries science. Ultimately, Wahlberg said, this curious tale of fish breaking wind in the waters of the Atlantic delivered two important messages. Firstly, that 'a slight squeeze from the herring [showed] you can really change a country's foreign policy', and secondly, the public would do well to ignore politicians, especially those prone to incendiary rhetoric. If anyone wanted to fact-check the science at home, he added, they need only purchase a herring from a local market, submerge it in a bowl, put their ear underwater and squeeze the fish to hear 'this beautiful concert' for themselves. *Beastly Britain* does not officially recommend this.

Movements and Migrations: From Shoals to Spawning

Marked by a striking iridescence, Atlantic herring have a blue-green metallic sheen to the back of their bodies, with silver scales at the sides and white bellies. This coloration provides a double camouflage in that their darkling profiles are hard to see from above (think airborne seabirds) and their underbellies tricky to distinguish from the background sky when looked at from below (think cetaceans and larger fish). Their light-reflecting 'shimmer' actually defies the laws of physics in using two different types of guanine crystals, meaning that sunlight bounces off the fish from all angles and loses nothing to polarisation. This reflectivity trick, which is also used by sprat and sardines, makes them harder to see by the likes of cod, seabirds, dolphins, whales, tuna, salmon, swordfish and halibut, all of which enjoy a herring snack. A further survival advantage comes from a fine turn of speed, which allows the fish to propel itself swiftly through the water – up to ten times its body length per second – courtesy of slimline aerodynamic contours, seven well-placed fins (including a forked tailfin anchored to the ribs by tiny bones and muscles) and a proven technique that involves flicking the tail from side to side.

Arguably, however, it is when the herring move as a shoal – their typical pattern – that their most mesmerising optics are revealed. Twisting through the water in vast groups up to 1 cubic mile in size, this 'body' of several billion fish creates the impression of a shape-shifting marine murmur. The moving army of translucent scales, stolen tails and glassy glances is amazing to behold. This performance of the light fantastic is also pretty useful for confounding would-be predators – perhaps one of the reasons the herring has become one of the most abundant marine species in the world. Though not entirely foolproof. Various species have developed complex strategies to earn their fish suppers. Swordfish swim into the 'bait-ball' and slash the shoal with their serrated noses, gannets dive-bomb at speeds of up to 50 miles an hour (their skulls protected from impact damage by a cranial air sac) and humpback whales perform elaborate 'carousel attacks' which start with blowing air bubbles to herd the shoal into an ever tighter bundle and culminate in a lunge attack from deep beneath, where members of the pod explode skywards and gobble up thousands of fish at a time.

The shoal also functions as an effective hunting unit. Typically feeding at night, herring seek out small crustaceans, krill, fish larvae and zooplankton – hoovering up smaller species by an open-mouthed filter-feeding system or grabbing larger delicacies with their jaws and using sharp inward-facing teeth to stop their prey escaping. Copepods, a kind of plankton, can present as tricky customers. These are not only tiny but can leap out of danger up to eighty times before becoming exhausted, using the large antenna on their heads to warn of approaching fish. The herring have this figured out, though, and swim in parallel lines to effectively block the plankton from plotting out escape paths. On calm moonlit nights when the herring are hunting, a combination of the phosphoric glow of their prey and the light bouncing off their reflective scales creates quite a light show.

One of the most intriguing parts about the natural history of the Atlantic herring relates to its movement, migration and mixing habits which, for many centuries, remained a source of mystery. It was assumed they wintered and raised young in the waters of the Arctic Circle before travelling south in a spring migration, but we now know their movements are – in the words of Donald S. Murray, author of *Herring Tales* (2015) – more akin to a life of 'constant travel'. As a metapopulation, the herring engage in giant circular perambulations, a sympatric symmetry of silvery movement in which different communities travel together before dispersing to discrete spawning sites. In British terms, this practice is carried out by two populations. The first of these is the North Sea fishery – the mainstay of the British catch – which contains the Buchan/Shetland shoal (which operates off the coast of north-east Scotland to south-western Norway), the Dogger Bank herring (which travel between Whitby on the English east coast across Dogger Bank to Jutland) and the Downs/Southern Bight population (which moves from the Dover–Dunkirk strait to the middle of the North Sea). On the other side of the country, the territory of the North-East Atlantic fishery includes the waters off Devon and Cornwall, around the coastline of Ireland (from Dunmore to Donegal) and western Scotland (off the Firth of Clyde and around the Western Isles). Subtle differences in the behaviour and morphology of these two metapopulations identify which group they hail from. A particularly curious community – the Blackwater shoal – do things entirely differently. Smaller than their North Sea brethren, they have one less vertebra on their backbone and buck the long-distance swimming trend to spawn every spring in the Thames Estuary and roam only as far as the North Kent coast.

Herring are one of the only species for which subpopulations spawn at different times of year, creating a successive wave of reproductive frenzy in the waters off Britain's coasts quite unlike any other. The cycle is based on a combination of seasonal and geographic variations and triggered by changes to the number of daylight hours and the occurrence of plankton blooms. The North Sea populations are autumn spawners, with the Buchan shoal kicking off in August–September, Dogger from August to October and Downs from November through to January. The Atlantic shoals are also autumn/winter spawners, while the Western Isles herring have shifted seasons back and forth over the course of the last century. Historically spring-spawners in inshore waters, this local population collapsed in the 1950s and, when it rebounded, switched to an offshore autumn spawning habit. Western Isles herring have been in decline since the 1970s, but recently (2018) biologists witnessed signs of a new spawning group, this time in historic inshore waters and in springtime.

Wherever the location, the process is the same. Sexually mature at about three–four years of age, spawning time sees the adult herring migrate to their specific patches, where the females approach the seabed to lay thousands of eggs, the older fish leaving the first layer and younger ones following on. Buchan females leave up to 67,000 and Downs 42,000. The males, whose genitals have grown to one-fifth of their body weight, then attend to the task of fertilising the deposited eggs with milt (sperm). The depth of the spawn is dependent on the local habitat: in Greenland local herring lay their eggs in 5 metres of water, whereas the North Sea population dives to the sea floor some 200 metres down.

Once fertilised, the clusters of eggs attach themselves, courtesy of a sticky mucus coating, to stones, sand, rocks, gravel or vegetation. This practice of creating an 'egg carpet' on the substrate is a reproductive tactic quite different from that used by most fish. Location is all-important. The eggs need to have enough oxygen from underwater currents, be in water no warmer than temperatures of 19°C and (ideally) be camouflaged from the attentions of haddock and other predators. Anthropogenic factors, toxins in the water, extreme weather systems and bottom-trawling have a huge impact on their pathology. The eggs – translucent, with two coal-black eyes – hatch two to three weeks after fertilisation to become larvae or fry, 5-millimetre-long translucent blobs with large eyes, equipped with a tasty yolk sac for sustenance. When the fry is about 15 millimetres long, it switches to munch on phytoplankton and copepods. At 17 millimetres long, they start to grow a dorsal fin, followed by other fins and a tail by the time they are 35 millimetres. Aged a year old, the fry measure 10 centimetres in length and, for the first time, look like little herring. Aged three, they move from inshore nursery populations to join the adult shoals further out to sea.

The Grand Fishery: Beastly Britain Through a Fish-eye Lens

Beastly Britain is an island irrevocably shaped by the herring fishery. As a staple source of food and a valuable commodity, this fish has been caught, traded and served at table for thousands of years, arguably perhaps from as early as 3000 BC. Around the coast, from Caithness to Caister-on-Sea, Stornoway to St Ives, communities engaged in a maritime dance with the 'silver darlings' that spanned the centuries. Writing in *Britain, or, a Chorographicall Description of the most flourishing Kingdomes, England, Scotland, and Ireland Brittania* (1610), William Camden went as far as to describe the residents of Tenet (Thanet), Kent, as *amphibii* because of their close relationship with the sea.

This effervescent fish swam into the lifeways and culture of coastal communities in elementary ways. On the Isle of Man, fisherfolk talked of an ancient time when the fish of the seas gathered to decide who would be in charge. Grey Horse the Shark, Dirty Peggy the Cuttle Fish and Athag the Haddock tried it out, to no avail, after which the committee of the deep looked to Brac Gorm, the Mackerel. When he arrived, however, all adorned in bright colours, the other fish thought him a fake and so crowned Skeddan, the Herring, as 'King of the Sea'. Another Manx tale told of the crafty witch-wren, an avian bird spirit who terrorised the shoals in ancient times and whose ritual hunting on St Stephen's Day furnished feathers for the herring boats to take to sea as lucky charms. Roman historian Solinus recorded in AD 240 that the residents of the Hebrides lived on herring and milk, while, in the Northern and Western Isles archaeological remains of ancient middens (kitchen food dumps) and Gaelic place names attest to the importance of the fish for Norse settlers, who left huge piles of herring bones dating to AD 1000 and gave a fish-flavoured identity to coastal inlets such as Geodha a' Sgadain ('herring cove') on the Isle of Lewis. Today, you can retrace the route of the Old Herring Path around the shores of Loch Hourn, a stony, engineered track built 125 years ago by Highlanders to transport fish catches to the village of Corran.

In England, the first formal mention of *Clupea harengus* in the historical record dates to AD 709, from the chronicle of the monastery of Evesham, where the fish appears as an item of revenue, later known as 'herring silver'. The epicentre for all things herring, though, has to be Great Yarmouth, whose association with the 'silver darlings' stretches back to the formation of the town. According to J.W. de Caux's *The Herring and the Herring Fishery* (1881), Roman soldiers stationed at Gariannonum ('the mouth of the Yare') acquired a taste for the fish from the locals and took it back to Italy as a 'dainty dish', while the landing here of Cedric the Saxon in AD 495 'gave fresh impetus' to the development of a fishery. Whether this was true – or whether, as others contend, a group of early medieval fishermen took to using the coastal spit as a useful haul-out spot – Yarmouth had a fish-fuelled identity by the mid-seventh century. *The History and Antiquities of Great Yarmouth* (1772), written by antiquarian Henry Swinden, notes that St Bennet's Church (built in AD 647) had a 'a godly man placed in it' by Bishop Felix of East Anglia 'to pray for the health and success of the fishermen that came to fish at Yarmouth in the herring season'.

Over the next few hundred years, the reputation of the Yarmouth fishery developed apace, with merchant vessels from Scandinavia, Holland, France and Italy journeying to the herring-rich waters off coastal Norfolk every autumn to cast their nets, provision their crews and sell their wares. By the time of the Domesday Book (1086), the town was recorded as housing 92.5 households, putting it among the largest 20% of settlements in England. A buoyant trade in fresh and dried herring (traded as 'red herring' – more on this later) shaped the growth of the town, from its tall 'fish-houses' incorporating space for residential use and business matters of salting, curing and storage to its extensive marketplace and town walls built on the back of *Clupean* commerce.

Prosperity cooked up enmities as well as foodly fortunes. The nearby fishing port of Lowestoft eyed up their wealthier neighbour with envious eyes in a provincial spat which went on for centuries. Equally protracted and decidedly more violent was the conflict that emerged with the Cinque Ports, the Kent–Sussex confederacy which attracted various Crown privileges (tax exemptions, legal allowances, fishing rights and shipwreck salvage) in return for naval services. Tensions flared over the 'den and strand' allowances of Portsmen who had set up a fishing camp at the mouth of the Yare and came to exert considerable power over the lucrative herring fair which ran from Michaelmas to Martinmas and had become a fixture of the Yarmouth calendar by the late twelfth century. In 1297 Kentish boats ambushed the East Anglian port, burned twenty-something ships and killed the fishermen on-board while, at the Battle of Sluys (1340), ships belonging to the rival factions set about fighting each other instead of the French. Edward III seemed content with Yarmouth's contribution, nonetheless. Despite the in-fighting, the forty-five boats from Norfolk (London, incidentally, sent twenty-five) discharged their duties admirably enough for the battle to be won. As a result, the King bequeathed the town a stunning coat of arms, on which were depicted three chimeric beasts sporting the head of a royal lion and the tail of a herring.

From the late medieval through to the early modern period, the 'Grand Fishery' (as the North Sea herring trade came to be known) exerted a profound effect on the geopolitical landscape of northern Europe, as governments, monarchs and commercial interests clamoured for control over this most valuable marine resource. Fortunes were made, alliances forged and wars waged on the back of the herring, the demand for which increased exponentially due to a combination of factors, including population growth, urbanisation and the radiating influence of the Roman Catholic Church, the latter particularly important for its prohibition of meat eating at Lent and other fasting days. Fish, an allowed protein for the faithful (if you could afford it), found itself highly prized.

Particularly important in this pelagic tussle were the Dutch. In 1295 Edward I affirmed the rights of boats from Holland to fish in British waters 'unmolested', and by the fifteenth century they had assumed a formidable command over the trade. During the 1600s – the zenith of Dutch power – it was said that up to one-fifth of the population was connected to the herring business. Amsterdam was founded on the bones of the 'silver darlings'. This primacy was based on various things: mercantile networks, the political (and military) power of an ascendant republic and a savvy system of fisheries regulation and management. Of particular importance was the development of large 'factory ships' (the *haringbuis*) and massive nets (*vleet*) as well as a novel technique of curing the catch that allowed for herring – an oily commodity that spoiled quickly – to be kept for longer. Reputedly pioneered by Willem Beukelszoon, a fifteenth-century Zeeland fisherman, this process (known as *kaaken*) saw the herring plunged into casks of salt and stirred vigorously for an hour, before being removed and gutted. The stomach, heart and gills were removed, but liver and pancreas left inside the fish to release flavoursome enzymes. Once prepared, the fish were packed tightly in barrels, each layer separated by a bed of salt, and left for a year to infuse.

The truly revolutionary twist from the Dutch was to take the pickling process on deck, meaning that large trawling outfits could marinade on the move. Accordingly, rigs from the Low Countries were able to track the vast shoals of North Sea herring all the way down the eastern coasts of Scotland and England, netting and processing their catches at sea and returning home several months later with holds stuffed full of pickled herring. The system had notable advantages – it satisfied burgeoning European demand for table fish (which Dutch inshore fishermen were struggling to keep up with), kept clear of pirates operating out of Dunkirk and avoided seaport closures which were an occupational hazard of trading in the English Channel during periods of Anglo-French hostility. Choreographing this mercantile migration, of course, were the seasonal circulations and life cycles of the shoals themselves: the fish were at their most fatty, and therefore most delicious, when they were sexually mature and about to spawn.

At its peak in the seventeenth century, up to 2,000 busses (as the Dutch boats were known) a year patrolled the waters of the British east coast, drawn by the shoals which were in such abundance the sea seemed to boil with them. Their presence exerted a significant impact on the places which served as operational stop-off points: the Shetlands and Buchan Ness from late June until mid-September; Great Yarmouth in the autumn, where the annual herring fair kicked off a two-month stint from 21 September with 'Dutch Sunday' and ritual blessings for a bounteous yield; and the East Kent coast from late November. The season ended every year on 31 January, at which point the *haringbuis* seamen went home to work in other jobs or fished for cod and sole on Dogger Bank. When Daniel Defoe visited Yarmouth in 1722, he described a town in the vibrant throes of the Grand Fishery, with prodigious catches of 'silver darlings', sailing boats stacked sideways like, well, sardines, and throngs of people on a quay he dubbed the finest in England.

The Scottish Ascendancy: High Times and the Herring Lassies

In 1751 the so-called 'herring poet' John Lockman published a treatise entitled *The Shetland Herring and the Peruvian Gold-Mine: A Fable*, in which he agitated for Britain to increase its *Clupean* catch and to prise command of the Grand Fishery from the Dutch. A hypothetical conversation between a fish and a subterranean hoard of precious metals, the 'calm Tenant of the Deep', urged thus: 'Wake BRITONS from their dangerous Sleep [and] swift to *Industry* awake.' A campaigning advocate for the value of herring, Lockman took to giving away salted fish with his poems to punters at Vauxhall Pleasure Gardens and was Secretary of the Society for the Free British Fishery, an organisation established in 1750 that lobbied to create a start-up fleet of British busses. The Society folded after twenty years due to poor administration, a series of bad fishing seasons and the actions of French privateers in the Channel, but change was nevertheless in the air. The 1800s augured a new turn in the herring story of Beastly Britain when the baton of commercial prowess indeed passed from the Netherlanders to a domestically grown fishery dominated by the Scottish. By the early twentieth century, the British commercial industry was landing close to 577,000 tonnes of the 'silver darlings' a year and employed 35,000 workers: the largest herring labour pool anywhere in the world.

This new era of *Clupean* commerce resulted from a range of factors, identified by environmental historian Bo Poulsen as 'interactions between a very dynamic natural system and a highly dynamic anthropogenic system'. Weighing into the equation was a raft of legislation which, since the early 1600s, had been introduced by a succession of British monarchs to counter the maritime power of the Dutch. Acting on the concerns of fishermen, political analysts and mercantile interests who were troubled by the size of a

Netherlands fleet that had grown from around 100 boats in the thirteenth and fourteenth centuries to somewhere in the region of 2,000, James I issued a Royal Proclamation in May 1609 that imposed fishing licences for all non-British craft operating in the seas of the kingdom.

The Proclamation generated a huge diplomatic row, including retaliatory measures against British cloth, and proved impossible to enforce, but it was a landmark moment in establishing a new age of regulation that was backed up by the persuasive powers of the Royal Navy. In the Battle of Buchan Ness (1652), sixty-six frigates commanded by Admiral Robert Blake faced off against 600 busses and their military escorts in a three-hour fight which resulted in heavy casualties and the sinking of Dutch boats. The argument smouldered on for a century and a half, at the root of which was a collision of two leviathans of marine legal code, namely the rights of national sovereignty over the deep blue and its resources (*Mare clausum*, as defined by British lawyer John Selden) versus the freedom of the seas (championed by Dutch counsel Hugo Grotius as *Mare liberum*). These angry jurisprudent beasts went on to raise their heads above the waves in many international fishing wrangles, from the Cod Wars with Iceland in the 1950s to post-Brexit fishing disputes over European Community rights to harvest aquatic resources.

On the domestic front, government bounties and the creation of the Fishery Board (1809) provided pecuniary incentive and advocacy for the developing industry, while the establishment of a new Crown Brand (which standardised barrel sizes and required a stamp on every cask, indicating when and by whom the herring had been cured as well as a signature from a government fisheries officer) lent the product an air of premium quality. Added to this was the cooking-up of a novel preserving method. The result of a public competition organised by the Arts Society of London in 1819, the top recipe was judged to be that of J.F. Donovan, a proficient pickler from Leith, who ditched the

Dutch salting technique and pioneered a new treatment which relied on the brining of fresh herring straight from the boats. This so-called 'Scotch cure' swiftly became the industry standard.

Expediting the process were technological innovations in the shape of railways, steam power and, especially, the development of fast, agile boats with half or full decks, equipped with large lugger sails, drift nets and, later, steam-driven capstans and able carry a sizeable cargo. Foremost among these was the Scottish herring drifter (colloquially known as the 'Zulu'), which was seen in great numbers in the ports of Alba at the turn of the twentieth century and was evocatively described by sailing writer Herbert Warington Smyth in *Mast and Sail in Europe and Asia* (1906) as a 'great brown pyramid'.

Where the Dutch had built North Sea dominance on a premium product captured from distant seas, the ebb and flow of herring–human geographies now favoured the new Scottish fishery. Piracy, warring European states and the proximity of the herring shoals themselves tipped the balance in favour of a rapid-reaction fleet grounded in a local, onshore processing industry. Added to what Poulsen calls this 'relative spatial advantage' was an alignment to global contemporary trends in consumption. Not only was there a waning demand for soused herring in the Low Countries (which affected the Dutch traders), eager Russian and German consumers were won over by cheaper pickled herring from Scotland and new markets for salted fish were emerging in the slave plantation economies of the Caribbean and the American South.

The herring boom transformed the fortunes of Lerwick, Banff, Wick and other Scottish coastal communities, described by Neil Gunn in *The Silver Darlings* (1941) – which chronicled a doomed romance set against the drama of the Highland Clearances – as 'a busy fabulous time'. Each summer, Wick harbour was crammed full of more than 1,000 boats (legend had it you could walk across without getting your feet wet) while the town's curing sheds, cooper's yards and whisky distilleries were alive with activity. It also transformed maritime subsistence economies in all places where the herring shoals swam nearby. Accordingly, a wave of commercial good fortune rippled around the British coast in fishing harbours from Berwick-upon-Tweed to Padstow, as local fleets expanded to capitalise on government bounties and a buoyant export market gobbled up 75% of the fishly hoard, some 2.5 million barrels a year.

Making a livelihood from the fruits of the sea brought euphoria and enervation, often in the same moment. As one fisherman put it, 'I have seldom seen anything which was quite so physically and coldly lovely . . . sheets and sheets of shimmering silver. My back was soon aching, my hands and arms torn and bruised with the net. But throughout the long hours which it took to haul in the net, I was never tired of watching the harvest.' Precarity – financial and meteorological – was never far away for the small boats heading out from safe harbour to waters that could be unpredictable as well as provident. On 18 August 1848 around 800 boats headed out from the Moray Firth for a day's herring fishing, only to be met by a sudden storm which blew up overnight; 124 boats were sunk, most of which were trying desperately to get back to land, and 100 lives were lost.

Where the Dutch trade had focused on a ship-based system of harvest and processing, the domestic industry adopted a choreography of catch, clean and cure that was equally agile but based on the movement of people over land rather than sea. As the Scottish industry expanded, a colourful labour migration followed the routes of the spawning herring and their chasing fishing fleets. Perhaps the most interesting group of migrant workers were the 'herring lassies', Scottish women who trailed to the Shetlands and mainland Scotland (Lerwick, Stronsay, Wick and such) as well as the Isle of Man and east-coast English ports (especially Yarmouth and Lowestoft) every season from the 1840s. At the peak of the industry just before the First

World War there were some 6,000 of them. Drawn largely from the Highlands and Islands, the 'girls' (who were often young and unmarried but always referred to as such despite their actual age) were hired by agents from curing companies, who toured Scottish settlements hawking the herringboon lifestyle and arranging terms of employment, transport and boarding. Specially commissioned trains were laid on to take the lassies to Yarmouth and Lowestoft, a fifteen-hour overnight journey that collected approximately 300 recruits at a time from various places en route and transported them to East Anglia for the start of the season.

The lassies worked for twelve hours a day, six days a week, starting at 6 a.m. with a tidy-up of the curing stations. After topping up existing barrels, they had a breakfast of porridge and awaited the crews who had fished overnight. Once the boats landed, the herring were taken on shore, tipped into containers, sprinkled with salt (which made them easier to handle), transported by cart or lorry to the curing yard and poured into long, shallow troughs or 'farlins'. Here was where the herring lassies took over. Three girls worked in each team, two labouring with dextrous velocity using sharp knives ('cutags') to gut the herring and throw them into creels according to size (maties full, maties, and maties small), while the third packed the cleaned fish into barrels, placing them carefully in a uniform pattern, bellies up, heads pointing outward, salting between each layer. Each barrel counted roughly 700 fish and an efficient gutter despatched up to sixty fish a minute. When the catch was bounteous, the working day delivered a maelstrom of moving fish that went from deck to basket, farlin to barrel in shoal-like symmetry. Over two days in the 1867 season, it was said that 3,500 herring lassies in Wick gutted 50 million fish.

The lassies cut a striking presence on the harbourside (see Fig. 20). Dressed in shirts with rolled-up sleeves, they wore shawls over their shoulders to protect from the weather and long skirts covered by oilskin aprons. Wellington boots protected their feet and the all-important 'cloots' (tightly bound bundles of rags) their fingers. When the catches were late, or non-existent, they wandered the quaysides singing songs, looking for fishermen from their home towns to chat to or knitting socks and jumpers, a hobby, they said, that kept the fingers in tip-top condition. The girls commonly boarded together in bed-and-breakfast accommodation, three to a room. The decor was sparse. Carpets and rugs were often taken up and walls covered with newspaper, the main reason being that the girls spent most of their day covered in fish guts, blood and scales and landlords were keen to stop their guest rooms from taking on a certain *je ne sais quoi*. Outside of their duties at the curing yard, the lassies enjoyed the 'bright lights' of the port and its entertainments come Saturday night. As Elizabeth Bain, a herring lassie from Nairn, quipped: 'O for Yarmouth bustle and hurry, Time for nothing but making money, But still it has its little joys, Hippodrome, theatre, Gem [game] and Boys.'

Travelling, working and playing together created a close community of women who were known for their hard graft, good spirits, lively banter and supportive camaraderie. The job was typically intergenerational, with mothers passing on the tradition to daughters. For many, it was a rite of passage, a ticket to new places and experiences, a way to make money and – amidst the fish guts and salt-stinging wounds – entry into a world of female comradeship, independence and confidence. Speaking of similar opportunities for female workers during the herring boom in Iceland in the early twentieth century, Anita Elefsen, director of the Siglufjörður Herring Era Museum, commented how female curers, *síldarstúlkur* in Icelandic, called this the time of 'herring adventure'. Mary MacDonald from Lewis, who worked in the Scottish industry during the 1930s, recalled how she 'saw a lot of the world. I went to Lerwick, Stronsay, Lochmaddy, Yarmouth, Lowestoft, Peterhead and Fraserburgh.'

A strong sense of collective identity in the migrant community of female fish gutters made them a formidable force

HERRING

20. The 'herring lassies' followed the fishing fleets (who followed the herring) in an annual migration down the east coast of Britain in the 1800s and early 1900s. Here, a group of fisherwomen from Pittenweem, Fife – in the midst of a knitting session – pose for their picture in Great Yarmouth (c.1900).

when it came to labour rights. Historically, they were paid by the barrel – piecework which encouraged a speedy turnaround of catches and serviced the rapid processing of a fish that spoiled quickly – which meant the lassies could earn more than the dockers (but not the fishermen) when the nets were full. However, a collapse in demand from Germany and Russia brough hard times for the herring fleets in the 1930s, with two-thirds of the lassies laid off and the rest on a pay freeze. Well aware of their vital importance to the herring trade, the Yarmouth lassies decided to down knives and strike for an improvement to their pay of 10d a barrel. A number didn't join, but a jocular visit from some of the younger militants (who brandished a seawater hose as well as stalwart arguments for the cause) convinced them to join the action.

Pathé News recorded on film the solidarity of the gutters with a grainy reel of placard-wielding strikers, captioned by their trademark shout: 'A shilling on the barrel we want, and a shilling on the barrel we'll have. And we'll not go back until we get it!' The curing companies hired mounted police from London to intimidate the strikers, who remained undeterred and pelted them with stones and old herring. After a week, their demands were met, they got the shilling and went back to work – a landmark victory won by female workers operating by collective action, and one which has largely remained untold in chronicles of the labour movement. As historian Sam Davis puts it, these strikes have remained largely 'hidden from history', because they do not fit easily into the dominant interpretations of the history of trade unions and industrial relations of the period.

History on the Table: From Red Herring to Bloaters

One amusing piece of cultural bait, which shows how this marine animal has swum powerfully through the subsistence and storytelling cultures of Beastly Britain, was a folk song. Known variously as 'The Herring Song', 'The Red Herring' and 'The Jolly Herring', the earliest version of this ditty dated to 1831 and was sung in hostelries all along the coastal fishing line. Depending on the version of the song, these fish were successively chopped up to become all manner of different things. Eyes became fine lamps, puddings and pies; fins, needles and pins; the head, fine bread. Gills became sails; the back, money in a sack or a lad called Jack; the belly, a girl named Nelly. The delightful tune paid heed to the financial boom time attached to this species and the usefully rhyming qualities of its body parts. Beyond an anatomical celebration of all things *Clupean*, folk singers said, it provided a great excuse for a drinking song. Some versions crafted the herring into an ever more outlandish beast which sported hair and legs. In a Northumbrian variant, 'Herrings Heid', it had become a monstrously huge catch some 40 feet long.

Such tales spoke to this animal's critical subsistence function and to its culinary adaptability. Across the dinner tables of northern Europe, herring provided a bounteous army of regional delicacies. The Dutch eat them raw and whole: grab the fish by the tail, hold aloft, open your mouth and lower it in. Add a smattering of gherkins or onions to complement the strongly flavoured flesh. The Baltic states favour the rollmop, a pickled herring wrapped around a pickled onion or gherkin, while the Swedish speciality of *surströmming* consists of lightly salted fermented herring (when the tin is first opened, the smell is not for the faint-hearted).

The British menu sports an equally diverse complement – a good number of which are pie-based – from the Manx minced herring pie filled with almond paste, fish roe, dates, gooseberries, rose water and saffron to the West Country 'stargazy' with its striking circle of heads sticking out from the undulating crust as if it were a choppy ocean. Many coastal communities ate them fresh, so-called 'green' herring, which probably related to the iridescence of their scales (which is particularly pronounced when just out of the water). In Scotland, fresh herring was often fried in oatmeal as a breakfast staple.

In the years before mass refrigeration, if herring was to be transported or kept for any length of time before eating, the trick was to soak or smoke it in something. This brings us to the famous 'red herring', a term used to describe a common medieval treatment in which a fish was dry-salted, washed and then smoked for several weeks. This smoking process created the distinctive coloration and preserved it for up to a year. *A Plain Cookery Book for the Working Classes* (1852), written by Charles Elmé Francatelli, Chief Cook to Queen Victoria, recommended that fish treated in this way were soaked in water for an hour before cooking to reduce their salt content. Drawing on the mercantile contours of an imperial export trade connecting London to the Caribbean, he heartily endorsed a Jamaican recipe which fried the fish in chilli, lemon juice, onions, tomato, garlic and thyme and served them up with yams and plantain.

'Red herring' was – and is still – hurled about as a humorous term to depict a ruse or a false start. The phrase was thought to have been first used in an 1807 article for the *Political Register* by radical agitator William Cobbett, who referenced the traditional use of the fish as a smelly bait to train foxhounds, then flipped it to create a metaphorical critique of the mainstream press peddling 'fake news' of Napoleon's defeat. A recent literary discovery by academic James Wade at the National Library of Scotland, however, suggests its etymology might be much older. Wade stumbled across the term in the *Collection of Romances and Religious Material, Mostly in Verse* (c.1480), a compendium of writings from fifteenth-century Derbyshire churchman Richard Heege, who had copied out in full a series of scripted comedy routines from a travelling minstrel. One of the skits, 'Mock Sermon', started with the entertainer cursing (then toasting) his audience, before launching into a story about three kings who ate so much, a herd of twenty-four oxen burst out of their stomachs. Armed with swords, the beasts set about chopping each other up, until only three remained. These, the minstrel quipped, were the 'red herrings'. Extracting a deeper meaning from this fishy punchline seems pretty tricky, though the audience presumably found some kind of hilarity in there. Wade offered a couple of possibilities as to what this surrealist slice of medieval stand-up might have been saying: beware the gluttonous habits of the elite and don't let the absurdities of pageantry distract from what is really going on at the royal court.

Aside from the 'red' variety, traditional culinary products of the British herring industry included whitebait, kippers and bloaters. Whitebait are simply young herring (or sprat) caught as fry. Legend has it that Richard Cannon, a fish seller from Blackwall, convinced the Lord Mayor of London that this was an entirely different species as a way to corner the market for himself. As for the kipper, this is simply a herring split butterfly-style and gutted (but with head and tail intact), soaked in brine and cold-smoked over wood chip embers for twelve hours. Although smoking was widely used in Britain for centuries, this style of preparation is most connected with fishmonger John Woodger of Seahouses, Northumberland, who, in the early 1840s, so the story goes, left a prepared herring out overnight in a room with a stove by mistake. Behold, a new way of curing fish was born.

Counter-claims to glory could be found in Yarmouth, Peel, Craster and Mallaig, each of which sported their own variants on the smoking process and supported fine smokehouses that serviced a roaring trade in fishy delicacies through Victorian and Edwardian times. A great social leveller, typically served with black pudding or in kedgeree, the kipper claimed pride of place on breakfast tables across Britain, from working-class homes to the inaugural menu of the Savoy Hotel when it opened in 1889. In the First World War, dyes were added in place of the traditional smoking process to save time and increase production of this protein-rich staple. Brown FK ('for kippers') was a cocktail of synthetic sodium compounds which is today banned by the European Food Standards Authority due to its toxicity.

And so to the bloater, a method of herring preparation that sported numerous regional variations but was most commonly associated with the East Anglian producers. Bloaters were herring brined whole and ungutted and then lightly smoked. Their sale in Great Yarmouth can be traced to around 1600, though it became most popular from the mid-1800s and was much loved by holidaymakers, who sent home boxes of the plump silvery souvenirs in their thousands. An Edwardian postcard dating to the early 1900s gave a visual flavour of this local delight by depicting a string of fulsome herring alongside the caption 'Just a line from Yarmouth' (see Fig. 21). Less salty and smoky than the kipper, *Cookery for Private Families* (1845) by Eliza Acton

21. A favourite postcard to send home from a holiday in Norfolk in the early twentieth century. Captioned 'Just a line from Yarmouth', this image shows a row of fine 'bloaters' – the salted and lightly smoked herring for which the town was famed. The postcard was produced by Alfred William Yallop, a local photographer and owner of the Royal Studio.

recommended cutting off the heads and tails, opening the herring up at the back, and heating them in front of the fire or on a stove (but not, presumably, with a salamander). Once cooked, Acton said, they could be rubbed with butter and seasoned with black or cayenne pepper or served as is. Nutritious and delicious.

Stormy Seas for the Fish That Made History

It has not exactly been plain sailing for the humble herring in recent years, nor for the coastal communities that traditionally fished them. Over the course of the twentieth century, the taste for salted fish waned and, after the Second World War, a new age of high-tech vessels equipped with electronic shoal detection systems, huge ring nets, on-board winches and vast holding tanks left little room for the driftermen and the herring lassies. The last Scottish steam-powered drifter, the *Cosmea* KY21, went in pursuit of the North Sea fishery off the Norfolk coast for a final voyage in 1956. Herring lassies were rare by the early 1960s and had disappeared entirely from British quaysides by 1968. A vastly enhanced capacity to harvest the fruits of the ocean, meanwhile, carried out by Norwegian, Danish, Dutch and Scottish pelagic trawlers, precipitated a global collapse in herring populations. Fish stocks dropped by 50% in the North Sea from the 1950s to the 1960s and the lowest ever catch of British herring was logged in 1977. From dietary staple and marine cash cow, the 'silver darlings' became an endangered species.

A blanket four-year ban was placed on the fishing of Atlantic herring in the North Sea in 1977 to service its recovery, after which followed the European Common Fisheries Policy (1983) and a system of licences and landing quotas. As well as trying to find a workable compromise over the choppy conundrum of *Mare clausum* vs *Mare liberum*, there was a bigger fish to fry: namely, the very survival of a keystone species which had not only powered the commercial fisheries of northern Europe, but also served as a critical nutritional agent in a healthy ecological network that connected tiny plankton to giant cetaceans. As Callum Roberts highlights in his *An Unnatural History of the Sea* (2007), the problem of overfishing in the present day is, essentially, a historical one, rooted in a powerful (and highly problematic) myth of inexhaustibility that governed attitudes to maritime resources from medieval times to the mid-twentieth century. Significant steps have been taken to improve species and habitat protection, but the old adage 'plenty more fish in the sea' may have a shorter shelf life than you might think.

Issues of pollution, anthropogenic climate change and overfishing continue to threaten global fish stocks, which, some scientists argue, could collapse as early as 2050. For their part, herring numbers around Beastly Britain are stable. They are, however, swimming in plain sight, obscured not so much by their reflective powers as changing culinary preferences. Too much fishing is a problem. But, some argue, so is too little. If the herring was restored to our menus (much of the domestic catch today is sent for fishmeal, animal feed or electricity biomass generation), it might count more defenders. Inexpensive to buy, with a Marine Stewardship Council stamp of approval, and good for our health courtesy of its load of Omega 3 oils, a number of chefs, from Delia Smith to Rick Stein, champion its return. Chef Richard Corrigan, for one, flies the flag for a pelagic patriot that never runs out of options or fails to impress: 'It's a British fish, it's a cultural phenomenon. No one does it like the Brits when it comes to a smoked kipper. I'd have kippers every day seven days a week. I smile after having a kipper.' Perhaps a reprint of the classic *New Herring Book: Scores of Simple Recipes* might be in order to help whet our collective palate. Published in the 1940s and written by Mrs Arthur Webb for the Herring Industry Board, this handy guide presented all manner of mealtime options. Fried, baked, boiled, grilled, poached and steamed. Bloater fritters, fried in batter and grated cheese. Even 'Herrings à la Française' fillets rolled with salt, pepper, nutmeg, lemon and minced parsley and baked in buttered paper parcels. Webb served up valuable advice on how to deal with the smelly afterglow of a kipper supper: wipe the pan with paper and rinse in cold water. Even better, add mustard to the dishwater. Most importantly, she hailed the herring as the 'fish that made history'. They may have fallen into obscurity, but beneath the iridescent camouflage of the silver darlings exists a whale of a tale.

What Lies Beneath

CHAPTER 7

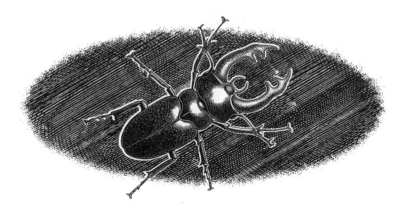

Stag Beetle

At distance it sounds like a Spitfire. Then, in the twilight, a striking sight looms out of the sky: a dark armour-clad winged insect in ungainly flight. More like a jumbo coming in to land in a force 9 gale, to preserve the aeronautical allusion. Stag beetle season is here, signalled by the long days of high summer.

When I lived in the west of England they were the stuff of legend – the unticked entry in *I-Spy Creepy Crawlies* and a beast known only in the plates of the *Observer Book of Common Insects and Spiders*. In the east, however, every summer still carries the possibility of a stag beetle extravaganza. For a few nights in June, the dusky air might be suddenly enlivened by their buzzing: resting females on the warm ground, males on guard on their hind legs, antlers tilted skywards in triumph. The Terrier's erstwhile cat brother, who had never seen one of these antlered marvels before, had a brief boxing spar with one once but decided to go inside in the hope of the fridge being open.

Subterranean Spectacular

In the UK, the European stag beetle (*Lucanus cervus*) remains one of the most striking species in our complement of native wild beasts. Britain's largest beetle and the largest terrestrial insect in Europe, it is one of 1,200 named stag beetle species worldwide – including the Chilean *Chiasognathus grantii* or Darwin's beetle, so named because Charles, an enthusiastic beetle collector, reputedly licked one as it came out of a tree stump to see what it tasted like – and one of some 4,000 different beetle species in the British Isles. The earliest trace of these members of the *Coleoptera* (the order of beetles) dates to the Holocene, where their imprint was found in fossil deposits at Sweet Track, Somerset. Typically located in ancient woodlands and hedgerows (their favourite food is decaying oak boughs) and in light soil where burrowing is easier, the stags have in recent years made highly successful homes in our parks and gardens. Their range extends across the south and south-east of England, with particular pockets or 'macro-colonies' in London and the Home Counties, East Anglia, the south coast and – a bit of an outlier – the Severn Valley. Historically, the beetles spread further north (though not into Scotland or Ireland), but habitat loss, predation and various other factors have seen their numbers drop over the last hundred years. Today, they are red-listed (threatened) across most of Europe and much of the UK, where they are categorised as nationally scarce and identified as a priority species under the Wildlife and Countryside Act (1981).

The life cycle of a stag beetle is truly remarkable. It starts life as an egg, wherein it grows for three weeks, before hatching into a grub. In this form, it lives underground for three to seven years, during which time it sheds its skin five times. White with an orange head and a yellow opaque body, the waxy, otherworldly larvae are up to 11 centimetres long and are typically found curled into a 'C' shape. Feeding off decaying wood up to half a metre beneath the surface, this is the form the stag beetle spends most of its life in. If you are lucky to find one sequestered in the soil, it is quite something to behold.

The world that lies beneath is a lively and intriguing place, where tree roots entwine and fungi communities extend through vast mycorrhizal networks. Acoustic recording equipment has discovered that stag beetle larvae communicate with one another with a rasping sound (called stridulation) made by rubbing their hind and middle legs together. The nature of their time underground, especially the quality of forage (dead tree roots, leaf compost, old stumps and rotting logs), determines their size as beetles. The larva pupates to take on its adult form for only a short few months, May to August, when the adults engage in one singular quest: to find a mate. Neither male nor female eat solid food once they have emerged from the chrysalis. Their only sustenance comes from drinking the sap from trees. Males buzz about in search of female suitors, who are typically ground dwellers. Once mating has been accomplished, the males die. The females retreat back underground to lay their eggs in familiar soil and then also expire. Another cycle begins.

In adult form, these are large and distinctive insects, with black heads and thorax and a chestnut-brown shiny wing case. Males are up to 7 centimetres long, females 5 centimetres. Their name comes from the appearance of the male, whose oversized mandibles look akin to antlers and are particularly impressive when seen in flight from below, their gloriously ungainly profile stark against the sky as the light fades. This is the time of day when they are commonly seen – when the sunbathing business of the day switches to the critical task of flying around in search of a mate. The mandibles are up to 3.5 centimetres long, about the same as the length of an adult male's body. No wonder this beetle's aeronautical habit seems rather cumbersome. Walking, mind you, also seems a bit of a challenge with such an appendage protruding from your head.

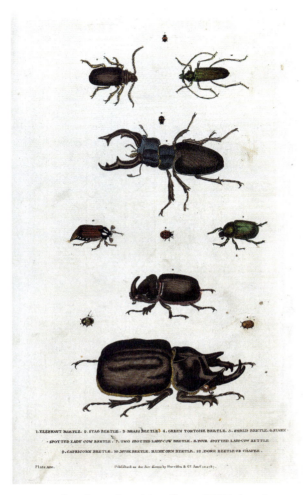

22. A coloured etching from 1787 showing twelve beetles of the order *Coleoptera*.

Many people assume that – because of their alien and armed appearance – these mandibles pack a ferocious bite, but in fact they are harmless. Although they appear pincer-like, the antlers are not in fact claws but much more akin to horns. Where the horns do come into their own, however, is during contests over female beetles. Then, they are used to prove strength and dominance, with males standing on their back legs or opening their antlers wide to show off their prowess and locking horns in dramatic wrestling contests with rivals. These fights are all-action – with gravity-defying lifts, spins and upended bodies, though neither party is usually damaged – more *World of Sport* Saturday-matinee wrestling than *Fight Club* uber-violence. At times, stag beetles have been known to use their formidable antlers against predators, as one amateur entomologist from the Home Counties discovered when he came outside one evening to hear his cat, who had been playing with a male beetle, scuttle off with a plaintive meow. As he noted (to reader and to feline), these amazing beetles are 'fast and powerful, and deserve respect'.

Antlered Anecdotes:
Tales of a Strange and Horned Beetle

A step into beetle genealogy positions the stag among the family of the scarabs, a group that counts more than 30,000 species and can be distinguished from other beetles by their heavy oval bodies and plated antennae. They can be found in all environments aside from oceans and the polar regions, and include the dung beetle and (the largest of the bunch at 12 centimetres long) the African Goliath beetle. Various human cultures revered the scarab, including the Egyptians, who painted images of them in hieroglyphs, produced amulets, seals and jewellery shaped in their image and placed them in funerary hoards. They were worshipped as an incarnation of the sun god Khepri or Ra and associated with the rising dawn and with ideas of transformation and resurrection. In other cultures, too – from the Chinese to the Celts – the scarab was seen as a powerful symbol of life, death and renewal: perhaps a reflection of the fact these critters were typically seen emerging from the soil.

Turning specifically to the stag beetle, it's not surprising that this otherworldly insect has dug its way deep into our collective consciousness, bursting out of the ground every year in a landmark moment of metamorphosis to remind us of its presence in flight and fight. In Japan, stags were known as the *kuwagatamuji*, named after the *kuwagata*, the pointed helmet of the samurai: a reference to their armoured casings and fighting stance. Pliny the Elder in his *Natural History* alluded to a beetle with 'horns of a remarkable length, two-pronged at the extremities, and forming pincers, which the animal closes with its intention to bite', and in Roman culture the stag was celebrated for both medicinal and culinary properties. Pendants made of beetle shells were worn by children to ward off certain diseases and to stop bed-wetting, while their bodies might be boiled up in wine and consumed to treat ague. The juicy larvae even made it onto the dinner table as a crunchy delicacy. Evidence of historic beetle remains preserved at various sites, including Oxfordshire, Lancashire and Rutland, suggests such uses were customary in Roman Britain. For the ancient Greeks, meanwhile, the linking of the stag to rebirth and transmutation was bolted to a cautionary morality tale on the dangers of trash talking. Here, the beetle was regarded as the embodiment of the shepherd-musician Cerambus, grandson of Poseidon and famed for playing a seven-stringed lyre – which looked like the head and antlers of a stag beetle. Legend has it that he so impressed the water nymphs and Pan, Lord of the Forest, with his sweet music that they looked out for his sheep. However, Cerambus was a mercurial creative type and one day chose to question the standing of the nymphs, who responded by allowing the sheep to perish in a snowstorm. The musician was turned into a stag beetle and consigned to roam the forest floor, poking about in leaf litter and detritus for eternity. The unfortunate part of this for Greece's beetles was that children took to decapitating them to fashion their own seven-stringed lyres.

In European folklore, stags equally maintained an association with magic and myth, often in the context of dark and elemental forces. In the New Forest, Hampshire, local folklore referred to them as the devil's imps and saw them as ill omens that would damage the harvest. Sadly, because of this, when they were seen they were pelted with stones. In similarly trickish fashion, stags reputedly emerged in the summer to steal cherries from Kentish orchards. My mum, recalling her Wiltshire childhood, remembers her and her friends taking care not to disturb any stags they found under stones, for fear of starting rainstorms. In Welsh they were the *chwilen gorniog*, or the horned beetle, and were often considered part of the generic English moniker *billywitch*, which comprised other beetles, including the chafer.

Such legends undoubtedly drew for inspiration on the stag's appearance – alien, formidable, horned, dark and mysterious – which seemed to invite a devilish association. Such was also the case in various other countries across northern Europe, where the 'devil's beetles' were laden with demonic portent and said to carry fire. In Germany, the *Feuerschröter* (fire beetle) was particularly feared for its (supposed) habit of carrying hot coals in its antlers, which it dropped on the roofs of houses in order to burn them down. In a similarly incendiary vein, these animals were said to be able to summon thunder and lightning and were often connected with the Germanic god Donar or Thor. Rather like the salamander and the burning logs, this possibly related to observations of the animal found after lightning strikes of veteran oak trees, the stag's favourite habitat. In the Vosges, it was said that a beetle head worn on a hat repelled both thunderstorms and evil forces.

Sketches of a Stag: Renaissance Art and Science

The years of the Renaissance prompted a fervent enquiry into the natural world and its workings, as artists, naturalists and philosophers drew on a new humanist sensibility to document the non-human world. With a self-confident belief in the power of reason and empirical observation, they fostered a new spiritual and intellectual climate and a desire to unlock the 'truths' of nature. An age of global exploration, new thinking in medical science and technical innovations in surveying, drawing and astronomical instruments created what historian Brian Ogilvie calls a new 'science of describing'. Many in this emerging coterie of naturalists ignored the world of the insects as 'lower forms', but a few turned their attention to the many- and the no-legged beasts. Because of their large size and remarkable appearance, however, the stag beetle did receive some scrutiny, with early treatises on natural history blending classical reference, folk mythology and a studious gaze to craft a vivid impression of this most charismatic *Coleopteran*.

In Renaissance art, stags were used as devotional motifs, a spiritual mash-up that saw pagan references to death and rebirth and classical notions of the beetle carrying messages to the gods tweaked with a Christian sensibility. *God the Father and Hermit Saints* (c.1360s), by Italian illustrator and architect Giovannino de' Grassi, depicted a stag beetle leaving the company of oak trees and stags of a deer variety in the woods to fly towards a vision of the Creator communing with hermits, while an altarpiece for Cologne Cathedral designed by Stefan Lochner featured a beetle sequestered on the grass in front of the city's assembled patron saints. The most striking Renaissance image, however, was crafted by German painter Albrecht Dürer, whose 1505 watercolour offered a painstaking illumination of the insect as a botanical subject with a nod to its legendary and mysterious imprint. A tiny canvas, only 14 by 11 centimetres, it was not far off from being life-size. As a biological study, meanwhile, it was singular: the beetle as fascinating centrefold, the curious beauty of its armoured body captured on a blank background. The perspective was intriguing: viewed from the back, it is as if the stag was going about its business, watched undetected by the human viewer, while its studious detail – art historians contend – was most probably a reflection of the author practising for close anatomical life drawing. It could easily walk off the page.

Dürer famously said that 'art is omnipresent in nature, and the true artist is he who can bring it out'. This canvas did that and more, immortalising the stag as a magnificent beast worthy of close inspection. Lifting its head aloft to display its wondrous mandibles, Dürer's animal carried off an air of horror as well as natural history. It cast a shadow on the page that gave it a dose of living Gothic allure and channelled something of the monster imaginary in its hooked legs and serrated antlers – an apparition from the depths of the forest which connoted visions of strange and terrifying entities from the netherworld. In 1999 Californian artist John Baldessari was commissioned by the J. Paul Getty Museum in Los Angeles (where Dürer's canvas hangs) to revisit the famous work. A reflection of the artist's long-standing interest in Pop art, human classification of the natural world and playful attitude to scale, *Specimen (After Dürer)* supersized the stag to B-movie proportions and angled the canvas on the wall to put the beetle on a flat surface onto which it appeared to have just crawled. Stopping the insect in its tracks was a giant metal pin, which punctured the thorax (and the canvas itself) at a sharp angle, affixed to the wall in the style of the Victorian entomologist with an added slasher film riff. Visitors to the gallery, Baldessari said, might want to connect with their inner arthropod: 'to project yourself into the position of the bug and imagine yourself in some other world, being pinned to the wall as a specimen'.

Thomas Moffett's *The Theater of Insects: Or Lesser Living Creatures* (1634) presented a multi-volume survey that drew attention to this neglected animal order, collating extant work from key scientists of the day Conrad Gessner, Thomas Penny and Edward Wotton. Born in Stratford, East London, and both physician and naturalist, Moffett was well known for his interest in silkworms and especially arachnids (he is sometimes credited as the source of the 'Little Miss Muffet' nursery rhyme, an incident said to derive from a spidery encounter that befell his daughter). His compendium certainly reflected a keen entomological eye. Studiously put together and vividly illustrated with woodcut drawings, the book is popularly regarded as the first written in English to focus on insects as a subject. It covered the *Coleoptera* in some detail, opening with the point that beetles are 'bred of putrid things and of dung' and it 'chiefly feeds and delights in that'. Other defining characteristics included living under ground and eating wood and buzzing in the air as they flew. *The Theater of Insects* also paid heed to a few yarns about beetles – classical legends of them being used as messengers to deliver the talk of the gods to humans, their hatred of the smell of roses and love for 'stinking and beastly places'.

Moffett placed the stag at the top of the beetle hierarchy, seeing it as unrivalled 'for the shape of its body, length and magnitude' and drawing attention to its horns, 'cloven pincers' which, he noted, could deliver a nasty nip and were used rather like a crab or lobster used its claws. The stag's mouth was described as 'gaping and terrible, with two very hard crooked teeth'. When gnawing on wood, it was said to grunt like a pig. The beetle, he went on, was prized by 'vain astrologers' for its connection to the lunar cycle ('said to be dedicated to the Moon, and the head and horns of it wax with the Moon, and do wane with the Moon') and its head could live on after the body had been severed. Other allusions to the feeding habits of the adult were more factually accurate, if descriptively unpleasant: it 'feeds for the most part in a clammy fat juyce coming forth of the oak'. Moffett also noted its historical medicinal properties. The beetle's antlers might be worn (around the neck or as a protective amulet) and its body boiled up in wine and imbibed to alleviate fever.

Insect Mania: Catalogue, Collection and Coleopteran Clothing

The fascination for natural history that blossomed during the Renaissance gathered speed through the eighteenth and nineteenth centuries to metamorphose into a veritable craze of naturalist enquiry. This reflected the emergence of various intellectual movements, from Romanticism to natural theology, that invested Nature (with a capital N) with scientific, divine and intrinsic meaning and regarded it as a cathartic antidote to modern industrialism. Also weighing into the equation was the new affordability of devices such as the microscope, as well as the rise of learned societies and amateur clubs that chattered energetically about all things animal, vegetable and mineral. Amidst this broader nature-mania, insects attracted particular interest for their alien aesthetics, feats of strength, bodily transformations (and thus ideas of 'improvement'), systems of social communication, work ethics and community order. Others read their importance in socioeconomic terms, seeing the value in understanding the impact these tiny critters had on agriculture (usually as pests), their role in causing and curing various medical afflictions and (later) their connection with sanitary cities and public health initiatives.

Small and striking, insects offered, to boot, a wonderful opportunity for collection and display – think glass cabinets of row upon row of butterflies – and, by virtue of being largely overlooked by the scientific establishment, fertile ground for those looking to claim a slice of taxonomical posterity. As leading entomologist Reverend William Kirby saw it, the joy of looking at the insect order at once honoured the skills of a divine Creator and the technical wonders of the microscope, with an added enticement of biotic curiosity: 'Insects, indeed, appear to have been Nature's favourite productions in which to manifest her power and skill, she has combined and concentrated almost all that is either beautiful and graceful, interesting and alluring, or curious and singular . . . To these, her valued miniatures, she has given the most delicate touch and the highest finish of her pencil.'

An early figure in this world of catalogue and collection was George Edwards, an English naturalist best known for his work on birds. The so-called 'father of British ornithology', Edwards travelled in Europe in search of unusual avians to draw and also sought out the exotic captives which were all the rage among wealthy collectors in London. Like many of his naturalist peers, he was a trained physician as well as a skilled artist. Edwards's most famous work, *A Natural History of Uncommon Birds* (1743–51), presented a four-volume survey focused on species beyond the British Isles that remains notable for its beautifully crafted and coloured subjects set in their particular ecologies with wonderfully drawn pine cones, stumps, lizards and butterflies. Available to buy on subscription, it set the stage for an explosion of interest in illustrated studies of bird life. The closely studied descriptions of birds in the follow-up three-volume set, *Gleanings of Natural History* (1758–64), meanwhile, were used by Carl Linnaeus to revise the taxonomical details of an estimated 350 species in the tenth edition of *Systema Naturae*. Why, you might wonder, does Edwards – a twitcher by inclination – appear here? A keen example of the way in which some of the animals of *Beastly Britain* roared and soared in the margins, hiding in plain sight, *A Natural History* contained portrayals of all manner of insects as supporting acts in his study of 'exhibiting figures', including a particularly memorable image of stags (see Fig. 23). In this striking drawing, two giant beetles crawled over a map of Britain and north-western Europe, atop of which appeared to hang a supersized mandible as celestial armorial ornament. Look closely, however, and there is more going on than surrealist *Coleopteran* horror. The map depicted areas where Edwards had travelled as a naturalist, while accompanying images celebrated his show-stopper beastly collections

23. A somewhat surreal etching from ornithologist George Edwards (c.1746), in which two stag beetles crawl over a map of Britain and north-western Europe underneath what appears to be a large mandible. Dig deeper, though, and there is a logic to be found in all this. The so-called 'beetle map' showed the places Edwards had travelled to in the years between 1716 and 1730, while the critters showcased here were some of his prized finds from further afield: two stag beetles from Borneo, the bill of an Egyptian ibis (and not a mandible) and a Jamaican hummingbird.

from beyond the map: stag beetles from Borneo, the bill of a Egyptian ibis and a Jamaican hummingbird. As Edwards noted in the accompanying text: 'The uncommon mixture of a geographical sheet and the figures of natural things may not at first be comprehended by every reader.' This, he added, 'obliges me to give a little explanation'.

Stags typically gained a few references in general studies of the *Insecta* published in this period, though the style of these varied enormously. William Kirby and William Spence provided a guidebook to the emerging field in their *Introduction to Entomology* (1815), which lambasted those who saw insect fanciers as 'mere triflers' and instead emphasised the value of all God's creatures and the useful findings delivered to modern society by an entomological vocation. Sections of the book were thematically arranged – metamorphosis; injuries to agriculture and property; medicinal benefits; habits, diet and reproduction; social structures and habitations – and offered a useful illustration of the priorities of the age in terms of species hierarchies. Stags gained coverage in the *Introduction* for their woody appetites, striking mandibles and armoured coats (hard to put a pin through, the authors noted in a later edition). Jan Swammerdam's *The Natural History of Insects* (1792) reported that the adults emerged from worm larvae to take on a 'very beautiful appearance', were common in Kent and Suffolk and could give a nasty nip from their long pincers, while Frank Cowan's *Curious Facts in the History of Insects* (1865) assembled for readers the known corpus of 'facts' on these species to present a smorgasbord of 'legends, superstitions, beliefs and ominous signs'. The stag was here characterised as a legendary critter with associations of fire and devilry, and one whose decapitated head could survive long after its body had died. Positioned as a titan of the insect world, Cowan reported the account of a Cambridge professor who claimed the beetle was able to carry a wooden wand a foot and a half long in its powerful jaws (even flying with it), before ending with a gruesome anecdote that noted the custom of Victorian children to capture the beetles, tether them to small sticks and make them drag their loads along the ground as if they were tiny oxen.

Perhaps the most intriguing figure to weigh in on the natural history of the stag in this period was Reverend John George Wood, whose wildly popular *Common Objects of the Country* hurled scurrilous accusations of foul play at the hedgehog residents of Beastly Britain. Beetles got their fifteen minutes of fame in another of his publications, *Insects at Home* (1872), which presented readers with a 'tolerably comprehensive' account of all British species. Here, the stag was documented through egg, larval and adult stages, its body 'dissected' on pages and plates, and its behaviour and diet explained.

Episodes of Insect Life (1879), published seven years later, took a different tack in aiming to promote a 'kindly feeling' towards the order of creepy-crawlies. Wood admitted this was a work of 'scientific facts and fanciful invention' in which anthropomorphism sat alongside a shrinking-humans-to-size mentality to improve the public-relations profile of the nation's *Insecta*. In this work, the stag was described as a 'gigantic forester' that could be stumbled across in the lanes of southeast England every summer. Wood took pains to point out that – while many saw them as monstrous – these were harmless beasts. He didn't stop there. Perhaps, the parson urged, one might better come to an endearment with this animal by bringing it into the home and getting acquainted with it. Accordingly, the book offered an anecdotal vignette in which the author recalled his own experiences playing beetle host.

The 'goliath of British coleoptera', as it turned out, was 'playful as a fawn' – supping syrup from sugar-coated bread, slurping raspberry juice and tossing a cotton ball on its horns for amusement. It only showed 'impatience under confinement' on two occasions, apparently, both during a thunderstorm. Otherwise, the beetle lazed happily under the shade of a leaf during the day, before venturing outside at dusk for a fly-around. An accompanying image showed a delighted young girl gazing upon her two pets – both playing with balls of cotton wool – the first a kitten, and the second (in size the larger of the two, somewhat inexplicably), a domesticated stag beetle (see Fig. 24). There was one note of caution, however.

> Apropos of this Goliath of British Coleoptera. Though reputed to live on sap, we have never, during the six weeks of his captivity, seen him extract it from leaf or branch by pressure of his pinching jaws. His preferred and chosen fare is the syrup from sugared bread, and the only leaves he cares for are those of which the surface is bespread with honey dew. He seems, in short, to dispense gladly with all labour incidental by nature to procurement of food, and, provided always that he be defended from the unwelcome intrusion (by a leafy canopy) of daylight, seldom evinces restlessness, not even of an evening,—his time when at liberty for taking wing.
>
> On two occasions only has he shown impatience under confinement, and these have been previous to and during thunderstorms, when atmospheric influence has urged to the most energetic efforts at escape.

24. An illustration from the Reverend John Wood's *Episodes of Insect Life* (1879), which shows a young girl playing happily with her two pets: a (very small) kitten and a (very large) stag beetle.
The caption reads, 'There's a pet for you!'

Ladies should beware – although these were 'wonderful and admirable creatures', they might now and then mistake a finger for a juicy twig. A blend of science and folklore, species observation and homely sentimentality, *Episodes of Insect Life* voiced the preference of a good many Victorians to look upon a natural world rosy in tooth and claw.

Nineteenth-century nature fancy found its way into cultural life in predictable and not so predictable ways. Middle-class parlours were adorned with taxidermy fox and fish cabinets, lepidoptera-covered fire guards brightened the hearth and ferns unfurled deliciously in specially designed glass cases (in fact, the pteridomania that swept the UK even saw ferns make it onto the design of custard cream biscuits – take a look at the motif when you next eat one). As citizen science vocation and consumer fad, artefacts from the natural world brought biotic vitality and good taste into the 'great indoors' during a time of rapid urbanisation and industrial growth.

Beetles were part of this decorative matrix in various guises. How about a metal bootjack shaped like a stag to aid in shoe removal by the door? An ornamental whimsy and a shout-out to British iron manufacturing prowess, the beetle's antlers seemed perfectly designed to grasp onto the heels of even the most reluctant piece of footwear. As entomological specimens, meanwhile, stags were commonly to be found in the dens and billiard rooms of nineteenth-century houses – masculine spaces in which the biggest and most ferocious-looking of Britain's beetles were placed near the trophy deer heads that were equally prized by the sporting naturalist. Like Baldessari's beetle, stags were pinned to boards, laid out in rows of family groups, labelled with taxonomic classifications and housed in wooden cabinets, decorating rooms with *Coleopteran* presence and signalling the scientific erudition of the homeowner by the ordered aesthetics of taxonomic display. In the collection of essays *The Poet at the Breakfast Table* (1882) by Oliver Wendell Holmes, 'Scarabee', a nerdy entomologist, paid heed to the provenance of the beetle as a particularly important talisman of masculine scientific expertise: 'Lepidoptera and Neuroptera for little folks; Coleoptera for men, sir!'

Victorian beetle mania resulted in some bizarre products. Festive greetings cards from the late 1800s featured all manner of surreal nature-themed images, from cheese mites sending festive salutations as they munched through a slab of Stilton to marching blue tits carrying matches aloft and promising to 'lighten your Christmas hours'. Stag beetles featured highly in this world of curious, critterly merriment – carrying mistletoe through snowy landscapes and waltzing with frogs as a green damselfly played tambourine. In the realm of high fashion, meanwhile, the burgeoning fad for all things *Coleopteran* saw stags (along with various other insects) appear on women's jewellery, hats and dresses. Sometimes, these took the form of brooches or pins made in the image of beetles in goldwork or gemstones, often playing on contemporary fascination with Egyptology and borrowing that culture's famous use of the scarab as a good luck charm. In other cases, the actual insect body was immortalised in copper alloy or enamelled onto a mount. Things took a decidedly strange turn when live beetles started to appear as sartorial accessories, tied to threads or housed in minute cages: the ultimate dinner party talking point. In one anecdote from the early 1890s, a Mrs DeJones sported a diamond tethered to the back of a beetle, which crawled across her decolletage as an animate necklace.

In a piece called 'Art in Dress' for the magazine *The Art Amateur* (1882), Mary Gay Humphreys castigated the modish practice of invertebrate adornment. While the use of insects was less cruel than the contemporary fad for wearing bird-headwear, it was no less detestable. 'Wasps, hornets, caterpillars and cockroaches will all be able to nestle soon near the damask cheek of our fashionable beauties,' she railed. 'What next? Adder necklaces, a lobster-brimmed hat or a mackerel "sitting on its tail" around a sun bonnet!' In the main, however, the insect imprint on the world of period fashion was seen as entertaining whimsy or sophisticated spectacular. In one of the landmark moments of *Coleopteran* fancy, Victorian actress Ellen Terry wore a beetle-wing dress in her opening night at the Lyceum Theatre. The green crocheted garment, iridescent from the 1,000 wing cases from the jewel beetle that had been stitched into it, gave a particular Gothic shimmer to the villainy of Lady Macbeth, whom Terry was playing in the 1888 season. Costume designer Alice Laura Comyns-Carr noted she was 'anxious to make this particular dress look as much like soft chain armour as I could, and yet have something that would give the appearance of the scales of a serpent'. The dress went down a storm, making this version of *Macbeth* a sell-out in London during its six-month run. Incidentally, no jewel beetles were harmed during the making of the dress, as their wings naturally fall off as a part of their life cycle.

The satirical magazine *Punch* had a lot of fun with this creepy-crawly fashion, seeing part-human, part-insect creations in every crowd. However, there was also a deeper cultural context behind these sartorial manifestations. Exotic creations from the far reaches of empire and the British backyard gloried in the primacy of imperial science and the fascinating beasts revealed by exploratory zeal, intellectual enquiry and new technology. Equally, threaded into costumes of this critterly fancy was a lurking fear, one born from the sheer otherness of the insect world that manifested itself in chicken-sized gnats in Lewis Carroll's *Through the Looking-Glass* (1871) and invading armies of the six-leggeds in H.G. Wells's *Empire of the Ants* (1905).

In Richard Marsh's *The Beetle* (1897) the tables were turned and *Coleopterans* emerged as nefarious mind-control specialists, the eponymous lead wriggling free from the scarab carcasses of an Egyptian tomb to take control of various human bodies and to threaten the integrity of British parliamentary democracy. The science fiction thriller went down a storm with readers, its dastardly tale of insect takeover playing to contemporary anxieties about evolutionary science, the mystical arts and the emasculation of the industrial, male body. In the first year of printing, it sold more than Bram Stoker's *Dracula*, also published that year.

From Trip-hop Star to a Proper Geezer: The Stag Beetle Today

Today, 70% of stag beetle sightings come from towns and cities (largely in south-east England), where the species seems to have found a niche habitat based on the deadwood payload of suburban greenery and the heat island effects of a built environment. Reporting to the *Entomologist Record* in 1987, one delighted naturalist saw a whopping forty wriggling larvae in rotting stumps at the base of an old elm in Surbiton. Astonishingly, nearly a third of all British stags are hosted in London. Wimbledon and Putney Commons, Epping Forest and Richmond Park represent special spots of activity, vestiges of old woodlands and open grounds that have become critically important spaces for an invertebrate whose national range has experienced a contraction since the 1960s due to the removal of treescape ecosystems, the exponential growth of road infrastructures and agricultural (and other) uses of pesticides. *Lucanus cervus* presents something of a conundrum – a beast whose subterranean requirements rely on the layered detritus of ancient woodlands but which seems quite at home in urban shrubbery. Much like the fox, which has successfully moved from the countryside covet to find rich pickings in suburbia, Britain's largest beetle has pulled off a similarly spectacular metamorphosis to take command of the capital's parks and gardens. Back in 1959 E.F. Linssen wrote in *Beetles of the British Isles*: 'the stag beetle could well serve as the insect emblem of London.' For Penny Metal, the creator of a wonderful project called *Insectinside* which explores the hidden 'life in the bushes' in a Peckham park, this most distinguished animal presents as 'a proper south London geezer, dressed up to the nines in a sharp, shiny suit tinged with purple, brandishing a fine set of red antlers held aloft with pride', lounging around, sparking fights, looking for the ladies and 'demanding respect as Britain's largest beetle'.

Given its urban stylings, the stag's most famous recent cultural trace is not as incongruous as one might think. *Mezzanine*, released by trip-hop artists Massive Attack, might well have opted for the fox as the Bristol urban hustler of choice. However, the stark monochrome of their 1998 album instead went for the stag beetle. The brainchild of 3D artist Robert Del Naja, art director Tom Hingston and photographer Nick Knight, the image emerged from Naja's arachnid dreams of the time, developing interest in patterns inspired by the insect body and an opportune photoshoot in the Natural History Museum. With a dose of the Gothic horror long associated with the stag, the image spoke about transformation – another established beetle motif – and one that seemed an ideal fit for the creative direction the band was taking. *Mezzanine* is one of my favourite albums. Menacing, brooding, darkly melodious, its opening track 'Angel' comes alive (to me at least) with the sound of a tapping beetle wandering through the substrate of the score. As music journalist Sam Willett puts it, 'the predator that lurks on the cover of the album perfectly represents the moods locked in the album – it's in-your-face, confusing, demonic, and eerie. It's startling at times and soothing at others.' Perfect terrain for the stag.

For all their swaggering armoured style, however, we need to look after our stags. They may be doing quite well in subterranean suburbia, but their future still looks precarious. The destruction of old-growth woodlands, as well as a historical desire on the part of humans to 'clean up' park, forestry and garden ecosystems, massively impairs beetle population health beneath the ground, while predation (especially from magpies, cats, kestrels, foxes and carrion crows), together with collisions with cars and lawnmowers, are major culprits of mortality once they emerge as adults. Despite their seemingly impermeable exoskeleton, these beasts are actually rather vulnerable, especially to vehicles with much tougher shells. Climate change and, with it, super-heated or unpredictable summers also make for a tougher season for Britain's beetles.

If you are lucky enough to have a garden, don't keep it too tidy, think about creating a stag wood pile or 'loggery' in a quiet corner and be extra careful when digging in the dirt and using a mower. Check the pond in the summer in case of downed flyers and, if you disturb one of the larvae, put it back in the same place (they don't enjoy being relocated). Another way you can help this species is by getting involved in some citizen science. Since 1998 the People's Trust for Endangered Species has organised a Great Stag Hunt, which runs for six weeks in July–August and encourages people to adopt a local route, walk it several times over the course of the survey and record their beetle sightings. The event has been a wild success. Thousands now take part, making their own micro-journeys, as Wilson advised in *Biophilia*, from appreciating a species and learning about it to helping conservation efforts. In 2017 more than 6,000 stags were identified. Huge, amazing, scary, beautiful and lovely were the most common descriptors used by respondents. As more and more Britons joined up, interestingly, beetle numbers steadily climbed, a signal of their increased visibility rather than a take-off in population terms. In 2020 the pandemic-inflected survey delivered a whopping 14,000 sightings (the result of people being at home and noticing nature around them). In 2023 the figure was 9,300. This coming August, why not take a *Coleopteran* pilgrimage around your neighbourhood? You might see a stag and, along the way, a host of other creatures. If you spy one of these spectacular beasts on a road or pavement, do scoop it up and put it somewhere out of sight of predators and away from traffic. Don't heed J.G. Wood's advice and take one home (as a protected species, they are prohibited from being kept as pets). Instead, perhaps spend a moment marvelling at this country's largest beetle, which Wood described impeccably: 'So solid – so compact – so perfect – so permanent.'

CHAPTER 8

Flea

Are you feeling itchy yet? Chances are by the time you finish this first paragraph, you will be. Fleas certainly inspire a cognitive impulse to scratch. An actual bite from one of these parasitic insects, of course, produces a physical response. The allergens generated by its saliva cause our bodies to flood an affected area with protective histamines, leading to the appearance of a round welt at the puncture site, accompanied by swelling and an infernal itching sensation. Even the idea of a flea bite inspires a fair share of unease, a psychological discomfort with the notion of uninvited creepy-crawlies jumping on board whenever they feel like sucking our blood. More than that, this tiny jumper sports a host of unpleasant historical associations with all things unclean: from the mid-nineteenth-century term for a dirty bed that has been hurled at unfortunate schoolmates across many a playground ('flea bag!') to the epidemic diseases with which this species is commonly associated, most notably bubonic plague. This chapter plots the vampiric history of the flea in Britain, taking a look at its physiology, imprint in literature and science, reputation as a disease carrier and athletic profile as a circus performer, before ending with a surprising twist. By the latter years of the twentieth century, the human flea had actually become something of an endangered species, summarily eradicated from our modern homes by vacuum cleaners and insecticide products.

The Natural History of a Jigger

Not a great deal is known about the ancient natural history of the flea, though we do know a supersized one of their kind feasted on the (cold) blood of dinosaurs in the Jurassic period, 165 million years ago. This ancestor of the modern flea, of which fossilised examples have been found in China, was up to ten times as large as its descendants (some 20 millimetres long) and lacked a capacity to jump but instead had claws on its legs to hang onto reptilian scales and serrated tubes on its mouth to ingest the blood of prehistoric victims. At some point in its evolution, the species moved on to mammals (probably peccaries or guinea pigs, as it first originated in South America) and later birds. Belonging to the arthropod division (species with an exoskeleton) and classified as an insect (an animal with six legs and a segmented body), it is most closely related to woodlice, centipedes and ticks, though it was once assumed to be a wingless fly.

Most fleas are dark brown in colour, with flattened bodies that allow them to slide between the hairs of host animals. Their external armour plates, known as sclerites, are rather like those of a lobster, made of a material called chitin which is incredibly hard, and are flanked by rows of bristly backward-facing hairs to allow them to stick to host bodies. At its far end, the flea is no less remarkable. These animals are characterised by a set of powerful and overdeveloped back legs which have several segments, hooks at the end and an inbuilt spring mechanism. Drawing on a protein called resilin, when the tendons are bent this creature can jump incredible distances. A typical flea is able to leap 18 centimetres vertically and somewhere in the region of 33 centimetres horizontally: pretty impressive for a critter that is only 3 millimetres long.

Belonging to the order of *Siphonaptera*, fleas encompass some 2,500 species of parasitic insects that survive by consuming the blood of host animals. Astonishingly, there are 62 different varieties in the British Isles. They can lay dormant for long periods between meals, waiting for a juicy host to appear before leaping to hungry life: this is one of the reasons why an outbreak appears so virulent. Some have eyes, others don't, but all share a formidable range of mouthparts, including a proboscis designed to pierce a victim's skin and a suction tube to extract blood. Food is necessary to sustain the flea metabolically and also to mate successfully, the act of which involves the male flea inseminating the female with a penis two-and-a-half times the length of its body (Miriam Rothschild, flea aficionado, noted: 'Any engineer, looking objectively at such a fantastically impractical apparatus, would be heavily against its operational success').

After coupling with multiple partners, the female lays her eggs twenty-four hours later, which emerge as larvae two to twelve days after that. Some are finely attuned to the life cycles of their host animals. Rabbit fleas, for example, only lay eggs in a burrow when the resident rabbit is pregnant, thereby ensuring that there is a ready meal in place for the adult fleas once they emerge at the pupal stage and are on the lookout for their first blood-suck. All share a vampiric habit and an ability to feast on pretty much any warm-blooded creatures, though most are actually quite fussy about their haemoglobin of choice, meaning there are (by preference) cat fleas, dog fleas, rabbit fleas, bat fleas, armadillo fleas and even elephant shrew fleas. A few, however, are more flexible in their eating habits, most famously the oriental rat flea, which notoriously transmitted bubonic plague from rats to humans through the medium of lunch.

Vampire Mites at the Margins: Scratching Around for Fleas in British Culture

Aside from its notorious claim to fame as a carrier of plague (more on this later), two particularly bold contentions have been made that suggest the flea punched far above its weight in its ability to shape the course of human history. In the first of these, we travel back 2 million years, a time when our primate ancestors began to engage in group socialisation, the rationale for which, according to anthropologist Robin Dunbar, was rooted in the grooming practices of higher primates. From combing through each other's fur to remove fleas, lice and other parasites, he argues, came the impulse for more sophisticated forms of communication, from which evolved language. The second claim relates to an equally important evolutionary milestone: the emergence of the hairless ape roughly 1.5 million years ago. Scientists have posited various reasons for why we as a species shed most of our fur – was it a function of keeping cool on the hot African plains after we emerged from the primeval forest, or to better enable us to forage for food in aquatic environments where hair offered little insulation? No one knows for sure but, according to scientist Mark Pagel, we might well have ditched the hairy look to reduce the ability of parasites, including fleas, ticks and lice, to cling to our bodies.

And so to *Pulex irritans*, the human or house flea, the variety with which we have been most closely associated. Classified by botanist Carl Linnaeus as a wingless insect in his *Systema Naturae*, it was taxonomically connected with us by name and by its favoured homely habitat. In terms of a longer etymological trail, the word 'flea' was Old English in origin, first appearing in an eighth-century language glossary and with linguistic roots in the German term *flauhaz* and Proto-Indo-European *plúsis*. Particularly interesting was the way in which the Old English 'flea' referenced the similar 'flee' (thereby conjoining the idea of a sharp exit with the jumping tendencies of these tiny insects). *Lop*, which was commonly used in Yorkshire, Lancashire and Cumbrian dialect to refer to the tiny parasites and reflected a Norse lineage brought to these shores by the Vikings, also employed a neat demonstration of word–object association, being derived from the Danish/Norwegian *loppe* or to leap. In the naming of the flea, etymological flourish seemingly collided with natural history observation to make for some fascinating turns of phrase. Similar linguistic stylings were found in French, where the word for flea (*puce*, also from *plúsis*) denoted the colour purple, a tone particularly favoured by Marie Antoinette that resembled the bloodstains left on skin, clothes and furnishings after a fleabite.

There is no doubt that *Pulex irritans* got well and truly under our skins – more so, arguably, than any other in *Beastly Britain*. Our ancestors spent not an inconsiderable amount of time trying to guard against this tiny critter whose taxonomic nomenclature tells us a lot about how humans typically regarded fleas: irritants. Every 1 March (St David's Day and an important date in the flea calendar), households up and down the land readied themselves for parasitical assault and, depending on where you were located, the advice varied from opening all doors and windows to closing them tight. One story from Devon in the 1890s warned of 'the black army' that 'always came down Exeter Hill, in Swarms'. Some said the Devil himself put bags of fleas on people's doorsteps on 1 March. If you left the door open when it should be closed, or vice versa, it seemed that our forebears had a few techniques up their sleeves to fend off infestation. Put common fleabane in vases and never bring violets into the house were two popular recourses.

25. Look closely at this bucolic image of rural labourers resting up after a hard day's work gathering hay stooks, and you will see a woman plucking fleas from a man's head.

Anglo-Saxon communities tried to eradicate them by locking away clothes in airtight, dark chests and laid sheepskins near an affected bed in order to try to lure fleas away from places where they slept. Large numbers of the tiny parasites were preserved in excavations from Roman York, suggesting that the elaborate public health and bathing rituals for which this culture was known did not make it immune from ectoparasitical woes. *The Good Wife's Guide*, written in the late 1300s by an elderly man to his young spouse, presented novel ways to banish fleas and thereby ensure a happy medieval household. The bedroom could be scattered with alder leaves to trap the little critters; a trencher (a flat loaf of bread used as a plate) with a lighted candle in the middle could be placed on a table and doused with birdlime or turpentine to which fleas got stuck; a white cloth might even be placed on the floor to which fleas were said to be attracted, then bundled up and shaken outside.

Sixteenth-century poet-farmer Thomas Tusser recommended a good sweep of the chamber, followed by wormwood decorations in March as a remedy against the flea in his *Five Hundreth Pointes of Goode Husbandrie* (1577). For the early modern nobility, stoles were worn around the shoulders as flea-deflecting devices and comfort dogs served the same purpose in beds (Cavalier King Charles spaniels were a favourite of Mary, Queen of Scots, and Charles II, from where their name derives). Queen Christina of Sweden even went as far as using 4-inch-long miniature cannons against *Pulex* insurgents, while eighteenth-century fashionistas sported ivory or gold flea traps, cylindrical pendants worn around the neck into which a few drops of blood were placed, along with honey or fat that 'stuck' hungry fleas. Perhaps the least reliable of all anti-flea concoctions, however, was detailed in the *Royal Cornwall Gazette* from June 1856. Reporting on the recent Bodmin Horse Fair, the paper cautioned readers against the 'sovereign remedy' offered on one trade stand. When purchasers got home and opened the box, there was nothing inside, except a short note which read 'Catch 'em and kill 'em!'

For all this everyday parasitic activity, perhaps even because of it, the flea didn't inspire much attention beyond remedies and eradication advice. Sparser still were positive responses, one intriguing outlier being an old Norfolk anecdote from a Cromer fisherman in the mid-1800s, which advised: 'When you see my shirt alive with fleas, then there is certain to be a good tidy lot of fish.' In the main, though, these tiny critters were ignored or, at best, flicked away as nuisances. As naturalist Harold Russell pointed out in the opening lines of his 1913 study *The Flea*: 'So far as I am aware, no book, devoted to what is known about fleas, has ever been published in English.' We have a scattering of idioms – notably, to send someone away with a 'flea in their ear' (a curious phrase which originated in medieval France with a meaning connected to amorous feelings or devotional revelation that morphed into a term for rebuke or anger when it landed this side of the English Channel) as well as various stand-in monikers for filth (flea pits and the like) – but, generally, references to fleas were relatively scratchy when compared to the cultural imprint of other species. Perhaps these tiny critters were too remote from our mammalian experience, too small to notice, or people just wanted to forget about them. To find them in the historical record, then, you have to look closely, peering into the margins of artistic and scientific enquiry where a few commentators found a subject of pariah-like intrigue typically defined by three qualities – an appetite for blood, diminutive size and amazing athletic ability.

Fleas were formally classified as the order of *Siphonaptera* in 1825 by zoologist Pierre André Latreille, but their association with blood-sucking went back much further. Aristotle believed (erroneously) that the flea originated in decaying animal manure, 'the lowest degree of putrefaction', while medieval writer Albertus Magnus thought the six-legged beasts emerged, ready to bite, from 'moist warm sand when it suddenly comes into touch with the warm bodies of animals'. For Shakespeare, the flea was ravenous and foolhardy in its mealtime aspirations: 'That's a valiant flea that dare eat his breakfast on the lip of a lion,' noted the Duke of Orleans in *Henry V*. Arguably the most famous take on the biting qualities of this insect, however, came from metaphysical poet John Donne. 'The Flea', his three-stanza poem written in the 1590s, played mischievously with themes of sex, blood-sucking and morality, with an amorous fellow remonstrating to his lover as follows. A tiny parasite had fed on him and then her ('it suck'd me first, and now sucks thee') in an act that – he was sure she'd agree – was neither sinful nor shameful. With the blood of the two humans happily mingling in the body of the satisfied flea, he argued, what was morally wrong in the two lovers sharing body fluids by sleeping together?

The second verse took the momentum up a notch, with the narrator pressing on with his point to describe an entwined holy trinity of engorged flea and two human paramours. Creating an elaborate metaphor around the flea's 'living walls of jet' as a conjugal bed, he pleaded with the lady to spare its life. It would, he argued, be an act of both self-murder and sacrilege to squish it, 'three sins in killing three'. The object of his affections nonetheless went ahead and crushed the insect, at which point the narrator performed a tricky sleight of hand, circling back to his original argument, with an added twist. Truly, the lady had experienced no collapse in her physical or moral integrity from the flea-killing spree. Indeed, such would also be the case, he pointed out, if the two lovers were to have sex ('Just so much honour, when thou yield'st to me, Will waste, as this flea's death took life from thee'). Published after Donne's death, 'The Flea' was wildly successful, combining period cultural preoccupations with sex, religion, justice and death with a whimsically lewd conceit that toyed with a tiny parasite as a device of seduction. That all of Donne's readers would have been very familiar with fleas and their biting ways made the metaphysics of the poem even more delicious.

The Power of Magnification: Mapping the Miniature

It fell to a piece of technical equipment – the microscope – to open the flea to a new kind of human gaze that focused in on its second defining trait: size. In fact, when this whimsical new technology emerged, it was colloquially known as a 'flea glass' for its newfangled ability to magnify the minuscule. The first microscope was said to be invented by Dutch optical specialist Zacharias Janssen around 1600, but only really came into its own as a scientific instrument a half-century later. Galileo Galilei was probably the first to scrutinise *Pulex irritans* through a microscopic lens as part of his inaugural studies of animals in miniature, written up as *Apiarium* (1625). Writing to a friend of his investigations, he noted having 'contemplated a great many animals with infinite admiration' through the use of a scope, of which the flea was 'the most horrible'.

Micrographia (1665), compiled by Robert Hooke, was rather less derogatory and, in its fine-drawn lines of magnification, was the first to put the flea on the scientific map. A remarkable study of an organic world in miniature, what he called 'minute bodies', Hooke's study illuminated the fantastical possibilities of a natural history spied through the glass. In the preface to this survey, he waxed lyrical on the possibilities for nature study with this new scale in view: 'By the help of microscopes, there is nothing so small, as to escape our inquiry; hence there is a new visible World discovered to the understanding.' Alongside the various objects that were examined and then drawn for Hooke's collection, the presentation of the flea was striking for its painstakingly accurate lines and its captivating mash-up of science and art.

Pictured in a fold-out four-page spread, *Pulex irritans* was depicted in side profile view, with its armoured thorax, extended legs and proboscis etched with forensic precision. The scientific specimen seemed to come to life – reanimated by an instrument lens and a human eye to create a new object of insectoid fascination (see Fig. 26). The Enlightenment aesthetic of rationalism set out in *Micrographia* was hugely important, but so too was its style. Hooke's flea was not only eye-wateringly detailed, but also had personality in its intimately drawn lines. It was clothed in an alien exoskeleton which Hooke called a 'curiously polish'd suit of sable Armour, neatly jointed' and stared out of the page with a penetrating look from its one visible eye that locked the reader's gaze. Moreover, with a nod to the 'more-than-human' aegis that seems much more twenty-first than sixteenth-century in its way of thinking, Hooke even made a stab at viewing the flea on its own terms. While most contemporaries saw little value

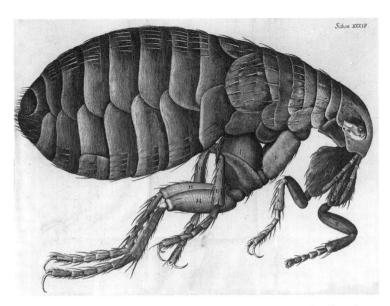

26. Robert Hooke's famous 'zoomed-in' depiction of a flea from *Micrographia* (1665).

in *Pulex irritans* – Dutch expert in optics and microbiology, Antonie van Leeuwenhoek called it a 'small and despised creature' – Hooke believed 'the strength and beauty of this small creature, had it no other relation at all to man, would deserve a description'.

Under the microscope, the flea was seen (perhaps for the first time) beyond the parameters of pest. Supersized under glass, its sheer difference made it intriguing. Irish author Jonathan Swift's *On Poetry: A Rhapsody* (1733) had fun with this period fascination for ever-decreasing scales of scrutiny in a short ditty about the tiny, hungry parasite: 'So, naturalists observe, a flea Has smaller fleas that on him prey, And these have smaller still to bite 'em, And so proceed *ad infinitum*. Thus every poet, in his kind Is bit by him that comes behind.' According to art critic Jonathan Jones, in forwarding a new way of seeing the non-human body – a textured, up-close biotic landscape of wonderment

– *Micrographia* made ripples far beyond the realms of scientific study to become 'the first great work of British art' and inspired a legion of artists from John Constable to Damien Hirst.

One of the most intriguing canvases that drew a line of artistic descent from Hooke's study was William Blake's *The Ghost of a Flea* (1819). In this rather macabre painting, the poet and artist combined his interests in vampiric imaginings with a signature fascination for producing small-scale artistic pieces to offer an existential take on *Pulex irritans*. Where Hooke went for scientific realism, Blake took the microscopic conceit and flipped it into a fantastical and otherworldly dimension. Inspired by an interest in the spectral, the canvas featured a grotesque demonic figure with a long probing tongue drinking from a cup of blood, beyond which was a sky full of shooting stars. It was, Blake said, the likeness of a flea spirit which had come to him during a séance with astrologer friend John Varley to reveal esoteric truths about its species. Appearing in human-vampire-reptilian form, the flea imparted a conversation he had with God at the time of creation, in which the deity had wanted to make him the size of a bull, but went instead for a minuscule scale, 'when it was considered from my construction, so armed – and so powerful withal, that in proportion to my bulk (mischievous as I now am) that I should have been a too mighty destroyer'. The demonic flea also told Blake that in his kind were contained the souls of men who were 'by nature bloodthirsty to excess'. Playing with ideas of monstrosity and magnification in equal measure, the canvas paid heed to long-standing associations between bloodsucking, bestial desires and devilry. Pictorially speaking, *The Ghost of a Flea* measured a mere 21 by 16 centimetres, but it was thoroughly grand in design.

And so, to the third quality by which the flea was commonly referenced – its athleticism. Writing in *History of the Earth and Animated Nature* (1774), Oliver Goldsmith devoted less than a page to the tiny insect, though the attributes he did flag were telling – its 'blood-thirsty disposition' and its agility. The latter, he contended, enabled it to leap onto a host with great stealth and, post mealtime, depart at great speed to avoid being squatted. Oddly enough, the phrase 'fit as a flea', which became popular in the 1800s, drew more on alliterative device than the insect's jumping capabilities for inspiration – rehashing the much older idiom 'fit as a fiddle' where 'fit' was used to denote a specific purpose rather than describe a physical condition. One family, meanwhile, who were very much focused on an entomological gaze were the Rothschilds. Lionel (Walter) Rothschild built a vast zoological collection at his private museum in Hertfordshire (established 1889), which included 2 million butterflies and 30,000 beetles, whereas Nathaniel (Charles), his brother, collected some 260,000 flea specimens and named around 500.

The most significant figure in this family tree of flea fancy was Miriam, Charles's daughter, born in 1908 and an avid childhood collector of butterflies and beetles. Aged seventeen, she finally persuaded her father to allow her to study zoology at evening class and, despite the extreme limitations placed on women working in science, became an accomplished naturalist and a leading authority on the flea. Biomechanics were her particular specialism. Working with more than 6,000 slides in her independent lab (she noted 'Once you have a microscope, life is never long enough'), Rothschild conducted revolutionary research on the insect's miniature gymnastics to discern how the protein resilin was stored in its muscles and, along with a spring in the thorax, allowed an enormous release of kinetic energy. She documented how these tiny parasites could jump some 30,000 times without stopping and, in a six-volume *Catalogue of Fleas* (1953–83), provided an accurate and evocative description of a species defined by its athleticism: 'insects which fly with their legs'. A naturalist who combined scientific rigour with an emotional connection to the natural world, Miriam regarded the flea as 'beautiful' and said that looking at them produced a feeling in her as euphoric as smoking cannabis. She remained thoroughly captivated by the species, even keeping fleas in plastic bags in her bedroom so that she could 'see what they are doing and so children do not annoy them'.

Writing (with Teresa Clay) for the Collins New Naturalist series, her *Fleas, Flukes and Cuckoos* (1952) demonstrated keen credentials in nature study and a dry humour that even managed to garner popularity for a range of parasitical species derided by humans. The book described the skylark as a 'flying zoo' due to its many parasites and took misanthropic glee in imagining a tapeworm as long as a cricket pitch curled up in a Hollywood film star's colon. As well as the gendered constraints of professional science, Miriam's practice was limited by the technical impossibility of capturing a jumping flea in five seconds of film. Since then, however, scientists using sophisticated camera and computer equipment have finessed her conclusions. Using image-capture technology able to record 5,000 frames a second (as well as a group of hedgehog fleas kindly donated by St Tiggywinkles Wildlife Hospital), researchers from the University of Cambridge (2011) showed how the tiny jumpers push off from the floor using their feet, catapulting themselves skywards by a combination of remarkable leg biomechanics and rubbery-protein propulsion. If only for a fraction of a second, these *Siphonapteran* superstars can reach speeds of up to 1.9 metres per second, a rapid burst of acceleration which subjects their bodies to an equivalent gravitational force of 135G (humans pass out around 4 or 5G).

Bubonic Plague:
Rats, Fleas and Multi-species Migrations

The start of this story goes back to AD 541, when, in the time of Justinian, a plague raged across the Byzantine Empire.

Most likely emerging in China, the epidemic spread along the Silk Road to India and North Africa, from where it hopped across to Europe, bringing with it an affliction that caused fever, delusions, red swellings in the armpit and groin, necrosis, septic shock and an 80% mortality rate. Many at the time believed this to be a divine punishment on the emperor, but modern scientists working with DNA samples have confirmed that this was indeed the first recorded outing of bubonic plague.

Carried by various species of wild rodents, the pathogen *Yersinia pestis* could remain relatively inactive for a long time, confined to a particular species reservoir (typically black or brown rats) and limited by natural immunity in those populations. However, if the bacilli leaped across to other animals – cats, dogs, ferrets and humans – courtesy of an infected flea, things got a lot more complicated. In the case of the Justinian epidemic, this jumping-off point came from a vibrant east–west mercantile trade that allowed infected rats and their fleas to catch a lift on ships, travelling from port to port. The fleas used their famed athletic ability to leap from dead rodents onto human hosts with catastrophic results. This entanglement of multi-species migration created a perfect storm for zoonotic disease transfer. At the height of the epidemic, up to 5,000 people a day died in Constantinople. Bubonic plague took some time to arrive in Britain, reaching these shores around 664, and spread from the south of England to infect all regions except Scotland. A third of the population of Ireland lost their lives. Bede's *Ecclesiastical History of the English People* (731) called it a 'cruel devastation'.

The second bubonic plague pandemic was even worse. Emerging in Europe in the mid-1400s (and reappearing sporadically until the nineteenth century), it killed 25% of the continent's population, somewhere in the region of 30 million people. Known as the Pestilence and later the Black Death, the disease travelled (again) through mercantile trade routes, this time from Asia Minor and the Near

East through the Black Sea ports to the Mediterranean. Here, too, *Yersinia pestis* was the culprit, spread once more by infected fleas travelling on maritime rodents, from which source it was communicated overland by human as well as rat hosts. The Black Death famously made it to England in 1348, landing with a ship from Gascony that docked at Weymouth Port (Melcombe Regis). Two sailors were reputedly carrying the disease as they disembarked to take refreshment and digs at the site of today's George Inn on the harbourside. A eulogium written by a Malmesbury monk a few years later documented the infectious routes of the pestilence: from Dorset at midsummer, Bristol by mid-August, Gloucester, Oxford and London later that calendar year and Wales and Ireland in 1349.

Medical practitioners at the time blamed miasma (bad or fetid air that came from decaying matter or corpses), an imbalance in the body's four humours, astrological and geological phenomena (comets and earthquakes), curses or divine retribution. Curative strategies took various forms: spiritual prescriptions in the guise of prayer, amulets and ritual flagellation; animal-based remedies such as plucking the feathers from the back of a pigeon (or chicken) and tying the bird to afflicted areas of the human body to 'draw out' the toxins; and the imbibing of various potions, including a heady brew made from the powdered horn of a unicorn, cocktails of crushed emeralds, opium or arsenic and a blend of 'four thieves vinegar' containing wine, vinegar and several spices. The latter was probably the best option. Though it had no curative benefits, it would at least not kill you.

Taking an olfactory approach, other treatments focused on cleansing the atmosphere with incense or herbal posies or on social distancing via quarantine. The sinister costume of the plague doctor, with long black cape and strangely beaked mask, was designed to offer protection from fetid air (and unwittingly probably deterred the odd flea or two), while a popular song from the time, 'Ring a Ring o' Roses', remains the most evocative cultural artefact of the Black Death. This ditty evocatively captured the mood of the time with its references to the round welts (roses) that bubonic plague produced on the skin, the floral prophylactics sold by quack doctors to guard against infection (posies) and the extreme infectiousness and mortality rate of this most-feared disease (we all fall down). The plague remained in circulation for the next few hundred years, notably flaring up the year before the Great Fire of London, where it killed 60,000 in the capital. In Derbyshire, residents of the village of Eyam began to fall sick in autumn 1665 following a shipment of flea-infested cloth from London, and took the brave decision to self-quarantine themselves to stop the plague from spreading.

Writing in *The Theater of Insects*, Thomas Moffett saw the flea as a critter of 'vexation to all' (especially those less fastidious about cleanliness), but breezily decreed them to be 'not the least plague'. An interesting choice of words, one might think. However, it was not until the late 1800s that fleas and pestilence were formally associated as bedfellows. This discovery came during the third plague pandemic which started in Yunnan Province, China, in mid-century and reached Hong Kong and Bombay by 1894. Despatched to the British colony in Hong Kong by the French government and the Pasteur Institute, Swiss-French physician Alexandre Yersin set about studying bacterial samples from plague victims under a microscope, where he discovered the pathogen *Yersinia pestis* residing in the swollen lymph nodes (buboes) of afflicted humans and rats. This research established, for the first time, a causal link between plague and the presence of rodents, though fleas at this stage were not in the picture. Yersin instead believed that the disease was spread through the inhalation or ingestion of bacteria from contaminated soil or faeces.

Four years later, Karachi-based French bacteriologist Paul-Louis Simond made a further breakthrough in understanding the relationship between bacteria, reservoirs, vectors and hosts in the spread of bubonic plague. Noticing the skin punctures on infected patients, he resolved to investigate the possibility of insect-borne transmission and so conducted an experiment in which an infected rat from the home of a plague victim was caged next to a healthy rat, with a few cat fleas thrown in for good measure. Both rodents fell ill and died. When autopsies confirmed the presence of a large quantity of bacteria, Simond was ecstatic, feeling he had solved a 'secret that had tortured man since the appearance of plague in the world'.

His peers initially remained sceptical, but corroborative research from the Commission for the Investigation of Plague in India (1905–7) and two British scientists from the Lister Institute soon confirmed his epidemiology. Tracking the route of *Yersinia pestis* from rat to flea in the *Journal of Hygiene* (1914), Bacot and Martin explained (in somewhat gruesome terms) how, when a flea bit an infected rat, it became both victim and transmitter of the pathogen. Once ingested, the bacilli lodged in the insect's oesophageal tract, multiplied and created a blockage. This provoked a frenzied attempt on the part of the flea to feed successfully and, as more and more blood backed up in the blocked proventriculus, it was forced to regurgitate partially digested material into its host, along with a dose of bacteria. Fleas had long been thought of as pests but, with this revelation, their long-term connection with blood-sucking assumed a pestilential significance. Carriers of a much-feared disease, they were now critterly persons of interest in the context of global public health. As Miriam Rothschild saw it, this was the moment when they 'stole to limelight' to become 'makers of history'.

It might reassure those prone to insomnia (or acaraphobia: a fear of insects that cause itching) to know that *Yersinia pestis* has not been active on these shores for the last 250 years and that, in most instances, it can now be successfully treated with antibiotics. Aside from a case connected to the Porton Down laboratory (1962), there have been only two outbreaks in the UK – one in Glasgow (1900) and one in Suffolk (1906–18) – both of which warrant a brief detour for their illustration of the public health coordinates of the flea in modern times.

The Glasgow case, falling during the third plague pandemic, was incredibly well documented by medical officials mindful of the virulence of a disease that historically followed the contours of the world's shipping lanes. Civic authorities not only attributed the outbreak to infected rats coming ashore from the busy port, but also suspected that humans played a role in transmitting the disease once it made landfall. Keen to stop fleas – gloriously labelled as 'the suctorial parasites of mankind' – in their tracks, they embarked upon a comprehensive public and environmental health campaign that limited human-to-human contact in the Gorbals, the overcrowded tenement district where the cases congregated, and carried out fumigation, disinfection, inoculation and contact-tracing measures using local hospital services. The port was closed, wakes cancelled and rodent catchers sent in. When the rats were examined, however, hardly any were found to carry *Yersinia pestis*. A salient example of a joined-up approach that connected human and environmental health, the outbreak was successfully limited to thirty-five cases and sixteen deaths. Meanwhile, research in 2019 by scientists at the University of Oslo confirmed the instincts of Glasgow's health experts to be correct: most instances of the plague came from secondary infection and moved through families. The rat had long been castigated as an animal criminal, but humans played an equally critical role in the multi-species matrix that facilitated the spread of bubonic plague.

In Suffolk, the cluster of cases on the remote Shotley Peninsula in the early twentieth century remains an obscure episode in plague epidemiology. Here, in September 1910, three adults and a child, who were living in neighbouring cottages near the village of Freston, came down with a flu-like affliction and each died several days later. Was it poison?

Pneumonia? Local GP Dr Carey suspected pneumonic plague (which was communicated by fleabite and also transmitted by humans from infected sputum), and called in bacteriologists from Ipswich and Cambridge as well as the district medical officer. Plague was duly confirmed as the cause, prompting funerals for the afflicted to be held in the open air and all contacts placed in isolation at a nearby workhouse. Four other outbreaks were subsequently identified on the peninsula, two of pneumonic plague – the first having occurred earlier, in 1906–7, but which had been erroneously recorded as pneumonia, and the second in 1918 – and two of bubonic plague – a family of seven from Trimley (1909–10) who, officials noted, lived in poverty in a flea-infested house, and a sailor from Shotley Barracks who contracted the disease from an infected rabbit which he trapped near Freston (1911). In total, twenty-two people were infected and sixteen died.

Where had the disease come from? No one knows for sure, but it probably arrived with plague-carrying rats or particularly energetic fleas sequestered in grain sacks that disembarked from ships docked on the River Orwell. Certainly, when a local rat, hare, ferret and cat were all found with plague pathogen in their systems, public health officials leapt on the idea of a rodent vector and launched an official campaign that endorsed the use of rat poison and the deployment of professional catchers paid at 2 pence a tail. Two scientists who previously worked for the Indian Plague Commission arrived with portable lab equipment in January 1911 and, over the next few years, somewhere in the region of 270,000 rodents (and their fleas) were killed for analysis. The results were unexpected. For sure, there was some evidence of plague, but it was not particularly widespread and seemed to tail off by 1914. Just as mysteriously as it had appeared, *Yersinia pestis* vanished. According to veterinary historian David Van Zwanenberg, one of the few people to look at the case in detail, the most likely conclusion was that this was an enzootic outbreak of plague (in other words, it circulated locally within the wild rodent population) that only momentarily made the leap to humans. Significantly, when the offending fleas did jump onto two-legged hosts, the isolated nature of a peninsula where life had changed little since the 1600s meant they did not travel far. What happened in Suffolk stayed in Suffolk. For his part, Van Zwanenberg could not decide whether this was 'a unique and curious episode' or a 'model for plague in rural England in past centuries'.

The Smallest Show on Earth: Micro-athletics at the Flea Circus

If bubonic plague presented the blood-sucking agency of the flea in grand, epidemic proportions, the flea circus drew on its other two habits – size and athleticism – for the purposes of rip-roaring family entertainment. It appears as somewhat ironic that, at the same time as laboratory scientists were scrutinising the flea's role as plague vector, *Pulex irritans* was playing star performer across town, wowing audiences with 'The smallest show on Earth'. And yes, the fleas were real.

Flea circuses started life in the early modern period as occasional vignettes created by jewellers and watchmakers to showcase their dextrous skills in working with small objects. In these scenes, tiny parasites were typically tied to carriages and chariots by silk or copper thread. One of the earliest mentions of this industry staple came from Thomas Moffett in the mid-1600s who talked about a flea that drew 'a coach of gold' which was 'in every way perfect' and equally balanced the 'Artists skill, and the Fleas strength'. This was probably a reference to the work of Mark Scaliot, a London blacksmith and watchmaker who produced a tiny lock and chain in gold that was so small it could be worn by a flea, a demonstration that played on the minuscule dimensions of *Pulex irritans* to illuminate the fine technical hand of *Homo sapiens*. Watchmaker Sobieski Boverick was particularly renowned for his elaborate flea-drawn contraptions which he displayed in his shop off the Strand and even took on tour. In 1743 he presented his parasitical perambulations to the Royal Society, being introduced to fellows by the eminent microscopist Henry Baker.

A fascination for all things miniature manifested itself on the Victorian entertainment circuit in a range of exhibits from intricate dioramas of famous battles to figures of religious saints posed in the eye of a needle. Part educational, part playful, always mesmerising, this shrunken world drew on technical ingenuity in optics and engineering, an interest in history, nature and invention, and a theatricality both scaled-up and scaled-down. *Pulex irritans* sat well in this micro-world of wonder – a tiny critter that already had form as a performer for the mechanical arts and whose biological traits lent it a quizzically oxymoronic quality. It was minute and fragile, yet Herculean in its ability to leap and to pull stuff. Everyone knew of fleas and they were easy to procure.

Demonstrating mastery over this tiniest of species – one which the Victorian circus pamphlet *All About Fleas* labelled as 'diminutive but diabolical' – also presented a reassuring sense of human command over the natural world. Moreover, despite their long-standing reputation as itch-inducing pests, in performance guise fleas seemed to present as naturally comic. The Victorians loved to indulge in a spot of anthropomorphism – demonstrated in the vignettes of stuffed frogs doing gymnastics and kittens taking high tea that were runaway successes at the Great Exhibition – but the flea's otherworldly quality lent it a certain edge. As *Micrographia* had shown, its minuscule dimensions and its alien look made a gaze into this particular insect's domain especially riveting. The fact that its body was clothed in human costume and engaged in tasks at once extraordinary and everyday heightened the amusement even more.

One of the leading entertainers in the nineteenth-century parade of flea-fancy was the Italian Louis Bertolotto, whose

27. 'Les animaux savants', an image depicting various fleas at work in a flea circus. Acrobats, swordfighters, musicians and carriage hauliers: these were some of the traditional roles which these diminutive actors were trained to perform.

'Extraordinary Exhibition of the Industrious Fleas' exemplified the set of the typical flea circus. First appearing in England in the 1830s, the 'Industrious Fleas' performed daily at the Cosmorama Rooms on London's Regent Street, stunning punters with their carriage rides, orchestra, swordfighting duels, fortune-telling abilities (in which a flea moved in circles before settling on a hieroglyph that 'read' the future for an enquiring onlooker) and signature move of pulling along a 120-gun galleon. The troupe appeared at various spots in England in subsequent years, including Birmingham, Plymouth, Bognor and Cambridge, where Bertolotto's book *The History of the Flea* (1835) was available to buy as a souvenir outside the exhibition room for

1 shilling. One of Bertolotto's exhibition flyers credited him with raising fleas from obscurity to become 'the great lions of the day'. It was a slogan that effectively captured the whimsy of the small-big world of the flea circus and pumped up the reputation of the parasite-wrangling showman.

The flea found its feet on the nineteenth-century entertainment circuit to become a popular attraction, appearing at livestock fairs and travelling sideshows, penny museums and music halls across the country to wild acclaim. Professor England's 'Royal Exhibition of Educated Performing Fleas' ('professor' being the favoured moniker of flea-tamers) featured as an attraction at Scarborough's People's Palace and Aquarium, London's Crystal Palace and the Southport Pavilion, offering, for the price of 3 shillings, a show of flea-borne strength. The show promised 'a most Gratifying, Instructive and Amusing Exhibition' endorsed by royalty and some 3 million satisfied customers. A reassuring addendum noted, 'The public are respectfully informed that each flea is securely chained'. Those who came along were treated to a series of set pieces in which 'our natural enemy' turned the sails of a windmill, pulled a carriage, chariot and wagon, walked a tightrope and, reinvented as 'man's best friend', was chained to a kennel as watchdog.

With so many acts touting flea-based entertainment, the competition to create a novel gimmick was intense. The 'Educated English Fleas' (perhaps a patriotic barb at Bertolotto's crew) thus included, in the 1890s run at Southport, an ingenious take on Buffalo Bill's Wild West show – the touring favourite of the hour – with a flea cavalry (labelled by one journalist as the 'midnight enemies of the human race') saving the Deadwood Stage. Also on the ticket was a Funeral for a Soldier Flea – an insectoid slant on death and ritual that played to the *memento mori* fascinations of the age with a tiny hearse and electrified model church. The Liverpool *Daily Post* was particularly taken by the philanthropic conceit of the latter, noting it as a 'wonderful triumph of human patience, moulding the intelligence of a low order of animal life into a superior phase of existence'.

What could the average flea expect from a circus life? A glance into the suitcase (the travelling habitat of the parasite actor) reveals a curious symbiosis between ringmaster and actor, a relationship perhaps best illuminated by the professor's adage: 'I live off them and they live off me.' Fleas needed feeding every few days to stay alive, a biological need which the flea-wrangler serviced by allowing members of the troupe to attach themselves to his forearm when he felt they might be peckish. Professor England told one reporter that a flea dinner took about twenty-five minutes on average and, while painful at first, was not at all 'irksome'. Each performer, on average, lived for several months. With a relatively short lifespan, it was important to start flea taming early. A man with keen insight into this art was Professor Len Tomlin, who worked at the Belle Vue Flea Circus which opened in Greater Manchester in 1836 and operated through to the early 1970s. Tomlin had started out as a watchmaker, before making the leap to flea instruction in the 1950s, a vocation which took him two years to master.

The flea's training regime began (ideally) when the fleas were about a month old. The first thing for a flea-tamer to engage in was close observation, as that way individual fleas could be matched to specific routines. Tomlin thus got to 'know' his recruits, 'the fleas that jump, fleas that will walk, fleas that will hold things for me such as the duellists, or the juggling flea, or the tightrope walker and the hopping fleas, they are naturally the ballerinas, the ballet dancers.' Not all fleas were alike – while some seemed keen to jump and others to walk, some were not inclined to do anything. As Tomlin put it, 'we get some lazy fleas, fleas that will just feed and won't work . . . just idle fleas.' Professor England reckoned on one in six fleas making the cut. From here, the training regime proper started with the flea being placed into a harness made of fine gold wire (in which it remained for all its life). This was a critical moment, according to Pauline, a flea-wrangler from the 1960s, as you needed a steady hand to hold the animal's legs with finger and thumb while looping the wire around its neck with forceps. This was 'quite simple when you know how', she said, although one wrong move and you 'decapitate your artist'. Over a period of time – England said a month – fleas were schooled to move in a certain way so they 'appeared' to pull things. Otherwise, the performance mechanics were really about glue and knots.

When Belle Vue closed, it was the end of an era: Britain's last flea circus was no more. Entertainment had moved on since the years of Bertolotto, with cinema and television auguring a new medium of popular entertainment. But the story had another twist. In a world of centrally heated, insulated, double-glazed homes, the flea's room to roam had shrunk. This was a critter that didn't thrive in humidity nor high temperatures. Vacuum cleaners sucked up their eggs and cleaning sprays sanitised soft furnishings, leaving few places to hide. The widespread use of insecticides, meanwhile, meant any infestations were treated to chemical warfare. As a species, we have long tried to put distance between us and the flea, using various remedies from sheepskins to spaniels, marigolds to mothballs, and, by the latter years of the twentieth century, we had succeeded. *Pulex irritans* was rare in Britain by the 1950s and had disappeared by the 1970s. One of the last of the flea tamers, Tomlin was forced to put ads for fleas (£1 for twelve) in the Manchester *Evening News* and increasingly relied on two pensioners collecting them on cotton wool placed beneath curtains at night and delivering them to him in jars. Some operators tried out cat fleas, but they just weren't as clever. Without its artistes, the show simply could not go on.

Today, the closest interaction we have with fleas is with cat and dog varieties, which many of us keep away with a monthly dose of insecticides. The value to our dogs and cats is not to be scratched at, but there are wider impacts here, too. Traces of neonicotinoids, the nerve agent used in topical pet treatments, have been detected in 99% of Britain's rivers and at levels far exceeding that which is recommended. Fish and birds feeding on insects by the waterside might just consume far more than they bargained for.

Ghosts and Monsters

CHAPTER 9

Black Dog

No animal history would be complete without mention of 'man's best friend'. The dog is, after all, the UK's most favoured pet according to a 2024 survey (some 13.5 million live with us, edging out cats at 12.5 million), with 36% of British households sporting a canine resident. This is a long-standing interspecies relationship. From domestication to the digital age, the forebears of Fido and Spot have walked to heel (well, sometimes in the case of the Terrier) with humans for at least 15,000 years.

From pastoral protectors to pedigree toys, dogs animate our physical landscapes and our imaginations in profound ways. So much so, in fact, that one of their number – the Old English or British bulldog – perhaps has the best claim to being the nation's signature animal (the lion, notwithstanding). Descended from the 'broad-mouthed dog' of Britain favoured by Roman soldiers for its fighting spirit and known by Julius Caesar as *Pugnaces*, the breed came to prominence in the bull-baiting sports of the 1600s and 1700s where it earned a reputation for stocky courageousness. An association with John Bull and star power on the emerging Victorian show dog circuit meant that it survived the Cruelty to Animals Act (1835) that outlawed baiting sports to inspire countless patriotic odes, Churchillian cartoons and insurance policies. The modern incarnation of the Old English has lost the aggressive traits of its ancestor, as well as its ability to tussle with bulls. Sadly, it is probably best known today for the brachycephalic health problems it shares with other inbred, short-nosed breeds.

A canine-centric history of these isles would easily run to many volumes. Instead, this chapter leaves the corporeal mutts of Beastly Britain to snooze in their beds and takes a decidedly spookier path: taking its lead from the abominable tracks of beastly etymology to venture into the fabular realm of ghosts and monsters. Striding (mostly without trepidation) into the British countryside in search of weird and uncanny pawprints, it travels across an expansive necro-geography (literally, a landscape of death) to find a scattering of skeletal traces and a surfeit of ghostly sightings. Just as flesh-and-blood dogs have animated literature from Edward Jesse's *Anecdotes of Dogs* (1858) to Virginia Woolf's *Flush* (1933), our enduring relationship with *Canis familiaris* is equally illuminated in the spectacular tales we have told of ephemeral and mysterious beasts. From the Welsh legend of faithful greyhound Gelert to Norfolk's fearsome phantom Black Shuck, dogs have carried our fears and aspirations; provided solace, company and assistance; earned a special place in many hearts; and inspired more than their fair share of spectral shivers. One might even say we are haunted by *Canis familiaris*.

Buried Bones and Ancient Companions

Humans domesticated dogs in the Palaeolithic era, the time of hunter-gatherers, before adopting a pastoral lifestyle (which saw the domestication of the sheep and pigeons visited in previous chapters), making them the animal with which we have the most enduring connection. The earliest evidence of the role of dogs as companion species in Britain takes us right back to the very origin point of home, or at least to the oldest house in the UK, at Star Carr near Scarborough. Dating to the Mesolithic period, c.8500 BC, this lakeshore settlement preserved in the peat contained bone evidence of various wild species used for food, craft and ritual purposes, including hare, hedgehog, boar, beaver and red deer. What was first deemed to be a seasonal camp (based on excavation work in the 1940s), archaeological studies now suggest Star Carr was a year-round settlement, an important landmark on the journey of our species from a nomadic to a sedentary lifestyle. This conclusion was substantiated by the discovery of post holes, wooden structures and a near-complete skeleton of a domestic dog (earlier surveys had labelled the canine remains as wolf). The presence of *Canis familiaris* was important for two reasons. Firstly, it validated a British timeline of animal domestication, evidenced by the fact this four-legged friend occupied a position in the community somewhere between hunting aide and pet. Secondly, it provided the best evidence so far of human occupation at the site. How so? As it turns out, in archaeological code, dog equals human, our shared past as companion species, meaning that evidence of *Canis familiaris* serves as useful proxy for the presence of *Homo sapiens*.

With Mesolithic-era human remains in Britain notoriously hard to come by, the discovery of canine body parts, even in the form of a few pieces of bone, provides all-important sources for historical reconstruction. Accordingly, the discovery of a lone dog tooth at a site of an ancient spring near Amesbury, Wiltshire, in 2016 generated much excitement. From this tiny fragment, forensic archaeologists were able to piece together the details of an ancient canine lifeway. The Blick Mead dog, named after the location it was found at, was an Alsatian-like adult canine that spent time with a group of humans camped at a settlement 2 kilometres from Stonehenge around 4900–4800 BC. Using oxygen isotype and enamel analysis, researchers discovered the water the animal routinely consumed as a pup came from somewhere near York, suggesting that the dog (and its humans) travelled a few hundred miles from their home to camp on Salisbury Plain. This was 2,000 years before the famous stone circle was built and an indication of the importance of the site as a ritual landscape of feasting and pilgrimage. Also preserved in this dental trace was a record of the animal's diet – fish, auroch (wild cow) and deer. Similar culinary fare to the traces of cooked bone found at the camp, this discovery intimated that two- and four-leggeds shared food at mealtimes. Who would have anticipated that a toothy find from 7,000 years ago would reveal an ancient example of dogs scrounging scraps from their human companions, not to mention providing evidence of what the BBC effusively described as the 'earliest journey in British history'.

Would-be archaeological detectorists are advised to take note: the ultimate prize of an entire dog skeleton from the deep past of Beastly Britain remains tantalisingly elusive. Those which have been found to date offer the briefest of glimpses into the oldest waggy tales on these isles. Enter, for the record, the evanescent animal histories of (whom I call) Sleepy Easton, Rusty, Hatch and Speke the Headless.

First stop on the trail of the skeletal hound picks up not far from Stonehenge, along the A303, in fact, then south towards Salisbury, where a fox terrier-type dog was found on Easton Down during excavations of an old flint mining site in the 1930s. Alongside the pottery remnants, a hammerstone tool and various ash pits (evidence of charcoal burning at the site) was the complete skeleton of a small dog. Nothing is known about Sleepy Easton, who was found head resting on its front paws and tail tucked between its legs, curled up in a sleeping position since Neolithic times.

Jumping forward to the late Iron Age, a young male terrier was buried with his master in a grave near Cirencester, Gloucestershire. In life, this animal quite possibly served as a guard dog for the Roman settlement of Corinium. Excavated as part of a dig in 2008, its skeleton was painstakingly put back together by Lancashire Conservation Studios and sent to Cirencester Museum in a box marked 'beware of the dog'. Put on public display in 2021, this Roman-era canine companion was named Rusty as a result of a popular vote (this happens to be the name of my childhood pet, a border terrier known for his affable nature, bin-raiding abilities and hatred of Merlin the Dachshund).

Next are two early modern canine celebrities. The first was a seadog, discovered when the *Mary Rose*, Henry VIII's flagship, was raised from the Solent deep in 1981–82. Named Hatch by the marine archaeologists who found him lodged in sediment outside the ship carpenter's cabin, this small male brown curly-coated terrier–whippet cross was aged between eighteen months and two years when the vessel sank. He probably spent all his life at sea employed as a ratter. Four centuries after his death, Hatch found a new lease of life performing as ship's mascot. He made it to Crufts in 2010 as VIP of the Kennel Club and even boasts his own X (Twitter) account.

Last but no means least on this list is Speke the Headless, a nearly complete dog skeleton now residing at Liverpool Museum that was discovered during archaeological excavations at Speke Hall, Merseyside, in the 1970s. His or her tale (we aren't sure which) is perhaps the most striking of all. Found under the floor of the billiard room and dating to around 1550, this animal lacked both a skull and a front leg, with few leads as to how it ended up in a sixteenth-century canine Cluedo scene. It remains unclear whether these severances occurred (immediately) before or after death – no lead piping was to be found – though it is most likely the dog was a pet whose head (and leg) literally rolled into obscurity as the result of building works sometime in the last four hundred years.

Imaginings of a Tragic Greyhound

A landmark in Britain's canine necro-geography, the grave of Gelert is said to be the resting place of a famous medieval Welsh hound. The story goes that, in the thirteenth century, Prince Llywelyn the Great, ruler of Gwynedd, went off on a hunt one day accompanied by his trusty pack of hounds. One of their number, a greyhound called Gelert, could not be found at the castle when the hunting horn was sounded and so the entourage left without him. Gelert was Llywelyn's favourite, loved by his master for his loyalty at home and his primal love of the chase. After a day of sport, the prince and his pack returned to the palace, only to find Gelert with his muzzle covered in blood. Llywelyn feared the worst and dashed to the nursery to check on his infant son, where he found the cradle messed up and the room splattered with blood. The babe was nowhere to be seen. Flying into a fierce rage, the prince set upon Gelert, plunging his sword into the greyhound's heart. However, as Gelert let out a dying howl, Llywelyn heard a baby crying underneath the upturned crib. Nearby was the carcass of a huge wolf, whom the trusty hound had bravely vanquished. Overcome by this tragic misjudgement, Llywelyn carried his favourite hunting partner outside the castle walls and buried him in a grave where all could pay tribute to this special dog.

Many did and in fact still do. Legions of visitors have been drawn to Beddgelert, the town where the grave is situated, which pays homage to the hallowed greyhound in its very name. Around Gelert's tomb, a pile of stones and a plaque retold the story, both dating to the 1800s when a cult grew up around the famous dog. One of the many poems and songs that commemorated the tragic fate of the faithful hound, William Robert Spencer's 'Beth Gelert: or the Grave of the Greyhound' (c.1800) offered a romantic eulogy to an animal described as 'a lamb at home, a lion in the chase'. 'Beth Gelert' (1846) by Richard Henry Horne retold the legend in full rhyming flourish, waxing lyrical about vigorous sport in the Welsh green valleys, the hound with a 'grim and anxious look' upon his master's return ('with a bloody jaw . . . A panting breast, a quivering paw!') and the dastardly wolf laid on his back ('ghastly and black!'). The legend also appeared in *Wild Wales: Its People, Language and Scenery* (1862) by George Borrow, a travelogue tour of the country which talked of a place of picturesque scenery and 'stirring and remarkable' history surpassing anywhere else in the world.

Borrow recounted the legend of Gelert as 'beautiful and affecting', though he also raised an eyebrow as to its rooting in objective truth. He was right. There was, indeed, a trick in this sorrowful tale. The story might be compelling, but its historical grounding is decidedly shaky. As Borrow pointed out, the town had been named after a sixth-century saint, pre-dating the greyhound saga by some centuries. The tomb of Gelert, meanwhile, was also of dubious provenance, constructed not in medieval times but in the late eighteenth century. In fact, the whole legend speaks not of medieval tragedy, but the shenanigans of an entrepreneurial pub landlord named David Pritchard, proprietor of the Goat Inn, who hit upon the idea of a shaggy dog story to draw in tourists. Llywelyn was connected to the local abbey, the town provided the 'hook' of a name and so all that was needed was a stirring houndly yarn. On that score, Pritchard had a vast folkloric archive to draw on, though perhaps most closely related were 'The Farmer and His Dog' from Aesop's classical fable (though, in that case, the murderous miscreant was a snake) and the legend of Saint Guinefort, a thirteenth-century French greyhound, whose story was remarkably similar (though Guinefort wrestled a viper as well as a wolf) and whose final resting place, a well near Lyon, had become a shrine around which locals left their babies to be healed.

A Very British Haunting

It was said that Prince Llywelyn the Great was haunted by the cry of Gelert for the rest of his days. He was not alone.

The howls of phantom canines seem to echo across these isles, sightings of spectral hounds looming out of the nocturnal ether with abandon. We are visited by the ghost of *Canis familiaris* more than any other animal. Scooby-Doo, as it turns out, is chasing his own tail. This is not a peculiarly British thing, but it is *particularly* British. Many countries have their fair share of supernatural dog tales, but there are more spectral hounds here than anywhere else in the world. Are we, as a nation, more prone to falling for tricks of the light? More fearful of the dark? A propensity for REM-pattern sleep disorders? Who knows.

An animal history of Britain can provide at least a few clues as to this ghostly draw. Dogs have worked, lived and travelled with us across many centuries, creating a powerful imprint on an everyday experience that is both familiar and familial. For folklorist Kathleen Wiltshire, aptly named author of *Ghosts and Legends of the Wiltshire Countryside* (1973), these beasts were best understood as spectral throwbacks, 'guard dogs of the pedlars and travellers of the Bronze Age'. Since ancient times, we have told tales of their ways and their woes to create a rich vein of houndly folklore that is embedded in our landscape and our language. Canine idioms, from the 'hair of the dog' – one-time medieval rabies treatment, now hangover cure – to Shakespeare's 'dog weary' and Chaucer's 'let sleeping dogs lie', pay heed to this shared past. Even the British weather has a canine feel, 'raining cats and dogs' relating to the habit of householders in Tudor times of keeping pet animals up in the rafters, from where they leapt down to escape water dripping from leaky roofs during heavy downpours. That the animal which has walked closest with us in life wanders freely on a paranormal plane is not all that surprising.

Delving a bit deeper into this ghostly profile, the spectral hound is typically a large animal. Often, but not exclusively, black in colour. Usually travelling solo. Some – like unfortunate Speke – are headless. Occasionally, they sport two heads.

Most have glinting jaws and large saucer-shaped or flaming-red eyes. They are often connected to specific locations (graveyards, woods and wastelands, ancient roads or paths) and sometimes are linked with particular people, deeds or habits. This is an irrevocably historical landscape, one that sustains and is sustained by the richly textured contours of an ongoing physical and imaginative encounter between *Homo sapiens* and *Canis familiaris*. In this supernatural dog-scape brought to life at twilight, temporal boundaries seem to peel away to reveal hallucinatory replays of times long past – moments in which dogs leap out of the night to pounce on unsuspecting travellers, pad gently along old trackways, stand in customary haunts or race by with supernatural portent: always disappearing into thin air.

This imprint is genealogical, culturally so, in its mapping out of companionship relations. Equally, it reflects the complex feelings we have towards wild, dark places and the beasts said to inhabit those realms. It is also, to an extent, physiological. The power of a large dog makes it both fearsome combatant and useful partner. As comparisons go, an Alsatian can bite down with a pressure of 238 psi, humans can make it to 160, crocodiles 5,000. Dogs also have a complement of highly attuned senses (their noses contain 300 million olfactory receptors, compared to our 5–6 million, and they can hear in twice as many frequencies as us). In fact, many believe that *Canis familiaris* is especially alert to supernatural signals. According to a recent Blue Cross survey of 1,300 British dog owners, 63% believed their pet had seen a ghost. The Terrier, for her part, is more cheese hustler than ghostbuster, though she did once wake up at 3 a.m. to bark inexplicably (and incessantly) into the corner of an upstairs room in an old cottage on the Hartland peninsula in north Devon.

In paranormal Beastly Britain, a few patterns emerge. The non-corporeal canine seems to subscribe to four main types. Tugging at the heartstrings more than tingling the spine, the first of these – devoted defender and faithful aide – needs little explanation, given the ties connecting humans and dogs across a long pastoral path. 'Man's best friend' in the living years (and the living room) translated into a similar relationship in the afterlife, with devoted protectors continuing to discharge their usual duties or mournfully protest tragic fates befalling their owners. As for the second – *Canis familiaris* as otherworldly messenger – throughout history dogs have had an important mythological association with death, patrolling the space between this world and the next and even taking on the spirits of restless souls. Cerberus, three-headed Hound of Hades in Greek mythology, guarded the River Styx to stop the living entering and the dead escaping, while Anubis of ancient Egypt served as dog-headed usher to those passing between celestial planes. Closer to home, the hounds of Annwn from Welsh mythology ran to and from the underworld with departing souls and cut a formidable presence in 'wild hunts' across the Celtic calendar with their white coats and red eyes. Climbers of the mountain Cader Idris were said to die if they heard the Annwn howl.

Moving on to the third of the roles – malevolent agent of spectacular violence – the usual contours of canine identity are flipped. Faithful becomes fearsome, the thin veil of domestication, separating civilisation from the wild, left in spectral tatters. Dog, in this mould, reverts to wolf, an animal which has long been seen as the ambassador for the 'howling wilderness' and, in folkloric terms, serves as the 'go-to' villain. From children's fairy tales of tooth-gnashing monsters in the woods to parables cautioning the faithful flock as to the dangers of devilish temptation, *Canis lupus* stalks the world of legend with a predatory presence, as tricky as the fox but much more menacing. In a British context, these animals were blamed for worrying stock, stealing corpses and ambushing unsuspecting travellers, a reflection of the real danger posed by predatory beasts to precarious farming communities and the ecocultural attitudes that crafted it as an arch-enemy species in a natural world supposedly in need of human control. Evocatively communicating the idea of the wolf as voracious foe, *A Book of Highland Minstrelsy* (1846) spoke of it as a beast with 'fangs so sharp and white' and 'pitiless eyes that scare the dark with their green and threatening light'.

Take another step off the forest path and we reach the last of the dog types – the wolfen shapeshifter able to take on different identities. This variant is probably most famously represented by vampire and werewolf traditions and, on these isles, often took the form of ghost dogs with human heads. These spectral chimeras talked, walked on two legs and sometimes transformed into people, all of which drew on anxieties about the liminality of the human–animal boundary and the primal bloodlust (shallowly) buried in the human psyche.

The Isles of Ghost Dogs: Mapping the Spectral Hound

Sightings of ghostly dogs populate the landscape of the British Isles, from Orkney to Penzance, Ballygar to Great Yarmouth. Canine folklorist Mark Norman's gazetteer of spectral encounters included 719 reports at last count, while Nick Stone's 'Mapping the Grim', an atlas of black dog tales, featured more than 500 pins. There are cold spots – Robert Trubshaw, author of *Explore Phantom Black Dogs* (2005), notes an absence of sightings in Middlesex and Rutland – as well as definite hotbeds of paranormal canine activity: East Anglia, north-east England and the West Country.

The first recorded instance of a ghostly hound is from the east of England. A report in the 1143 Peterborough edition of the *Anglo-Saxon Chronicle* described a devilish pack of hunters hanging out in the deer park, dressed in black, riding black horses (and goats) and accompanied by 'black and big-eyed and loathsome' hellhounds. Not far away, in the fenland marshes, lurks Black Shuck, one of the most prolific and long-standing of Britain's canine phantoms whose name probably derives from the Anglo-Saxon word for devil (*scucca*) and the local dialect for shaggy (*shucky*), and readily combines Christian and pagan mythology of the 'wild hunt' to create a fearsome spectre. A huge black dog with shaggy coat, fiery eyes (sometimes just one) and a bone-chilling howl, Shuck was an adaptable apparition, sometimes attacking lost travellers, sometimes warning of doom (death to those who saw him and told another soul) and has been variously spied padding abominably in churchyards, remote lanes and coastal spots over the centuries. His most spectacular appearance came during a storm in August 1577 where, accompanied by bolts of lightning, he crashed into Blythburgh Church in Suffolk, killed two parishioners, burned the hand of another and sent the steeple crashing through the roof. Scorch marks left by Shuck on the door remain visible today. Shortly afterwards, the 'strange and terrible wonder' offered a repeat performance at St Mary's Church, Bungay, 12 miles away, where he reputedly rampaged down the aisle, snapped the necks of two worshippers and departed in an incendiary tumult.

Notes and Queries (1850), written by antiquarian Reverend E.S. Taylor, was the first to commit Black Shuck to print, described as a 'dog-fiend' with 'fiery eyes and of immense size' that terrorised communities across east Norfolk and Cambridgeshire. Historian W.A. Dutt, writing in *Highways and Byways* (1901), spoke of how anyone who heard the beast's cacophonous howling felt their blood run cold. Lest readers be fooled into thinking Black Shuck was nothing more than a whimsical relic from a pre-industrial age, the majority of his sightings occurred after 1900 (152 out of a total 181, according to Lowestoft-based para-chronicler Mike Burgess). To some extent, this reflected the activity of folklorists working mid-century as collectors of ghostly tales. As prominent folklorist Theo Brown noted, many 'reliable witnesses' had to be encouraged to tell their stories, thinking them to be too fantastical or even dangerous to share. As time wore on, meanwhile, a Shuck sighting seemed to take on more of an ambiguous tone – traditional wariness of him as a visitor to be feared sitting alongside a bubbling popular fascination for all things cryptozoological that (even) beckoned him closer. Popular haunts of late have been the north Norfolk coast road between Salthouse and Cromer and the back lanes of Blakeney, where Shuck has been seen dragging a chain behind him and on one occasion appeared to have two heads (catching a rat in one pair of jaws, only for it to scurry out the other).

Today, the saga of Shuck rumbles on in interesting ways. In 2014 the bones of a huge male canine were discovered in a shallow grave at an archaeological dig at Leiston Abbey. Was this the burial site of a monastic pet or the earthly remains of the famous hellhound? On further investigation, archaeologists estimated the dog to be the size of a Great Dane, with an injury to one of its forepaws that meant it probably walked with a limp. By the time it reached the *Daily Mail*, however, the story had become 'Is this the skeleton of legendary devil dog Black Shuck? Folklore tells of SEVEN FOOT hell hound with flaming eyes.' In Bungay, meanwhile, spectral manifestations were everywhere to be seen at the Black Shuck Festival. Started up in August 2022, the annual event celebrates the signature Suffolk hellhound with stories, folklore and performances. According to anthropologist Jonathan Woolley, Shuck remains an especially timely beast, an animal for the Anthropocene whose visceral associations with disaster, deep time and deathly howls seem hauntingly relevant in a fenland landscape destabilised by climate emergency. These ghostly apparitions might just be the spectral shocks we need, he says, 'to warn us of impending disaster . . . pursuing us through wild places' to lay bare our environmental misdemeanours, our mortal vulnerabilities and instil in us a greater sense of environmental responsibility.

If Shuck was the neighbourhood phantom of the fenlands, further north lay the domain of three spectacular animals: Padfoot, the Gytrash and the Barghest, each of which was in

28. *Shadows of the Shuck*, an innovative artwork by Lauren Sharples that uses Tetra Pak milk cartons to sculpt an image of charismatic hound. The piece won first prize in the *Return of Black Shuck & Friends* exhibition at the Bell Gallery, Bungay, part of the 2024 Black Shuck Festival.

the habit of terrifying unfortunate travellers with their ghostly presence. Padfoot ambled silently (as its name suggests) along high roads near Bradford and Wakefield and often pulled a clanking chain as it trailed behind night-time voyagers. Writing in *Notes of the Folk-lore of the Northern Counties of England and the Borders* (1879), William Henderson described an animal the size of a small donkey, black with shaggy hair and large eyes like saucers which made a 'shog ... shog ... shog' sound when it walked. Anyone engaging the Padfoot apparently fell within its thrall and was unable to move. It was said to be a shapeshifter and also an omen of death. In one sighting dating to the 1400s, a monk from Byland Abbey witnessed a chain-dragging black dog change from a crow into a flame, then a goat and finally a man. In another tale, the Wakefield Padfoot was joined by a group of Gabriel's Hounds, a spectral phenomenon specific to the north of England said to have human faces, a glowing green aura and a yelping cry which issued forth a sentence of mortal doom on any that heard them fly over their homes. Many believed that the Gabriel's Hounds were the tortured, sky-roving souls of unbaptised children. Reverend J.C. Atkinson, writing in the *Cleveland Glossary* (1868), instead deemed them to be wild geese in night flight, honking in the darkening sky.

Another deathly harbinger from these parts was the Gytrash, a hound with shapeshifting abilities and a distinctive sound when it passed by. Writing in the *Yorkshire Folklore Journal* (1888), J. Horsfall-Turner described a large shaggy dog with saucer-eyes, and feet that made a 'loud splashing noise, like old shoes in a miry road'. Perhaps the most famous appearance of the Gytrash was in Charlotte Brontë's *Jane Eyre* (1847), where the eponymous heroine caught sight of what she thought was the terrifying dog spirit she'd heard the servants talking about, as she walked alone along a darkling Yorkshire lane. Suspense mounted as the shape came closer, a 'great dog' the size of a lion with a huge head. Behind it clattered a horse, on which rode a mysterious rider: this was no phantom but instead her first encounter with Mr Rochester.

The Barghest, meanwhile, a large and ferocious spirit dog that inhabited various haunts in North Yorkshire, Lancashire and County Durham, could change into all manner of other animals, from rabbits to pigs. Boasting a range of particularly impressive paranormal moves, it could manifest with or without a head, become invisible and even had the power to summon the local dogs of any given village with a howl before leading them on a barking funeral procession that augured the death of a parishioner. One Barghest reputedly killed a man who doubted its existence in a steep limestone valley called Trollers Gill near Wharfedale. Another made frequent appearances in Whitby, playing grim announcer in serving up nocturnal death notices with its chilling howls.

When Bram Stoker wrote of Dracula coming ashore at the town harbour famous for its herring and whaling fleets before metamorphosing into a large black dog, he probably had the local Barghest in mind. In one account from the 1950s, Devon clergyman Reverend Donald Omand visited Kettleness Point, a regular haunt of the beast, on the invitation of a spooked local schoolteacher. As the two men stood on the point, joking about Whitby's Dracula–black dog connection, a canine spectre appeared on the dark shoreline, which Omand dosed with holy water and words of sacramental banishment. Legend has it that the teacher never recovered from the experience and ended up in a psychiatric hospital. Omand, meanwhile, seemed to enjoy his brush with the uncanny and went on to perform exorcisms at various sites around the world, including Loch Ness and the Bermuda Triangle. The Barghest, for its part, seemed unperturbed.

In the mild, mild West, Britain's third ghost hound hotspot, a plethora of paranormal pooches were to be found roving among churchyards and burial mounds, along old trackways, in castle ruins and in eerie woods. Most, in common with the broader tradition, were spotted at night, a time seemingly most conducive to paranormal rendezvous. Meanwhile, for maverick folklorist Ruth Tongue, who collected yarns from the region in the mid-twentieth century, another temporal explanation was at play. Writing in *Odds and Ends of Somerset Lore* (1958), she alleged those attuned to the wanderings of spectral hounds had been born at certain times of day, so-called 'chime hours' that conferred a special ability to commune with ghosts, channel healing energies, talk to animals and move across worldly planes. There seemed some dispute when these hours actually were. Some said 8 p.m., midnight and 4 a.m. (the night times of monastic prayers), others identified the critical period as between midnight and first light, and Tongue herself championed a spectral 'sweet spot' from midnight on a Friday night to dawn on Saturday.

Celebrated in a poem and folk song from Olivia McCannon and Paul Sartin (2016), the Gurt Dog, which inhabited the Quantock Hills in Somerset, favoured nocturnal rambles on the moor when the moon and stars were obscured by clouds. True to its name, this beast was very large. However, this was not a creature to be feared like Shuck or the Barghest. Instead, this affable aide provided a valuable service in guiding travellers along their way: a rare example of a kindly canine apparition. Friend not fiend, local parents reputedly let their children play unattended and gather mushrooms in Gurt's Wood, safe in the knowledge he would watch over them. In McCannon and Sartin's salutation to the growling guardian, the narrator was rescued from the dark moor by a beast with a velvety muzzle that gently guided them homewards. Keen to thank the shaggy patron saint, the ditty ended with the wandering youth taking to the nocturnal moorlands once more to give the kindly beast a bone of thanks.

On the hauntingly beautiful landscape of Dartmoor, the contingent of paranormal beasts appeared rather less genial, the bleak moorlands with their stunted *krummholz* (windblown trees) and swirling mists seemingly ideal habitat for channelling infernal energies. As John Fowler, Devonian writer, eloquently put it: 'the real black hound is the Moor itself – that is, untamed nature, the inhuman hostility at the heart of such landscapes.' Along its north-eastern boundary, a ghostly Lady Tavistock boarded a phantom coach from her estate at Fitzford on a nightly tour to Okehampton Castle, accompanied by a greyhound with a solitary eye in its forehead. Legend has it that the coach stopped to offer a ride to any travellers it overtook. None seem to have accepted the invitation. At the end of the journey, the tale took a shapeshifting turn, with the formidable lady turning into a black dog to make the return trip.

The road over the high moor, an ancient route known as the Abbott's Way which continued on into Cornwall, was said to be frequented by the Wisht Hounds. According to

James Mothy's *The Tales of Cymry* (1848), these devil dogs were 'rough, swarthy and of huge size' and ran in procession behind a demonic huntsman who stole infants for his own dastardly pleasures (unless they slept with a piece of consecrated bread under their pillow). The Wisht had various hangouts and were commonly associated with the craggy hilltop of Dewerstone (said to be the home of the Black Huntsman himself) and the dwarf oak forest of Wistman's Wood (reputedly the hounds' kennel). On the southern side of the moor roamed the Yeth Hounds, said to be the souls of unbaptised children and led on wild hunts to the underworld by a headless (but still howling) leader: to hear their yell augured death within a week.

Hound Tor, one of the granite outcrops for which Dartmoor is renowned, resembles a dog's head (depending on how much cider has been drunk, admittedly). Legend has it that a group of witches turned a giant dog to stone here and, on certain nights, a phantom black beast continues to

29. Wistman's Wood, Dartmoor, the legendary home of the Wisht Hounds.

roam the rocks. The Terrier bravely undertook a close investigation a few years back, finding no olfactory traces of maleficence and some very delicious rabbit droppings (dog Maltesers, she says). Her impressions aside, the paranormal contours of Beastly Britain speak to a powerful connection between place and presence (*haunt* as habitation and *haunt* as visitation) that one can't help being mesmerised by. The potency of this storied landscape certainly had a lasting impression on writer Arthur Conan Doyle. After visiting Dartmoor and taking inspiration from a rich seam of Devonian canine legends, he penned *The Hound of the Baskervilles* (1901–2), a canine mystery yarn starring the famous detective Sherlock Holmes, who investigated the misadventures of the Baskervilles at their ancestral seat on Dartmoor. Doyle's hound ended up being a normal dog painted up with phosphorus to look otherworldly (the criminal, of course, was human), but it did shed some light on how Britain became the ghost dog capital of the world. With its spooky setting, criminal machinations and Gothic hellhound motif, *The Hound of the Baskervilles* encapsulated a fascination with death, storytelling and paranormal activity that became wildly popular during the Victorian period. According to folklore scholar Romany Reagan, sightings of ghostly animals as recorded by British newspapers leapt from just over 2,000 in the years between 1800 and 1849 to more than 18,000 over the next fifty years. Unless the gates of hell had been errantly left open at mid-century, the explanation had to be cultural. This was the heyday of spiritualism and a boom time for pet keeping in this country. Antiquarians eagerly collected ancient ghostly tales; superstitious Victorians saw phantasms beyond the gaslight; and sentimental dog owners eagerly communed with the spirits of beloved animals (dead and alive). Pedigree dogs great and small were welcomed to the fireside and a curiosity for all things paranormal reached a crescendo: a perfect storm for the spectral pack to run like never before.

Black Dog Tales of the Road

Moving beyond these spectral 'hotspots' and the iconic beasts identified with them, the UK at large abounds with tales of road hauntings. These are the most common of all spectral hound categories and what folklorist Theo Brown called their 'natural home'. What was it about the lonely road? Did these phantom canines favour well-worn tracks, in the habit of their ancestors lurking, as Mark Norman jokingly put it, 'all over the place, waiting to be seen?' Or was this a reflection of the generations of human traffic that frequented the trackways of Britain? We can't exactly leap onto a spectral plane to gauge the intention of the ghostly hound, to see the world through its fiery eyes. However, the folkloric detritus that has gathered along British verges over the centuries does illuminate the function of the road as a psycho-geographical artery. Roving along customary pathways of movement, a storied pack of ghostly black dogs paid heed to the historical travels of humans and other species over a long span of time and to the legion of tales that invested these routes with cultural meaning. As Brown noted, the black dog was 'astonishingly persistent, and perplexingly versatile, serving as an image for a very large assortment of situations'. In many of these tales, the finer details were rather sketchy (black dog appears, surprises traveller, then disappears into the night), thus making the peculiar coordinates of each haunting important as markers of identification. How else was one spectral dog to be distinguished from another without its signature roadway?

The Black Dog of Torrington, north Devon, presented a case in point. A large canine with shimmering eyes, this creature was spied many times along a 20-mile stretch of road leading to Copplestone. Those who regularly traversed the route were accustomed to seeing it, though they never tried to touch it or engage the beast in conversation. It was known by its place. Elsewhere, the details of the story fleshed out the spectral contours of a particular slice of tarmac. This imprint could be spectacularly malignant: see the story of the Dando Dogs owned by an iniquitous priest in St Germans, Cornwall, or the many beasts from Ardura, Mull, to Westerham, Kent, whose presence dealt travellers a deathly portent. It could equally be memorably mundane, such as the canine escort that accompanied a walker in Bwlchgwyn, Wrexham, on a nightly basis. At other locales, ghost dogs stalked roadways known for historical crimes or accidents: houndly reanimation adding immortal weight to a traumatic moment situated in place and in time. Mostly, these incidents related to murders, family tragedies and accidents but, on occasion, witnessed trauma through a more than human lens. In Stourpaine, Dorset, local folk spoke of a dog who one day escaped the clutches of a cruel master, only to be killed under the wheels of a passing wagon. In this sad waggy tale, its chain-rattling ghost was said to race out of the village and up Hod Hill, caught up in an eternal quest to find the kindly owner it knew as a pup.

Scattered across a storied landscape, black dog tales of the road created a powerful and lasting connection between phantom and place that passed into collective memory: a luminous map brought to life by ghostly glow. Beastly Britain resonated with paranormal energies connecting humans and dogs, present times to moments long past. These spectral yarns were everywhere to be found, and yet each one also had a unique quality for each of the communities who 'knew' their local dog or dogs. Many of us will know a tract of ground reputed to be a ghostly haunt, a tale passed down through the generations and whispered between school friends walking lanes by torchlight.

My own 'go-to' spectral coordinates are found in the Wiltshire countryside. Here, the canine complement includes the A350 beast that leapt out at travellers on the road from Lacock to Melksham, the unusual white hound with red ears that accompanied a pagan priest on midsummer dawn at

West Kennet Long Barrow, the 'devil' beast that ran with a headless horseman at Wootton Rivers and the (also headless) chain-clanking fiend of the churchyard at Bishops Cannings. Looming largest of all was the black dog of the A4, the old coaching route from Bristol to London, who patrolled a twisting stretch of road between Chippenham and Calne. Here, on (the usefully named) Black Dog Hill, two men had reputedly drawn pistols to fight over a local farmer's daughter (a similar yarn, it turns out, was told about Black Dog Woods, Chapmanslade, some twenty-odd miles away). When one was mortally wounded, his dog leapt into action and ripped out the throat of his adversary. The dog can be seen crossing the road late at night, eternally mourning his stricken master. Nearby stood the site of the Black Dog Inn (1745–1848) as well as Black Dog Halt, a railway station on the branch line built in 1863 by Lord Lansdowne to access his estate at Bowood. The Halt was closed in 1965, but the story of the bereft hound lived on. Every week when I travelled home from swimming club as a child in the early 1980s, jammed into the back of an old Mini with my tracksuited team-mates from Calne Alpha Four, I looked wistfully out of the steamed-up window, hoping for a fleeting glance of the infamous black dog. Sometimes, even, I'd hold my breath in an act of phantom anticipation for the beastly spectre described by a witness in *Wiltshire Notes and Queries* (1896) as the 'girt big black dog, all over bristly hair, flowing fire from his nostrils'. Reader, it never appeared.

CHAPTER 10

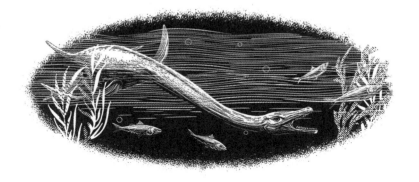

Plesiosaur

The last chapter of *Beastly Britain* gets up close with another creature of monstrous and magical proportions. If ghostly hounds mark the British Isles as a terrestrial landscape resonant with spectral howls, this final critterly entanglement journeys to the fossilised reaches of the distant past and to cryptozoological shorelines of mystery. From bones preserved in sandstone to speculations on the genealogy of a certain long-necked creature emerging from the peaty murk of a Scottish loch, the plesiosaur swims into the story to claim its place as one of the UK's most striking and iconic creatures.

Tales of the Deep: Ancient and Modern

Drawn in crayon and chalk by children the country over, the plesiosaur typically assumes the form of a classic sea monster, gliding through the water at speed, with a body of antediluvian immensity, elongated neck and mouth open in savage anticipation of capturing unsuspecting fish or hapless mariners. It is perhaps no surprise that it looms large in our collective consciousness. Britain is a country of coastlines – some 11,000 miles of it, according to the Ordnance Survey – which none of us live far from (Coton in the Elms, Derbyshire, claims to be the furthest, at 70 miles). Although many of the world's most fantastical marine creatures hailed from distant places – the Kraken of the Greenland Sea, the Cetea of the Indian Ocean – a combination of tidal and imaginary reach makes the UK a particular hotspot for monster folklore.

Britain boasts a lively cultural topography of watery fables to match its estuarine stretches and rocky inlets. Ancient tales told of courageous and conniving beasts that astonished, confounded and sometimes digested travellers on tidal bank, river edge and lake shore. The medieval saga of the Lambton Worm offers one enticing example. Set in County Durham, it told how an irreverent parishioner, John Lambton, played hooky from church on Easter Sunday to go fishing. He managed to catch a small eel-like creature with the head of a dragon and the face of a devil, gnashing teeth and a sticky, stinky saliva. Initially intrigued, he carried the creature off, but decided it was too hideous and too demonic for his liking and so threw it down a well. Years passed, during which Lambton went off to the Crusades and the creature grew to an enormous size. It preyed on local livestock and small children, occasionally uprooted trees in anger and took to coiling itself around a glacial moraine that came to be known as Worm Hill (the striation marks caused by its wriggling can still be seen). Various combatants tried to kill this giant, but every time it was sliced in two it re-joined together to fight another day.

Returning from the Middle East, Lambton resolved to make amends for his youthful rebelliousness by vanquishing the watery monster. A wise witch advised him to wear special bladed armour, designed to cut his adversary into tiny pieces, and to make sure he killed the first living being he saw after killing the monster, or his family would be cursed. Except Lambton forgot. In the delight of seeing monster-parts floating downstream in the River Wear, he forgot to blow the horn (the signal at which his father was meant to release a hunting dog, designed to serve as sacrifice to the curse). When his father galumphed into view, Lambton was unable to raise his sword in anger. Realising the error, he quickly returned to the family estate and killed the hound. However, the cursing forces were not fooled. Nine generations of Lambton men were said to have met grisly fates – drownings, deaths in battle and horse-riding accidents – until the spell was broken. As anthropologist Jamie Tehrani notes, this fable was not only about redemption, but also a cautionary tale about toxic masculinity out of control and the perils of ignoring sage women.

In other regions, tales of writhing beastly bodies were to be found in caves and coves, lakes and lagoons. A Knucker Hole (from the Saxon *nicor*, meaning water monster) near Lyminster, Sussex, led to an underground spring which served as home for a predatory aquatic creature which emerged to eat sheep, cattle and young women. The beast met its match – depending on which version of the yarn you read – at the sword of a peripatetic knight or courtesy of a courageous local lad who killed it with a poisoned pie (only to succumb himself). In Somerset, a giant dragon called Blue Ben was said to reside in a cave gouged out of the coastal shale, from where he slithered along a limestone causeway to reach the cool waters of the Bristol Channel, while in North Wales stories of horror and heroics circulated around the Afanc, a dastardly river monster that shape-shifted across many legends to appear variously as a serpent, dragon, giant beaver, platypus and demon. It cropped up in multiple locations, Llyn Llion, Llyn Barfog and Llyn yr Afanc, terrorising villages and causing floodwater torrents when it thrashed its tail in anger.

In the most widespread iteration of the legend, Afanc was connected with a pool in the Conwy River near Betws-y-Coed. Local villagers were aggravated by the beast, whose contortions regularly caused a deluge of water to flow down the valley, drowning animals and destroying crops. Having tried (and failed) to kill it on many occasions, the locals hatched a translocation plan. Ffynnon Lake in Eryri (Snowdonia) was selected as a good site – far from villages and with steep sides out of which the beast could not climb – but how to entice it there? A master blacksmith forged chains to contain Afanc, and Hu Gardan, a champion Welsh oxen drover, was enlisted to wrangle it north-west to Snowdon. The task of luring it out of its pool, meanwhile, fell to a young maiden known for her intoxicating song, who was to entice the creature out of its watery lair with soft melodies. It worked. Afanc came out, rested his head on her lap and promptly fell asleep. Waking up enchained, the monster kicked off, but the villagers were able to drag it to Yr Wyddfa (Snowdon) where the beast was released into its new abode with a roar. It still resides there.

Such monsters, it turns out, are not just the preserve of ancient legends. Instead, Britain's modern psychogeography is gleefully animated by a menagerie of weird and wonderful beasts that swim and slither in the waters of these isles. In living memory, a great number of people have seen (or at least claim to have seen) them. Documented by cryptozoologist Paul Harrison in *Sea Serpents and Lake Monsters of the British Isles* (2001), sightings from Skye to Skegness, Barmouth to Berry Head, impart tales of slithering bodies, tails, heads and humps emerging from the waves. Forget yarns of yore; in our time, a wander round the coast seemingly invited a brush with nature red in tooth and claw (or, more accurately, greenish-grey with tooth and flipper), lending a bone-chilling quality to the British seaside to match the bleakness of a northerly gale-force wind and a beachside kiosk closed for the season.

Off the coast of Norfolk, Rider Haggard's daughter Phoebe saw a 'thin dark line with a blob at one end, shooting through the water' and travelling at remarkable speed in July 1912. After checking out the story with the staff at his estate at Kessingland Grange, Haggard wrote to the *Eastern Daily Press* asking if readers had seen a 'peculiar creature' in the sea. The paper was inundated with responses from Cromer to Lowestoft – each of which spoke of a long black humped thing able to move through the water like a living torpedo. One summer day in 1935 a 20-foot monster with a similar profile was spotted off the pier in Herne Bay, Kent, prompting small pleasure boats to take pursuit (at a safe distance) and frantic swimmers to scarper out of the surf. An entire season of 'monster fever' broke out in Lincolnshire in the summer of 1966, where a spate of sightings of serpentine heads and humped bodies clustered around the Butlin's holiday camp.

In the south-west, particularly intriguing ripples played out in the shape of Morgawr (Cornish for sea giant), a creature said to be up to 40 feet long, grey or green in colour, with an elongated neck, snakely head and worm-like trunk, scaled or armoured skin, horns or tusks and even bristly hair. In 1838 John Hicks, a fisherman from Mevagissey, reputedly caught a 'great serpent', while seamen in Gerrans Bay in 1876 encountered a similar beast that showed 'signs of defiance', according to the *West Briton* newspaper. The mariners bashed it with an oar to dissuade it from coming near their pilchard nets, and later, when it swam near the boat, they captured it and brought it to shore. Locals gathered in Porthscatho harbour to marvel at the curious catch but, much to the consternation of the *Royal Cornish Gazette*, which saw the potential for a wildly popular tourist exhibit, the creature slipped away. Some say it was dashed to pieces on the rocks, but this was not the end of the story.

Morgawr's seductive silhouette resurfaced many times over the course of the twentieth century to spar with whales, gobble up sharks and spook any onlookers it came across.

Passengers on the *Phoenix*, a liner bound for New York, saw the 'reptile's head . . . [with] a fierce and most forbidding aspect' off Land's End in 1906. Seventy years later, in a March 1976 letter to the *Falmouth Packet* signed by 'Mary F', a bottle-green monster was spotted off Trefusis Point. Accompanying photographs portrayed the small black head of a creature with a neck akin to an elephant's trunk. She added: 'I would not like to see it any closer. I did not like the way it moved when swimming.'

Perhaps the most bizarre set of fishly tales was associated with artist, psychic and showman Tony 'Doc' Shiels, who spent the mid-1970s trying to summon the famous Cornish leviathan with the help of witches, self-styled 'dragon hunters' and TV camera crews. On Mawgan Beach in 1977 he was throwing sticks for his dog with the editor of *Cornish Life*, when a smooth dark head apparently emerged from the water. Both men confessed to feeling both fascinated and afraid at sharing a gaze with the monster. Morgawr looked in their direction, opened and closed its mouth, then lowered its body back into the deep from where it had come.

What were these unruly beasts, habitually emerging from Britannia's waves? Naysayers spoke of psychological delusions, pretensions to fame and fortune, overactive imaginations and inclement weather. Paul Harrison, however, described monster sightings as 'very real', in that most spotters remained convinced they had seen *something*. Perhaps these brushes with the beastly were encounters with known species: seals or basking sharks, eels, oarfish, giant squid or even whales (specifically their penises, which bore resemblance to the classic sea monster head/neck profile at distance). Equally, they could have been tricks of the light or flotsam and jetsam. More radically, might we dare to imagine there could be cryptids – legendary or extinct creatures – lurking off Britain's coasts? According to the *Daily Telegraph*, a 'monster' seen off Filey, North Yorkshire, in March 1934 could *only* be described as an 'unclassified, but awe-inspiring species'. Others dived deeper into antediluvian waters looking for answers. Harold Wilkins, who saw not one but two immense water beasts off East Looe, Cornwall, was sure they were plesiosaurs, while fisherman Tommy Graham from Maryporth had only one word to describe the creature he saw from a small vessel in 1933: 'dinosaur'.

Could a pod of plesiosaurs really have endured until modern times to gamely cavort in British seas? The notion was certainly entertained in nineteenth-century circles. Science writer Philip Henry Gosse, writing in *The Romance of Natural History* (1861), hypothesised that the sea serpent encountered by HMS *Daedalus* in South Atlantic seas in 1848 was likely to be a relic species of dinosaur. Biologist Thomas Henry Huxley wrote to *The Times* in 1893 as follows: 'There is not an a priori reason that I know of why snake-bodied reptiles, from fifty feet long and upwards, should not disport themselves in our seas as they did in those of the cretaceous epoch which, geologically speaking, is a mere yesterday.'

It seems unlikely that a sustainable population could have persisted – undisturbed and largely undetected – given the ferries, trawlers and all manner of leisure craft traversing coastal waters. That said, water covers 71% of the Earth's surface and only a fraction of the world's oceans have been explored. Who knows what might exist in these uncharted depths? Science fiction writer Ray Bradbury toyed with the tantalising prospect of a prehistoric survivor in his short story 'The Fog Horn' (1951). The beastly protagonist in his modern fable was a lonely soul who mistook the siren call of a lighthouse for a mate, surfaced to find his paramour more Sandtex than saurian and smashed it to smithereens. Elsewhere, various weird marine happenstances presented glimmers of possibility. The coelacanth, for instance, a species presumed extinct for 66 million years, was found alive in seas off South Africa in 1938, earning it the title of a 'Lazarus taxon', a species that came back from the dead.

What about the grotesquely captivating 'globsters' (unidentified carcasses) that wash up on seashores all over the world: could these be surviving animals from an ancient age? In 1808 a 55-foot creature dubbed the 'Stronsay Beast' was beached during stormy seas on the Orkney Islands. Experts from the Natural History Society, Edinburgh, scratched their heads as to what it could be and concluded it must be a new type of sea serpent, which they named *Halsydrus pontoppidani* or water snake of the sea. Others contended it was a basking shark (the decomposition pattern of which meant the lower jaws and dorsal fin decayed first, leaving a saurianesque body), while some – evocatively expressed in a sketch from Sir Alexander Gibson – opted for an antediluvian ancestry.

A curious body caught in fishing nets off New Zealand in 1977 by the Japanese trawler *Zuiyo Maru* provoked similarly sensational speculations. Documented in grainy photographs and sketches from Michihiko Yano, the boat's production manager, it presented the characteristic look of a classic plesiosaur with long neck and flippers. The leviathan lines of the 10-metre beast, along with crew testimony that talked of the 'capture of a Nessie-like carcass' inspired fervent popular interest (including a commemorative postage stamp) as well as striking scientific statements from Yoshinori Imaizumi of the Tokyo National Science Museum and Tokio Shikama from Yokohama National University, the latter of whom concluded: 'It has to be a plesiosaurus.' Marine specialists elsewhere (including the FBI) were more sanguine, thinking it far more likely to be the putrid remnants of a basking shark. Sadly, there was no body to settle the taxonomical mystery of the *Zuiyo Maru*, the crew having thrown the carcass overboard as it smelled so bad.

Back in Cornwall, finding the truth in Morgawr's tale involved similar contortions. As Harrison dug deeper into Cornish critterly chatter, most of which derived from the mid-1970s, he came across a strong dose of make-believe in the psychedelic haze. Doc Shiels as good as admitted he was 'Mary F', while his Monster Mind Experiment of January 1977 – designed to awaken the collective cryptids of the world through the power of several international psychics – seemed more than a little Paul Daniels. Eagerly endorsed by monster hunters with a 'want to believe' outlook, Morgawr was best described, according to folklorist Ronald James, as a fabulous example of 'fakelore': a beast brought into being by the power of storytelling that broke free of its moorings to frolic happily in local culture for the purposes of identity politics, tourist revenue and creaturely thrill-seeking.

Others, though, continued to subscribe to the idea of a prehistoric survivor out there in the surf, pointing to a handful of highly credible sightings in the mid-1980s and, particularly, to the testimony of John Holmes, ex-scientific officer at the Natural History Museum who, in 2002, produced a home video shot at Gerrans Bay a few years previously, which he believed showed the existence of 'a living fossil [and] . . . a group of plesiosaurs going around in the oceans of the world'. Media experts ruled the footage as genuine but refused to make any categorical statements as to the nature of the subject matter. The Cornish cryptid hasn't been seen since 1999, but its signature slippery contours can be viewed on Market Street, Falmouth, where a shapely bench with humped backrests pays homage to the famous sea monster. Who's to say a walker on the South West Coastal Path might not take a pause for fish and chips, gaze across the Channel and spot a saurian shadow gliding elegantly by?

The Jurassic Fantastic

British seas were ideal habitat for plesiosaurs once upon a time. Approximately 190 million years ago, the landmass of the British Isles was between 30 and 40 degrees north of the equator and the animal complement looked rather different. For one thing, much of the land was covered by a warm, shallow sea, populated by a range of species, including ammonites, belemnites and aquatic reptiles. This was the domain of the *Plesiosaurus*, an order of marine giants that evolved during the Triassic (215 million years ago) and contained more than 100 species. Unlike its closest cousin, the short-necked and long-nosed pliosaur, the plesiosaur was identified by its long neck, small head and broad, plump body. Up to 15 metres long, it was an impressive beast: a real-life, prehistoric leviathan of the deep.

Found in all the world's oceans and one of the most successful species of the Jurassic (200–145 million years ago), the temperate waters of what would be the British Isles delivered rich feeding grounds and habitat for the plesiosaur. Evolved from an earlier genus of marine reptiles called *Sauropterygians*, or flippered lizards, these ancient beasts were formidable predators, equipped with sharp teeth designed to capture and consume the fish, molluscs, squid and small reptiles that comprised their diet. Their bodies were covered with tiny scales and moved through the water courtesy of a small tail (which served as a rudder) and four bony limb-plates or paddles. Many marine animals use flippers for propulsion – think seals, penguins, sea lions – but what was remarkable was that the plesiosaurs had two pairs on board. We still don't know how exactly they operated (for instance, did the fore and rear flippers move separately or in tandem?), though scientists suspect they functioned rather like the wings of a dragonfly, capable of acting independently and working in phase to deliver both power and efficiency.

A deeper dive into prehistoric anatomy brings further surprises. Plesiosaurs were not actually dinosaurs. Technically, they did not share the upright stance (straight-backed bodies and perpendicular limbs) which set that group of reptiles apart from, say, lizards. They were also unlike most antediluvian marine animals in that they had no gills and instead surfaced from the deep to breathe oxygen. They birthed live young and were warm-blooded, making them much more akin to present-day aquatic species such as whales. The signature feature of the plesiosaur, its neck, offers yet more revelations. Taking up half its entire length and featuring up to seventy-six vertebrae, this elongated appendage is probably the plesiosaur's most distinguishing feature and one which gave it a certain monstrous quality. As depicted in nineteenth- and early-twentieth-century lithographs and museum models, it could be bent in all manner of serpentine flails, snaking out of the waves in elegant yet ungainly fashion.

Except that it couldn't. Recent anatomical studies have shown that, despite its super-stretchy look, the plesiosaur had rather a stiff neck, one which was able to move up and down due to the strong muscles which held it rigidly in the water, but it entirely lacked the capacity for rubbery contortions or swan-like gestures. As biologist Paul Scofield put it, the motion was more inverted giraffe than sock puppet. Biomechanically speaking, it remains hard to identify the genetic evolutionary advantage of having such a long neck. Palaeontologists surmise it could have been effective in hunting fast-swimming species or might have operated as a stealth device that allowed a 15-metre predator to creep up on unsuspecting fish (which presumably didn't realise the relatively distant marine body had a rather more proximate set of gnashing teeth). Perhaps, even, it allowed this species to bottom-feed for shellfish, lowering its head to the ocean floor like a JCB flipped on its back.

Fossil Mania

Plesiosaurs inhabited what would become British waters until 66 million years ago, when an asteroid collided with the Earth, causing global temperatures to plummet and food to become scarce. Three-quarters of living species became extinct. The plesiosaur went the way of the dinosaurs, unless you believe the cryptid hunters. Either way, that was not the end of its story. Fast-forward to the early nineteenth century, a time of industrial, demographic and socioeconomic transformation and one which was about to fall into the grip of fossil mania. Here, in the crumbling coasts of Dorset, the plesiosaur was about to (literally) burst out of the rock to become a beastly sensation.

Why here? The answer lies in the soil or, more accurately, in the geology. That shallow sea which covered much of Britain and supported a buoyant population of species eventually receded as the tectonic plate on which the UK sat moved north. When that happened, the sedimentary rocks and clay which formerly lay on the seabed were exposed, their textured lines revealing a chronology of organic deposits in the sandstone and oolite, tiny fossils, shells and skeletal remains: a veritable Jurassic Park preserved in prehistorically packed strata. Across south-western England, in fact, you find evidence of this ancient marine world in sandstone deposits full of tiny fossil shells. As a child, I remember eagerly taking off across the fields to go hunting in the local 'holy well' in Wiltshire. This magical spot was known for the tiny stars or crinoids with could be discovered around the spring, though intrepid fossilers ran the gauntlet of squelching mud as the freshwater also served as drinking spot for the herd of Friesians who were almost always in the field. No plesiosaur was buried here. For that, we have to go back to Lyme Regis.

Mary Anning, fossil collector, trader and palaeontologist, born in the Dorset town in 1799, was the first to discover an entire plesiosaur skeleton anywhere in the world. There had been fragmentary finds before, the odd vertebrate or skeletal remnant in a Lincolnshire quarry and documented by antiquarian William Stukeley (1719), but no one had found a complete specimen. An avid beachcomber, Anning was a familiar sight along the coast, especially after winter storms, gathering belemnites, ammonites and other fossils with her father Richard, who supplemented his income as a carpenter by selling geological curios on a table outside the family home. When Richard died, Mary and her brother Joseph continued the practice, scouring local Blue Lias and mudstone deposits for interesting finds. In 1811 the pair struck palaeontological gold by finding first the skull and then the skeleton of an *Ichthyosaur*, which they sold to a wealthy collector for the sum of £23.

Known for her daredevil excavations of the unstable cliffs, Mary was something of a maverick in the world of palaeontology, a poor, working-class, female, self-taught fossil hunter, though there was a surprising number of female geologists who contributed to the field in their own right (Etheldred Benett and Elizabeth Philpot, to name a couple) or operated with their more famous husbands as what historians Mary and Thomas Creese label 'wife assistants'. Later described by Charles Darwin as a paragon of 'stubborn English perseverance', Anning spent long hours working the coastline, skilfully unearthing new and important specimens, only for wealthy antiquarians and professional 'men of science' to claim the limelight for themselves. One of her associates, Anna Maria Pinney, remarked in her private diary of one such intrepid trip: 'We climbed down places, which I'd have thought impossible to have descended', before issuing an acerbic attack on the ways in which Mary's scientific acumen was sidelined: 'Men of learning have sucked her brains, and made a great deal by publishing works, of which she furnished the contents, while she derived none of the advantages.'

The discovery of the complete plesiosaur was a case in point. On 10 December 1823, Mary headed out as usual, leaving the harbour and trudging east across the sand and rocks to Black Ven, one of her favoured places for fossil hunting. It was here, two winters previously, that she had discovered a jumble of skeletal remains (most of which had disintegrated by the time she got back to her workbench) that Mary surmised to be from a long-necked and hitherto unknown marine reptile. These fossilised remnants were sold to Lieutenant-Colonel Thomas James Birch, a member of the Lincolnshire gentry and a frequent sponsor of the

Annings. This time, however, a shiny round object could be seen protruding from the Blue Lias and, after a whole night of careful excavation, Mary unearthed a remarkable prize: an entire skeleton belonging to a 9-foot sea beast with a small head, long neck and paddle-like limbs, the likes of which had been speculated on, but never seen before. She penned a note to one of her patrons, Sir Henry Bunbury, a wealthy baronet with antiquarian interests, both to record the details of the discovery and to tout for a sale. Accompanying Mary's note was a powerful image, a beautiful, intricately drawn ink in which every anatomical detail was picked out, nose to tail (see Fig. 30). Classically saurian in its proportions, Mary's 'rough sketch' absolutely satisfied her stated aim to give 'some idea' of what her astonishing excavation looked like.

Anning's discovery provoked lively chatter in geological circles. News travelled from Lyme Regis to London through the informal networks Mary had made with fossil collectors and palaeontologists. When the geological grapevine reached Paris, Georges Cuvier, arguably the most influential comparative anatomist of the day, declared the skeleton must be a fake, a chimera of a creature with an impossibly long neck. There was precedent here: bones from ancient sea monsters with dubious biological provenance were to be found in freak shows and museum venues across the country. Take, for instance, the wonderfully named *Gymnetrus Northumbricus*, a sea serpent with a striking cockatoo crest that was supposedly caught in the North Sea in 1849 and shown at London's Cosmorama Rooms on Regent Street, or, indeed, the replica ichthyosaur sold to the British Museum in 1834 by wealthy collector Thomas Hawkins. Something of an upper-crust confidence trickster – geologist Gideon Mantell labelled him as 'a very rich young man with more money than wit' – Hawkins's line in fossilised fraud was only revealed when curator Charles Konig put a scalpel through the plaster 'bones' of the specimen as he was readying it for display.

The Lyme Regis plesiosaur came under the scrutiny of a special meeting at the Geological Society on 24 February

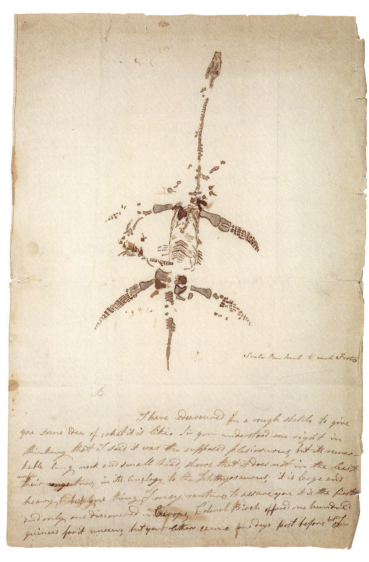

30. Mary Anning's famous sketch of a plesiosaur, sent with a letter to one of her patrons, Sir Henry Bunbury, in December 1823, and designed, as she said, to give 'some idea as to what it is like'.

1824. Anning was not invited: women were forbidden from being members and, besides, the idea that a poor, self-taught female fossil hunter might have something to contribute scarcely entered the closeted minds of the male scientific elite. Instead, the presentation was delivered by William Conybeare, clergyman palaeontologist and doyen of the British Geological Society, who had hot-footed it to Lyme Regis that winter to examine Mary's find. Together with fellow geologist Henry De la Beche, he had written a paper in 1821 on the anatomy and taxonomy of the beast they named *Plesiosaurus dolichodeirus* ('near lizard with a long neck'), based largely on bodily fragments unearthed by Anning the previous year. Now, too, he drew heavily on Mary's research, especially her notes and sketches. It was also hoped the sensational skeleton would make an appearance and, to that end, the Duke of Buckingham (who had bought the specimen for £110) travelled with his new acquisition by sea from Dorset. Bad weather in the English Channel meant they didn't arrive in time, but Conybeare nonetheless wowed the audience with an address entitled 'On the discovery of an almost perfect skeleton of the *Plesiosaurus*' and an evocative picture of prehistoric life. He spoke of a saurian beast swimming near the water surface, stretching its neck out 'like the swan and occasionally darting it down' to capture fish, before hiding in a kelp forest from predators, only its nostrils visible in the swaying seaweed. Mary was never mentioned by name, credit being given instead to the 'scientific public' that facilitated the discovery. The Society endorsed the skeleton as authentic. *Plesiosaurus* was formally identified and Cuvier ate humble pie.

Portraits of Deep Time

The prehistoric traces discovered by Anning and other nineteenth-century fossil hunters inspired a lively conversation about geological time and the creatures that inhabited an ancient Earth. Long after they had turned to sediment, plesiosaurs were trampling forth in metaphysical debates about the age of the world, the relationship between scientific and religious accounts of creation and between extant and extinct species. Scientists and theologians, philosophers and antiquarians all pondered where to place this curious sea monster and how to think on it. Henry De la Beche produced the captivating *Duria Antiquior, or, a More Ancient Dorset* (1830), which presented a vivid pictorial representation of the fossil finds of the Jurassic Coast (see Fig. 31). The first time 'deep time' was presented in visual form, the watercolour depicted a balmy stretch where a vast array of winged and marine reptiles soared above, and swam in the shallows of a prehistoric sea. The dominant message was 'eat or be eaten' and most creatures were in the throes of combat or seeking to avoid confrontation by hiding away. Of three

31. A fabulous scene from *Duria Antiquior* by Henry De la Beche (1830), which shows various prehistoric creatures in 'deep-time' Dorset. Three plesiosaurs are depicted in the picture, each of which are engaged in life-or-death contests with other ancient beasts.

plesiosaurs in the frame, one was stretching its neck out of the water to grab a crocodile's tail, the other doing the same to surprise a pterodactyl, while a third found itself trapped in a painful neck-hold courtesy of a biting ichthyosaur. Capturing a sense of antediluvian romance and horror, the drawing proved a hit among contemporaries. De la Beche had a lithographer run off prints, the proceeds of which were donated to Anning, who had just unearthed another plesiosaur skeleton, but was still struggling to make ends meet.

While De la Beche was enraptured by battles for survival in deep time, William Buckland, theologian and geologist, was trying to reconcile his Christian and scientific beliefs. *The Bridgewater Treatises* (1836) saw him explore such issues, along the way offering a fulsome description of plesiosaurian anatomy. Depicted as a 'strange' form that seemed to incorporate elements from a range of creatures, he described the sea beast as combining 'the head of a Lizard . . . the teeth of a Crocodile; a neck of enormous length, resembling the body of a Serpent; a trunk and tail having the proportions of an ordinary quadruped, the ribs of a Chameleon, and the paddles of a Whale'. Buckland ended his anatomical review with an extraordinary extrapolation on cross-species kinship: 'Even our own bodies . . . are brought into close and direct comparison with those of reptiles, which, at first sight, appear the most monstrous productions of creation; and in the very hand and fingers with which we write their history, we recognise the type of the paddles of the Ichthyosaurus and Plesiosaurus.'

Thomas Hawkins, fossil devotee and dealer based in Glastonbury, was also ruminating on how to affix the geological record to his spiritual worldview in *The Book of the Great Sea Dragons* (1840). Alongside plates depicting his geological collections lifted from Somerset and Dorset, sections of heavy primordial prose speculated on an ancient time of monsters, an epoch of the geological sublime which was forbidding, alien and dark, in his words 'an eltrichworld uninhabitate, sunless and moonless, and seared in the angry light of supernal fire'. In this antediluvian murk, a 'Spectral World' of 'poison fang and fury', the plesiosaur was one of a 'thousand hideous monsters' perennially locked in combat. The cover illustration showed two swimming plesiosaurs fighting an ichthyosaur, while another lay beached on the shore, its eye pecked at by two hungry pterodactyls.

Beyond the libraries and laboratories of the scientific elite, others were busily trying to imagine prehistoric worlds. Richard Owen, the first superintendent of the Natural History Museum and an acclaimed naturalist, coined the term 'dinosaur' (Latin for terrible lizard) in 1841 and it soon entered popular parlance. Across the country, local geological and naturalist clubs hosted lectures on all manner of topics, broadly encompassed by the 'lost age of the reptiles', while the reading public feasted on Jules Verne's underwater duel between plesiosaur and ichthyosaur in *Journey to the Centre of the Earth* (1864) and, later on, wondered at the captivating beasts in Arthur Conan Doyle's *The Lost World* (1912), living through the experience of the expeditioners as they encountered for the first time a captivating beast with a 'high serpent head ... barrel-shaped body and huge flippers behind the long serpent neck'. Reverend Henry Hutchinson – a clergyman and popular science writer – penned five books on geology in the 1890s alone to satisfy the public appetite for the prehistoric, combining anatomical descriptions, photographs of fossils, artistic descriptions and comical cartoons to animate the ancient past. His *Extinct Monsters* (1892) included a section on the plesiosaur, the 'long-necked lizard', in a study that aimed to 'bring to life' the 'lost creations of the old world' in a way that 'gazing at skeletons set up in museums' could never do. 'One longs', Hutchinson mused, 'to cover their nakedness with flesh and skin, and to see them as they were when they walked this earth.'

Those Victorians who wanted to get up close to the prehistoric found a few venues on offer. Middle-class tourists journeyed to Lyme Regis and wandered the cliffs with fossil hammers in hand and called at the Fossil Depot (as Mary's shop was known) to buy their own slice of the Jurassic fantastic. Anning's famous plesiosaur skeleton, meanwhile, was purchased by the British Museum from the Duke of Buckingham's estate in 1848 and placed on public display – alongside other sea giants – in the Marine Reptiles Gallery of the new Natural History Museum in South Kensington shortly after its opening in 1881. A guidebook to the exhibition galleries from 1890 contained a description and diagram of the impressive beast which splendidly swam along the walls of the museum alongside other fossilised forms, their prehistoric dimensions arrested in life-size frozen animation.

The place that perhaps came closest of all to a full-on immersive experience with deep time was Sydenham Hill, South London. Opened in 1854, this was home to the relocated Crystal Palace (created for the Great Exhibition), extensive landscape gardens and – evocatively captured in a period engraving from George Baxter – a prowling group of cement-rendered prehistoric beasts (see Fig. 32). The creation of scientific illustrator and sculptor Benjamin Waterhouse Hawkins – who had been commissioned by site owners, the Crystal Palace Company, to produce models of extinct animals in the grounds – the strange menagerie delivered 'state-of-the-art' palaeontological knowledge and provided an attractive commercial lure for the new theme park. Crafted in a workshop on site from clay moulds, the brick, steel and concrete beasts were placed in a 'geological court' at the far end of the 380-acre site, strategically positioned to give visitors something to set their sights on as they left the glasshouse at the top of the hill and walked down through Italianate terraces, roseries and grand water gardens. Situated on three islands, designed to represent Palaeozoic, Mesozoic and Cenozoic periods, were some thirty-odd 'true' dinosaurs as well as ichthyosaurs and plesiosaurs. Land-based animals peeped out from behind rocks and shrubbery, while aquatic species rested in shallow pools and on ledges, hydraulic pumps ensuing that

32. A primeval landscape of prowling dinosaurs can be seen in the foreground of George Baxter's print, 'The Crystal Palace from the Great Exhibition, installed at Sydenham' (c.1864).

water levels rose and fell to simulate the tide and to playfully reveal and obscure prehistoric bodies at different times of day. Three plesiosaurs featured in the ensemble, wallowing in shallow waters suggesting an amphibian habit, each depicted as slender crocodilian beasts with jointed flippers and impossibly bendy necks.

Science and sentiment, titillation and terror blended together to ensure the Crystal Palace monsters became a roaring success. On New Year's Eve 1853, before the park formally opened, Hawkins invited a group of well-to-do diners to take dinner in the belly of the model iguanodon, their liberal consumption of alcohol ensuring that loud bellows emanated from deep within the beast late into the night. The *Gardener's Chronicle*, which was never afraid to cast a critical gaze over what it regarded as improper horticultural adornments, eagerly endorsed the 'hideous giants of a former world' as wonderful complements to the park, while Charles Dickens effused about the 'Fairyland' of living ancients where 'gigantic creatures of lizard, toadlike, froglike, beastlike form grin at you, crawl at you, wind their hideous tails around you'. The opportunity to witness prehistoric Britain up close saw some 2 million visitors a year make their way to Sydenham for a thrill ride into deep time. The park was not cheap to enter – 20 shillings for a family of four – but its striking mixture of education and entertainment made for a winning formula. A testament to its cultural resonance, a cartoon in *Punch* magazine illustrated a slumbering man tucked up in bed after a wildly fascinating trip, fitfully dreaming of antediluvian visitations, including a plesiosaur perched uncomfortably on a bedside chair (see Fig. 33).

THE EFFECTS OF A HEARTY DINNER AFTER VISITING THE ANTEDILUVIAN DEPARTMENT AT THE CRYSTAL PALACE.

33. *Punch* magazine (2 March 1855) made merry with the fantastical dreams one might have after combining a visit to the Crystal Palace with a large (and probably boozy) supper.

The Crystal Palace models were the first examples of palaeo-art sculpture anywhere in the world and a prime site (perhaps even the first) for the exercise of dino-mania. Their fortunes during the early twentieth century, however, were about as precarious as *Punch*'s seated saurian. Battered by the elements and clambered over by generations of children eager to put their heads into perpetually gaping jaws, the stucco giants of South London needed constant maintenance. When the Crystal Palace Company went bankrupt in 1909 and the glasshouse was destroyed by fire in 1936, they fell into disrepair. Changing scientific understandings, meanwhile, saw the 'geological court' recast as an outdated relic – the heads were too big and bodies scandalously inaccurate. The extinct became obsolete, discredited by palaeontologists, overgrown by shrubbery and, even, bombed by the Luftwaffe (which managed to knock the head off one plesiosaur). Things began to look up in the early 1950s when the dinosaurs received mortar repairs and fresh coats of paint to menace in monochrome for a British Pathé newsreel entitled *Palace Monsters* (1954). A full renovation programme (2001) and a Grade 1 listing (2007) suggest they might just have survived another extinction event.

The Lacuna in the Loch: Nessie as Modern Monster

The final waymark along the monsterly shores of Beastly Britain takes us north, to the Scottish Highlands, where the most infamous of all water monsters resides. Loch Ness hosts arguably the most famous plesiosaur, quite a feat considering that Nessie isn't necessarily a plesiosaur and might not actually exist. Around the world there exist other bodies of water with mysterious serpentine occupants – Champ of Lake Champlain, Chessie of Chesapeake Bay, the Ogopogo of Okanagan Lake – and closer to home cryptids in the shape of Morag at Loch Morar and Lizzie in Loch Lochy, but none has the same spectacular reach as Nessie.

Loch Ness is 23 miles long and up to 230 metres deep. Created by a geological fault line, it holds 7,452 million cubic metres of dark, peaty water (more than all the English and Welsh lakes combined) and retains a link to the sea courtesy of the River Ness, which feeds into the Moray Firth. The earliest record of a water beast here dates to AD 565, when Irish monk St Columba came across a burial being conducted on the banks of the River Ness for an unlucky local swimmer who had been attacked. When the party tried to cross the watercourse, the hungry monster reappeared and was thwarted only by the saint's holy words and his cross held aloft. Related in Adomnán's *Life of St Columba* (c.700), a hagiography of the holy man which combined a hotchpotch of hearsay and hero worship, this was but one of many stupendous feats performed by the saint, from taming snakes to charming wild boar.

There were a few scattered tales through the centuries. In 1527 Duncan Campbell spotted a 'terrible beast' on the shore of the loch and in 1879 a group of children saw a 'small head on a long neck' protruding from the water. However, it was not until the early 1930s that sightings snowballed. Nessie was, put simply, a thoroughly modern monster. How so? Some might attribute the explosion in beastly tales at this particular moment to the Great Depression. When the certainties of modernity were challenged by stock market implosions, bank foreclosures and mass unemployment, the landscape of legend presented a wonderfully escapist realm in which to hide from a grim and mechanical reality. It also happened to be the time when a new road and hotels were built along the edge of the loch, making the area accessible (Nessie fans would say) and ripe for commercial development (the sceptics' choice). In any case, as the *Daily Express* pointed out, the fortuitous (and sudden) appearance of Nessie presented a boon for the region: Scotland's answer to the Taj Mahal, the Empire State Building, Primo Carnera (the hottest prize fighter of the hour) and the cartoon feature *Ripley's Believe It or Not*, all rolled into one. Moreover, as Daniel Loxton and Donald Prothero noted in *Abominable Science: Origins of the Yeti, Nessie, and Other Famous Cryptids* (2013), the flurry of encounters coincided with the release of the Hollywood blockbuster, *King Kong* (1933), which not only stirred a media frenzy around all things monstrous, but also featured a fight between the famous ape and a plesiosaur adversary. As the *Scotsman* astutely put it, this celluloid collision involving 'prehistoric monsters in contact with modern conditions' was just what the public wanted.

After a slow-burn newspaper item in the *Northern Chronicle* of August 1930, which reported how local fishermen were 'disturbed' by a 6-metre-long unidentified creature that left a wriggling wake, things really started hotting up at Loch Ness in May 1933. This was when the *Inverness Courier* carried an article that told how two local residents saw an unexplained beastie 'rolling and plunging for fully a minute, its body resembling that of a whale, and the water cascading and churning like a simmering cauldron'. Journalist Alex Campbell, who penned the piece, rated the sighting as credible, coming, as it did, from a local businessman and university graduate and, adding a bit of artistic licence and some extravagant prose, concluded the loch was inhabited by a 'fearsome-looking monster'. Later that summer, holidaymaker George Spicer and his wife saw a mysterious creature cross the road with a lamb in its mouth and disappear into the loch. Spicer's evocative description of the beast as 'dragon-like' in body with 'a long neck which moved up and down, in the manner of a scenic railway' spurred all manner of debate, not least from the *Chronicle*, which concluded this must have been a 'surviving variant *plesiosaurus*'. A handful of sightings followed over the next few months, along with corroborating photographs from Hugh Gray, who claimed to have seen the monster six times and managed, on one occasion, to capture a blurry form in the water, and Harley Street gynaecologist Robert Kenneth Wilson, whose April 1934 shot of a serpentine-necked creature poking out from the loch (the so-called 'Surgeon's Photograph') was front-page news in the *Daily Mail* and remains the most iconic footage of the Loch Ness Monster to date.

The cryptid phenomenon known as 'Nessie' (a term of endearment first used by the Edinburgh *Evening News* in January 1934 that won out against the *Daily Mail*'s 'Bobby the Sea Serpent') sparked a wave of monster mania in the decades that followed. Package tours and plush toys, popular ditties and consumer product endorsements made for a cash cow of beastly dimensions, while the countless captivating questions and few categorical answers that swirled around the loch created a fertile cultural ecology based on perpetual prognosis. Did the monster exist? Was it a prehistoric marine reptile, an otter, seal, eel, sturgeon or cormorant? How could a plesiosaur find enough to eat in the loch? Surely one animal could not have survived for so long? – ergo, there must be a family Ness. Cue the monster hunters, who formed a lively parade in the years that followed, often with the latest hi-tech in tow, and always resolved to settle the question of the lochian lacuna.

One of the first to arrive on the scene was actor and big-game hunter Marmaduke Wetherell, commissioned by the *Daily Mail* in the mid-1930s to find the beast, but who left in disgrace (either by accident or design) when the 'foot-prints' he supposedly discovered on the shoreline were found by the Natural History Museum to come from an altogether different beast: a hippopotamus-foot umbrella stand designed by taxidermist Rowland Ward and one of his signature pieces of 'animal furniture'. Wetherell's part in this drama was not over, however. Years later, in 1975, his son revealed the maverick monster hunter had created a 12-inch mock plesio-saur and floated it on the loch. This had been the animal captured in the Surgeon's Photograph. Wetherell's erstwhile employers at the *Mail* had been well and truly out-hoaxed.

Other investigators making a deep dive into Nessian waters included Rupert Gould, ex-naval officer and author of *The Loch Ness Monster and Others* (1934), and Constance Whyte, author of *More Than a Legend: The Story of the Loch Ness Monster* (1957). Gould toured the area on a motorcycle bought at Inverness, carrying maps, binoculars and a sense of objective 'detachment', to conclude the monster was one of the 'rarest and least known of all living creatures', most likely the descendant of a plesiosaur that found safe harbour in the loch (though he later decided Nessie was more likely to be a giant newt). Whyte, on the other hand, steered clear of speculating on the identity of the monster and instead focused on its cultural imprint, which amounted to a constant trickle of accounts (each, according to the dust jacket of her book, from persons of integrity) through to the 1950s. The 1960s and 1970s, meanwhile, brought all manner of devices to bear on the matter, from sonar waves to psychic powers, floodlights to submersibles. Tim Dinsdale, one of the biggest names in Nessie-hunting, spent a week on the lochside in 1960, having been inspired by reading about it in a popular magazine. His journey was epic: 'seeing' the monster on Day 1, then realising it was a tree; a long six-day interval in the cryptid wilderness without any sightings, followed by a 'flipper shot' on his last day, which he rapturously snapped on film. As he effused in the *The Loch Ness Monster* (1961), 'through the magic lens of my camera I had reached out, across a thousand years or more, to *grasp the monster by the tail*'.

Consumed by the idea of putting scientific flesh on the spectral skeleton of Nessie, veteran hunter Constance Whyte, along with conservationists Peter Scott and Richard Fitter, MP David James and broadcaster Norman Collins, created the Loch Ness Investigation Bureau in 1962. Using state-of-the-art wildlife filmmaking techniques and echo-imaging to document movement on and in the waters of the loch, the outfit produced some unexplained readings from an underwater 'acoustic net', but funding ran out in 1972. Other expeditioners carried forth the sonar baton, notably a series of projects through the mid-1970s sponsored by the US Academy of Applied Science and led by Robert Rines, which bounced sound waves off the floor of the loch and took underwater photographs. Enhanced by new image software from NASA, one of the resultant images showed a large grainy body and a fin, another what appeared to be two beastly forms. Enthusiasts got very excited and eagerly read the evidence as proof of a surviving plesiosaur, including Peter Scott, who gave the beast a scientific name to secure its protection as an endangered species. *Nessiteras rhombopteryx* ('Ness inhabitant with diamond-shaped fin'), as it turned out, contained a tongue-in-cheek taxonomical conceit, being an anagram of 'Monster hoax by Sir Peter S' and 'Yes, both pix are monsters, R'. Sceptics pointed out the images were probably from a saurian model used for a 1969 film, *The Private Life of Sherlock Holmes*, which had unceremoniously sunk to the bottom of the loch during filming.

The official Loch Ness sightings register runs, to date, to more than 1,100 reports. In the last fifty years, there have been more investigations, twists and turns, declarations of Nessie's truth, alive-ness and demise. Keeping the tale twitching was a lack of anything definitive; new reports switch-backed this way and that, sceptics and enthusiasts, science and storytelling reveal serving as beastly counterweights through the decades. Operation Deep Scan (1987) used a flotilla of boats to scan the entire body of water with sonar. They didn't find anything obviously monstrous, but they *did* plot an unexplained object moving in the murk 67 metres beneath the surface. In 2014 things looked bleak. Nessie had not been seen for eighteen months and the *Daily Star* sombrely reported on her death. Four years later, researchers from New Zealand performed a genetic sweep of the loch and found evidence not of saurian DNA but plenty of eel.

The story of Nessie, however, is not over. Perhaps it never will be. Stalwarts like Steve Feltham, veteran monster hunter of thirty years, continue to keep the dream alive: surveying the loch from the shore, eyes trained on the peaty waters of this most mysterious of beastly locations. Fresh fossil finds (2022) from further afield, meanwhile, highlighted the reaches of deep time as a fluid terrain, this time rewriting the accustomed wisdom on plesiosaur habitat to suggest the species was able to live in cold (Queensland) and fresh (Morocco) water. Both were boons to the Loch Ness Monster which, according to the *Daily Telegraph*, suddenly seemed 'more plausible' as a phenomenon. Post-COVID lockdown, in fact, Nessie seems to have re-emerged with fresh vigour. The Official Loch Ness Sightings Register lists twenty-five unexplained occurrences since 2021, many of which were spotted by avid watchers (from all over the world) of the twenty-four-hour-streaming Loch Ness webcams. Sonar readings taken during a Cruise Loch Ness excursion in October 2020 located a curious shape moving 500 feet beneath the surface and in October 2024 one of the Deepscan boat tours recorded a 'sizeable reading' suggesting 'substantial underwater presences or potentially large aquatic creatures'. With beastly chatter at an all-time high, Paddy Power slashed the odds of finding the monster from 10/1 to to 2/1 and a brand-new theory surfaced: this time from paranormal investigator Scott Ron Halliday, who contended Nessie might be a psychic shadow, a throwback to the Jurassic that only the most creaturely attuned were able to see.

The truth, as Fox Mulder of the *X-Files* regularly asserted, may be out there, but it shows no signs of immediate resolution. What remains firmly beyond doubt, however, is the continuing resonance of Nessie as an iconic monster and a classic, perhaps the classic, plesiosaur. Speaking on Radio 4's *Today* programme in February 2023, Paul Davis, geological curator of the Lyme Regis Museum, talked about the discovery of a new fossilised species on the Jurassic Coast, a crocodile that swam alongside plesiosaurs. These animals, he noted, were the ones 'that look a bit like Nessie'. It was striking that a professional geologist, in seeking to describe a real-life prehistoric marine animal, chose to reference a cryptozoological one. A creature that connects us to deep time, not truly wild nor a companion species, we imagine the Scottish beastie so clearly it almost glides into corporeal form. As journalist Daniel Cohen explained in *A Modern Look at Monsters* (1970): 'While there are many people who do not believe that the Loch Ness Monster exists, there is practically no one who would not be overjoyed to find out that it did.' The idea of a living fossil is mesmerising and quirky. It also serves as a form of beastly catharsis, a useful reminder that, for all our claims to brilliance, humans do not know everything and have not been everywhere. Anthropogenic impacts – from climate change to chemical contamination – present a raft of evidence to the contrary, but it is a wondrous thought to imagine a pod of ancient sea monsters diving out there in unfathomed fathoms.

Epilogue

I am in the chalk downlands, north of the resting place of Sleepy Easton and not far from where the 'devil beast' of Wootton Rivers runs with a headless horseman along an ancient droveway. Nearby are the broadleaved glades of Savernake Forest, where my great-grandparents lived for a few years in the early twentieth century. Family anecdotes record very little about their time in the small, rented cottage, aside from the antics of a goat which was in the habit of stealing a starchy feast of fresh laundry from the washing line. It is funny what we commit to posterity. Not details of bricks and mortar, but, very often, animal tracks. A reminder of more-than-human captivations in the present, at my feet wriggles the puppy kin of the Terrier, who is busily worrying a toy rat which requires many Attenborough leaps (Tiny Dog has learned this fast) to subdue its fabric-rodent ways. Nearby, a woodpecker drums hypnotically into the deadwood of a first-millennial veteran oak and bleating ovids complete the soporific pastoral. A sip of homemade sloe gin to fire up the cognitive cogs and I start to think about all things beastly.

From woodland to farmland, the air above to the substrata below, the backyard pond to the deep sea, animals are everywhere, entangled with us in a rich, complicated and symbiotic relationship that is ancient and enduring, complicated and captivating. The creaturely cast of *Beastly Britain* scurries, leaps, flies and slithers across the historical landscape, telling tales of treachery and transformation, harvest and heroics, farming and fancy. Each animal's story is entirely its own, shaped by the lifeways, habits and (often remarkable) abilities of each species, the spaces they inhabit and their distinctive relationship with humans over time.

Hedgehog, fox, sheep, pigeon, newt, herring, stag beetle, flea, black dog and plesiosaur – each stakes a claim to national greatness. But which is 'best in show'? The hedgehog rolls forward as the favourite among beastly-loving citizens drawn to garden familiars and nostalgic for childhood yarns. The fox trots closely behind, a charismatic mammal with a scarlet swagger that suits the countryside contours of a bucolic (imagined) past and a modern urban alley alike. We imagine *all* animals, but phantom dogs are seen here in concentrations unmatched anywhere in the world, perhaps a testament to a long, long domestic story of journeying that started in Blick Mead. And then there is Nessie, a cryptid beastie, arguably the most famous of all, whose serpentine form surfaces into view to connect deep time with a modern walk on the wild side. Perhaps if we grade these critters according to the magnitude of their historical agency, sorting the 'sheep from the goats' might get easier. In which case, some might favour the strongman champion of the fairground, the flea, which leaps athletically off the back of centuries of bubonic pathogens to claim top prize. Pigeon fanciers and military buffs flock (or march) towards a different conclusion, offering a regimental coo-coo and a quick flash of the Dickin Medal, while sheep and herring (respectively) stamp their hooves and FRT with abandon to signal their geopolitical reach in bygone times. Even the underdog entries – the newts and stag beetles – slither and buzz their way into idioms and art, literature and legislation. Which would you choose? Tiny Dog picks the Terrier, of course. I couldn't possibly disagree.

The bulldog and the lion, as it turns out, are only the advance guard. Get past them and the British past is alive with creaturely motion. A history brimming with beastly presence, the likes of which, once you know, you aren't likely to forget. The animal stories here grapple with the peculiar and the particular. Each are woven into a colourful tapestry of historical experience that spans political, economic, environmental and social worlds. The richness of these tracks is even more astounding when you deconstruct the scientifics of the 'British' animal. The label, taxonomically speaking, turns out to be a something of a misnomer, a red herring, even. There are actually very few species endemic to these shores (by which I mean exclusively found in this geography), a product, scientists say, of our closeness to continental Europe and the existence of ancient land bridges (notably Doggerland). In other words, the *Britishness* of all these creaturely tales is fundamentally rooted in history rather than biology. At once unexpected but somehow obvious, this final twist in the tale of *Beastly Britain* seems deliciously eccentric, dryly amusing, quite British, actually.

That history – of 'animals and us' – bites off rather more than one (or one book) can chew. Rather like that laundry-stealing goat of Savernake. However, in the cacophony of barks and snuffles that echo out across the chapters here, from the ghostly howl of the Wisht to the cordial chirps of a young hoglet, there is a common refrain to be heard. And that speaks, sometimes forcefully so, of the power of connections: of sanctuary and sustenance; room to roam; the threads binding landscape and identity; and the importance of taking notice. A glimpse into Britain's creaturely history reveals much about the bewitching ways of animal protagonists, their communities and capabilities, ancestral routes and abodes. It sheds light, just as much, on our species: from ingenuity and creativity to foibles and fallacies. Forget Reynard, *Homo sapiens* turns out to be an especially tricky character: one with quite a line in environmental wrecking and, at the same time, an effervescent fascination for other forms of animal life. This beastly past can be a 'desire path' if we choose to follow: to see the essential role played by animals in our ecology and culture and to nurture a home that is good for us all. In stone and story, from townhouse to *hibernaculum*, Beastly Britain has been made (and made better) as a landscape of many critters. We share these isles with a multitude of species, from the 220-leggeds (the centipede, incidentally) to the no-leggeds. More profoundly, tantalisingly, they share it with us.

Animal Tracks: A Select Bibliography

Below are some suggestions for further reading if you are interested in exploring more about the animal tracks of *Beastly Britain*. The first section contains general material on landscape and animals, followed by species- (chapter-) specific offerings. If you would like to do your bit to help the non-humans of these isles, a wealth of information can be obtained from local wildlife trusts, charities focused on particular species and broader conservation organisations.

General

Mark Avery, *Reflections: What Wildlife : A Curated Collection of Wondrous Wildlife Needs and How to Provide It* (London: Pelagic Publishing, 2023)

Joanna Bagniewska, *The Modern Bestiary: A Curated Collection of Wondrous Wildlife* (London: Wildlife, 2022)

Steve Baker, *Picturing the Beast: Animals, Identity & Representation* (Manchester: Manchester University Press, 1983)

Simon Barnes, *A History of the World in 100 Animals* (London: Simon & Schuster, 2020)

John Berger, 'Why Look at Animals?', in *About Looking* (London: Bloomsbury, 1980)

Stefan Buczacki, *Fauna Britannica* (London: Hamlyn, 2002)

Mary Colwell, *Beak, Tooth and Claw: Why We Must Live with Predators* (London: William Collins, 2021)

Diana Donald, *Picturing Animals in Britain* (London: Yale University Press, 2007)

Paul Farley and Michael Symmons Roberts, *Edgelands: Journeys into England's True Wilderness* (London: Vintage, 2012)

Chris Ferris, *The Darkness Is Light Enough: The Field Journal of a Night Naturalist* (London: Sphere Books, 1986)

Charles Foster, *Being a Beast: An Intimate and Radical Look at Nature* (London: Profile, 2016)

Erica Fudge, *Animal* (London: Reaktion, 2002)

Matthew Gandy, *Natura Urbana: Ecological Constellations in Urban Space* (Cambridge, MA: MIT Press, 2022)

L. Harrison Matthews, *British Mammals* (London: Collins, 1968)

Nick Hayes, *The Book of Trespass: Crossing the Lines that Divide Us* (London: Bloomsbury, 2020)

Hilda Kean and Philip Howell (eds), *The Routledge Companion to Animal–Human History* (London: Routledge, 2012)

Robert Kuhn McGregor, 'Deriving a Biocentric History: Evidence from the Journal of Henry David Thoreau', *Environmental Review*, vol. 12, no. 2 (Summer 1988), pp. 117–26

Roger Lovegrove, *Silent Fields: The Long Decline of a Nation's Wildlife* (Oxford: Oxford University Press, 2007)

Richard Mabey, *The Unofficial Countryside* (Wimborne Minster: Dovecot, 2010)

Arthur MacGregor, *Animal Encounters: Human and Animal Interaction in Britain from the Norman Conquest to World War One* (London: Reaktion, 2012)

Mary Midgley, *Animals and Why They Matter* (Athens, GA: University of Georgia Press, 1983)

George Monbiot, *Feral: Searching for Enchantment on the Frontiers of Rewilding* (London: Allen Lane, 2013)

Oliver Pike, *Wild Animals in Britain* (London: Macmillan, 1950)

Oliver Rackham, *The History of the Countryside* (London: Phoenix Giant, 1986)

Harriet Ritvo, *The Animal Estate: The English and Other Creatures in the Victorian Age* (Cambridge, MA: Harvard University Press, 1987)

I.G. Simmonds, *An Environmental History of Great Britain: From 10,000 Years Ago to the Present* (Edinburgh: Edinburgh University Press, 2001)

Keith Thomas, *Man and the Natural World: Changing Attitudes in England, 1500–1800* (London: Penguin, 1984)

Isabella Tree, *Wilding: The Return of Nature to a British Farm* (London: Picador, 2018)

Brett Westwood and Stephen Moss, *Wonderland: A Year of Britain's Wildlife Day by Day* (London: John Murray, 2018)

Tom Williamson, *An Environmental History of Wildlife in England, 1650–1950* (London: Bloomsbury, 2013)

Edward O. Wilson, *Biophilia: The Human Bond with Other Species* (Cambridge, MA: Harvard University Press, 1984)

Hedgehog

Pam Ayres, *The Last Hedgehog* (London: Picador, 2018)

Enid Blyton, *Hedgerow Tales* (London: Award Publications, [1935] 1986)

Liz Bomford, *The Secret Life of the Hedgehog* (London: Hamlyn, 1979)
Maurice Burton, *The Hedgehog* (London: Corgi Books, 1969)
Colin Dann, *The Animals of Farthing Wood* (London: William Heinemann, 1979)
Christopher Hart, *Hedgelands: A Wild Wander Around Britain's Greatest Habitat* (London: Chelsea Green, 2024)
Pat Morris, *Hedgehog* (London: William Collins, 2018)
Beatrix Potter, *The Tale of Mrs Tiggy-Winkle* (London: Frederick Warne, 1905)
Les Stocker, *St Tiggywinkles Wildlife Hospital: Jaws the Hedgehog and Other Stories* (London: HarperCollins, 1995)
Hugh Warwick, *Hedgehog* (London: Reaktion, 2014)
Hugh Warwick, *A Prickly Affair: The Charm of the Hedgehog* (London: Penguin, 2018)

Fox

Adele Brand, *The Hidden World of the Fox* (London: William Collins, 2019)
Roger Burrows, *Wild Fox* (Newton Abbott: David & Charles, 1968)
Emma Griffin, *Blood Sport: Hunting in Britain since 1066* (London: Yale University Press, 2007)
Stephen Harris and Phil Baker, *Urban Foxes* (London: Whittet Books, 2001)
Martin Hemmington, *Foxwatching: In the Shadow of the Fox* (London: Whittet Books, 1997)
John Lewis-Stempel, *The Wild Life of the Fox* (London: Penguin, 2020)
David Macdonald, *Vulpina: The Story of a Fox* (London: William Collins, 1977)
Allyson May, *The Fox Hunting Controversy, 1781–2004* (London: Ashgate, 2013)
Chloe Petrylak, *The Secret Life of Foxes* (Barnsley: Pen & Sword, 2023)
Brian Vesey-Fitzgerald, *Town Fox, Country Fox* (London: Cornell, 1965)
Martin Wallen, *Fox* (London: Reaktion, 2006)
D.J. Watkins-Pitchford, *Wild Lone: The Story of a Pytchley Fox* (London: Methuen, 1938)

Sheep

Clive Aslet, *Agricultural Societies and Shows: Past, Present and Future* (London: Wild Search, 2015)
British Wool Marketing Board, *British Sheep and Wool* (Bradford: British Wool Marketing Board, 2010)
Peter Clery, *Green Gold: A Thousand Years of English Land* (Chichester: Phillimore & Co., 2012)

Sally Coulthard, *A Short History of the World according to Sheep* (London: Zeus, 2020)
Laurie Graham, 'Keeping Score', *The History Girls*, 11 January 2013. Available online at: http://the-history-girls.blogspot.com/2013/01/keeping-score-by-laurie-graham.html
Stephen Hall and Juliet Clutton-Brock, *Two Hundred Years of British Farm Livestock* (London: Natural History Museum, 1989)
Eileen Power, *The Wool Trade in English Medieval History* (Oxford: Oxford University Press, 1941)
James Rebanks, *English Pastoral: An Inheritance* (London: Allen Lane, 2020)
M.L. Ryder, *Sheep and Man* (London: Duckworth, 1983)
Phillip Walling, *Counting Sheep: A Celebration of the Pastoral Heritage of Britain* (London: Profile, 2014)
William Youatt, *Sheep: Their Breeds, Management and Diseases* (London: Baldwin & Craddock, 1837)

Pigeon

Barbara Allen, *Pigeon* (London: Reaktion, 2009)
Andrew D. Blechman, *Pigeons: The Fascinating Saga of the World's Most Revered and Reviled Bird* (New York: Grove Press, 2006)
Mark Collings, *A Very British Coop: Pigeon Racing from Blackpool to Sun City* (London: Macmillan, 2007)
Courtney Humphries, *Superdove: How the Pigeon Took Manhattan . . . and the World* (Washington, DC: Smithsonian, 2008)
Colin Jerolmack, *The Global Pigeon* (Chicago: University of Chicago Press, 2013)
Martin Johnes, 'Pigeon Racing and Working-Class Culture in Britain, c.1870–1950', *Cultural & Social History*, vol. 4, no. 3 (2007), pp. 361–83
Jack Kligerman, *A Fancy for Pigeons* (New York: Hawthorn Books, 1978)
Rosemary Mosco, *A Pocket Guide to Pigeon Watching: Getting to Know the World's Most Misunderstood Bird* (New York: Workman Publishing, 2021)
Lev Parikian, *Taking Flight: The Evolutionary Story of Life on the Wing* (London: Elliott & Thompson, 2023)
M. Roberts and V. Gale, *Pigeons, Doves & Dovecotes* (Kennerleigh: Broad Leys, 2000)
Richard Van Emden, *Tommy's War: Soldiers and Their Animals in the Great War* (London: Bloomsbury, 2010)

Newt

Trevor Beebee and Richard Griffiths, *Amphibians and Reptiles: A Natural History of the British Herpetofauna* (London: HarperCollins, 2000)
Marty Crump, *Eye of Newt and Toe of Frog, Adder's Fork and Lizard's Leg: The Lore & Mythology of Amphibians and Reptiles* (Chicago: University of Chicago Press, 2015)

K. Etheridge, 'Loathsome Beasts: Images of Reptiles and Amphibians in Art and Science', in *Origins of Scientific Learning: Essays on Culture and Knowledge in Early Modern Europe*, ed. S.L. French and K. Etheridge (Lewiston, NY: Edwin Mellen Press, 2007), pp. 63–88

J. Foster, *The Ecology, Conservation and Management of the Great Crested Newt (Triturus cristatus)*, Scottish Natural Heritage Information and Advisory Note No. 92 (1997)

Richard Griffiths, *The Newts & Salamanders of Europe* (London: T. & A.D. Poyser, 1996)

R. Jehle, B. Thiesmeier and J. Foster, *The Crested Newt: A Dwindling Pond-Dweller* (Bielefeld: Laurenti Verlag, 2011)

Richard Kerridge, *Cold Blood: Adventures with Reptiles and Amphibians* (London: Chatto & Windus, 2014)

T.E.S. Langton, C.L. Beckett and J.P. Foster, *Great Crested Newt Conservation Handbook* (Halesworth: FrogLife, 2001)

Malcolm Smith, *The British Amphibians & Reptiles* (London: Collins, 1951)

Herring

J.W. de Caux, *The Herring and the Herring Fishery* (London: Hamilton Adams, 1881)

S. Davis, '"A Whirling Vortex of Women": The Strikes of Scots Herring Women in East Anglia in the 1930s and 1940s', *Labour History Review*, vol. 75, no. 2 (2010), pp. 181–207

John Mitchell, *The Herring: Its Natural History and National Importance* (Edinburgh: Edmonston & Douglas, 1864)

Donald S. Murray, *Herring Tales: How the Silver Darlings Shaped Human Taste and History* (London: Bloomsbury, 2015)

National Maritime Museum, *Fish and Ships: A Nautical Miscellany* (London: Unicorn, 2023)

Callum Roberts, *An Unnatural History of the Sea* (Washington, DC: Island Press, 2007)

A.M. Samuel, *The Herring: Its Effect on the History of Britain* (London: John Murray, 1919)

Mike Smylie, *Herring: A History of the Silver Darlings* (Stroud: The History Press, 2004)

Christopher Unsworth, *The British Herring Industry: The Steam Drifter Years 1900–1960* (Stroud: Amberley, 2013)

Stag Beetle

Frank Cowan, *Curious Facts in the History of Insects* (Philadelphia: Lippincott & Lippincott, 1865)

Adam Dodd, *Beetle* (London: Reaktion, 2015)

Arthur Evans, *The Lives of Beetles* (Princeton, NJ: Princeton University Press, 2023)

Norman Joy, *British Beetles: Their Homes and Habitats* (London: Frederick Warne, 1933)
William Kirby and William Spence, *Introduction to Entomology* (London: Longman, Rees, Orme, Brown & Green, 1815)
E.F. Linssen, *Beetles of the British Isles* (London: Frederick Warne, 1959)
Cannon Schmitt, 'Victorian Beetlemania', in *Victorian Animal Dreams*, ed. Deborah Denenholz Morse and Martin Danahay (London: Routledge, 2007)
Eva Sprecher-Uebersax, 'The Stag Beetle *Lucanus Cervus* (Coleoptera, Lucanidae) in Art and Mythology', *Revue d'Écologie (La Terre et La Vie)*, supplément 10 (2008)
Jan Swammerdam, *The Natural History of Insects* (Perth: R. Morison, 1792)
John George Wood, *Episodes of Insect Life* (London: G. Bell, 1879)

Flea

L. Bertolotto, *The History of the Flea with Notes, Observations & Amusing Anecdotes* (London: Crozier, 1835)
John F. Clark, *Bugs and the Victorians* (New Haven, CT: Yale University Press, 2009)
Boris R. Krasnov, *Functional and Evolutionary Ecology of Fleas: A Model for Ecological Parasitology* (Cambridge: Cambridge University Press, 2008)
Peter Marren, *Bugs Britannica* (London: Chatto & Windus, 2010)
Joe Nickell, *Secrets of the Sideshow* (Lexington, KY: University of Kentucky Press, 2005)
Miriam Rothschild and Theresa Clay, *Fleas, Flukes & Cuckoos* (London: Collins, 1952)
Harold Russell, *The Flea* (Cambridge: Cambridge University Press, 1913)
D. Van Zwanenberg, 'The Last Epidemic of Plague in England? Suffolk, 1906–1918', *Medical History*, vol. 14, no. 1 (1970), pp. 63–74

Black Dog

Sally Barber and Chips Barber, *Dark and Dastardly Dartmoor* (Exeter: Obelisk Publications, 1988)
Janet Bord and Colin Bord, *Alien Animals* (London: Granada, 1985)
Graham J. McEwan, *Mystery Animals of Britain and Ireland* (London: Robert Hale, 1986)
Mark Norman, *Black Dog Folklore* (London: Troy Books, 2016)
Elliott O'Donnell, *Animal Ghosts* (Brooklyn, NY: Sheba Blake, 2018)
Chris Pearson, *Collared: How We Made the Modern Dog* (London: Profile, 2024)
Robert Trubshaw, *Explore Phantom Black Dogs* (Orston: Heart of Albion Press, 2005)

John West, *Britain's Haunted Heritage* (Derby: D.B. Publishing, 2019)

Kathleen Wiltshire, *Ghosts and Legends of the Wiltshire Countryside* (Wiltshire: Compton Press, 1973)

Plesiosaur

Ronald Binns, *Decline and Fall of the Loch Ness Monster* (York: Zoilus Press, 2019)

Jan Bondeson, *Animal Freaks: The Strange History of Amazing Animals* (Stroud: Tempus, 2008)

John Cherry, *Mythical Beasts* (London: The Folio Society, 2021)

Tim Dinsdale, *The Loch Ness Monster* (London: Routledge & Kegan, 1961)

Shelley Emling, *The Fossil Hunter: Dinosaurs, Evolution, and the Woman Whose Discoveries Changed the World* (New York: St Martin's Press, 2009)

Rupert Gould, *The Loch Ness Monster and Others* (London: Geoffrey Bles, 1934)

Paul Harrison, *Sea Serpents and Lake Monsters of the British Isles* (London: Robert Hale, 2001)

David James, *Loch Ness Investigation* (London: Loch Ness Investigation Bureau, 1968)

Daniel Loxton and Donald Prothero, *Abominable Science: Origins of the Yeti, Nessie, and Other Famous Cryptids* (New York: Columbia University Press, 2013)

Sarah Perry, *The Essex Serpent* (London: Serpent's Tail, 2016)

Patricia Pierce, *Jurassic Mary: Mary Anning and the Primeval Monsters* (Cheltenham: The History Press, 2006)

Mark Witton and Ellinor Michel, *Art and Science of the Crystal Palace Dinosaurs* (Marlborough: Crowood Press, 2022)

Index

Aberdeen Bestiary, 157–9
Acton, Elizabeth, 193
Adams, Richard, 39, 77
Aesop, 29, 30, 35, 61, 257
Afanc, 275–6
agriculture, and animal shows/
    fairs, 99, 101–2, 107–8,
    127–8, 242–7; scientific and
    industrial, 38, 71–5, 80,
    104–9, 115, 125–6
Albarn, Damon, 142
Alderney, 41–2
Alken, Henry, 68
Allen, Barbara, 142
Alphonsi, Petrus, 89–90, 99
animal history, 2–6, 10, 251, 258
animals, and anthropogenic
    impacts, 5, 8, 84, 167, 177,
    183, 195, 302; in British
    landscape and culture, 2, 3,
    6–9, 56, 59, 79–81, 91–2,
    96–100, 114–15, 178; in
    children's literature, 35–9;
    futures, 5–6, 9; human
    perceptions of, 2, 3, 6–7, 8;
    and ideas of the wild and
    rewilding, 7, 9, 43–4, 46, 47,
    48, 74, 81, 84–5, 115, 141–2,
    148, 220–1, 259, 260, 263,
    302; in legend, story, and
    fable, 1–2, 7, 21–8, 29, 33–4,
    45–8, 58–9, 61, 190, 203–4,
    281; in literature and art, 10,
    30, 33–9, 46–7, 107–9; in
    medieval manuscripts, 3–5,
    23–6, 157–9

Anning, Mary, 284–8, 290, 292
Annwn hounds, 260
Anubis, 260
Archilochus, 18
Aristotle, 26, 159, 229
Atherton Hall, 126
Atherton, Lord, 126
Atkinson, J.C., 265
Atterby, Helen, 57
Augustine Priory, Canterbury, 96
Augustine, St, 156
Ayres, Pam, 14, 43

badger, 3, 18, 27, 28, 34, 37, 70
Bain, Elizabeth, 188
Baker, Henry, 243
Bakewell, Robert, 72–3, 106
Baldessari, John, 207, 215
Barghest, 263, 265–6, 267
Basil Brush, 46
Batty, Robert, 172
Baxter, George, 292, 293
beast, etymology of term, 7
Beaufort, 5th Duke of, 72
Beaufort, 10th Duke of, 73
Beche, Henry de la, 288, 289–90
Becket, Thomas, 101
Beckford, Peter, 74
Beckwith, H., 108, 109
Bede, 236
Bedford, 5th Duke of, 107
Bekker, Koos, 166
Belle Vue Flea Circus, 246–7
Berlin, Isaiah, 18
Bertolotto, Louis, 243–5, 247
Beukelszoon, Willem, 181

INDEX

Bewick, Thomas, 61
Bildt, Carl, 173
Bilsdale Hunt, Yorkshire, 72
biophilia, 9, 220
Birch, Thomas James, 285
Birmingham Roller (pigeon), 127
Bishop, Dave, 141
Black Death, *see* bubonic plague
Black Dog Hill, 272
Black Dog of Torrington, 270–1
black dog, *see* dog
Black Shuck, 252, 261–4, 267
Blair, Tony, 78
Blake, Robert, 184
Blake, William, 233
Blick Mead Dog, 253–4, 255
Blue Ben, 275
Blyton, Enid, 37
Boerce, Hector, 93
Bond, Simon, 40
Boorde, Andrew, 123
Booth, Frederick, 135
Borrow, George, 33, 257
Boverick, Sobieski, 242–3
Bradbury, Ray, 279
Brand, Adele, 81, 86
Brigid, St, 26
Bristol Zoo, 8
Britain, historical ecology and habitat, of, 6, 15, 34, 53–5, 92, 109–10, 145, 169–70, 274, 281–2
Brontë, Charlotte, 265
Bronx Zoo, 8
Brown, Lancelot 'Capability,' 108–9, 114
Brown, Theo, 270
bubonic plague, 3, 96, 101, 222–3, 225, 235–42
Buckingham, Duke of, 72, 288, 292
Buckland, William, 290
Buffon, Comte de, 65
bulldog, 251–2
Bunbury, Henry, 286, 287
Burgess, Mike, 262

Burns Committee, 78
Burrows, Roger, 58
Burton, Maurice, 19
Bushe, Thomas and Joan, 98
Buxton, T., 22

Camden, William, 178
Campbell, Alex, 297
Campbell, Duncan, 296
Cannon, Richard, 192
Canute, 70
Capek, Karel, 162
Carrier Pigeon Service, 133
Carroll, Lewis, 30, 217
Castle Combe, 99–100, 101
Caux, J.W. de, 179
Caxton, William, 65
Cerambus, 204
Cerberus, 260
Cerveny, Jaroslav, 62
Charlemagne, 95
Chaucer, Geoffrey, 102, 258
Christy, Miller, 25
Clapham, Richard, 56
Clare, John, 23, 33, 34, 35, 76
Clay, Teresa, 235
climate change/emergency, 114, 115, 167, 195, 220, 263, 302
Cobbett, William, 192
Cocks, Seymour, 77
Cohen, Daniel, 302
Coke, Thomas, 105–6
Coles, Major Adrian, 39
Collins, Norman, 299
Columba, St, 296
Columbarium Society, 126
Colwell, Mary, 47, 85
Comyns-Carr, Alice Laura, 217
Conybeare, William, 288
Cook, Colonel John, 74
Cope, Julian, 77
Corrigan, Richard, 196
Cotswold Lion, 94
Coulthard, Sally, 115
Countryside Alliance, 78, 79

INDEX

cow, 21, 22–3, 33–4
Cowan, Frank, 212
Creece, Mary and Thomas, 285
Cruelty to Animals Act (1835), 252
Crystal Palace dinosaurs, 292–5
Crystal Palace Show, 127
Cuvier, Georges, 286, 288

Dando Dogs, 271
Dangerous Wild Animals Act (1976), 42
Dann, Colin, 39
Dartmoor, 146, 267–9
Darwin, Charles, 56, 128
Davis, Paul, 301–2
Davis, Sam, 190
Davis, William Henry, 108, 109
Day, Francis, 172
Defoe, Daniel, 99, 102, 182
Dick, Philip K., 113
Dickens, Charles, 293
Dickin Medal, 137
Dill, Lawrence, 172
Dinsdale, Tim, 299
Dishley, *see* New Leicester
dog, bones and remains of, 252–5; breeds, 251–2; domestication, 251–4, 260; as favourites/ companion animals, 36, 100, 259, 260, 267; fleas, 28, 44, 228, 236, 247–8; ghostly forms of, 7, 252, 257–72; ghostly forms and the road, 270–2; legend, stories and fables, 252, 256–72; in literature, 252, 256–7, 265, 266, 269; names and associated idioms, 258; place in British culture and landscape, 251–5, 258–60, 261–72; taxonomy and physiology, 251–2, 259; training, 107; and wolf, 253, 256–7, 260–1

Dolly the Sheep, 92, 113–14
Domesday Book, 96, 180
Donne, John, 229–30
Donovan, J.F., 184
Dovecot, 123–5, 126, 139
Doyle, Arthur Conan, 31, 269, 291
Doyle, Charles Altamont, 31
Drabble, Phil, 112
Dürer, Albrecht, 206–7
Dutt, W.A., 262

Edward I, 102, 181
Edward II, 70
Edward III, 103, 180
Edward of Norwich, 71
Edwards, George, 210–2
Elefsen, Anita, 188
Elizabeth I, 34
Ellis, William, 107
Elwin, Whitwell, 128
Ely Abbey, 96
Ely Cathedral, 59
enclosure, 34–5, 104–5, 125–6
environment, and literature, 38, 59
Etheridge, Kay, 156, 157

Falstolf, John, 100
Feltham, Steve, 300–1
Ferris, Chris
Fessard, Claude, 119
Finnegan, Lorcan, 84
Fishy Evans's, Bath, 116, 139
Fitter, Richard, 299
flea, 7, 14, 28, 44, 64–5; bites and their effect, 222; and bubonic plague, 222–3, 225, 235–42; cultural perceptions of, 222, 228, 243; decline of human variety, 247; dog and cat treatments, 247–8; and flea circus, 242–7; and Glasgow plague outbreak, 240–1; historical remedies against, 226–8; and human

evolution, 225; and jumping abilities, 224, 234–5, 242; legends, stories and fable, 226–8; in literature and art, 229–30, 232–3, 243; mating and reproduction, 224; names and associated idioms, 222, 225–6, 228–9; natural histories of, 228, 231–2, 233–5; place in British culture and landscape, 225–30; relationship to rats, 236–9, 241; and Suffolk plague outbreak, 240–2; taxonomy and physiology, 223–4, 226, 229, 234–5; under the microscope, 230–3, 238, 243; and vampiric associations, 222, 229, 233, 234, 242
Forcett Hall, 126
Fortey, John
Foster, Charles, 85
Foster, Michael, 78
Fowler, John, 267
fox, 6, 10, 13, 27, 33, 34; adaptability and resilience, 47–8, 66, 80, 85; cultural perceptions of, 46–8, 57, 59, 61, 79–85; evolution and fossil record, 51–5; future for, 85–6; hunting ability and predatory nature, 47, 62–4, 65–6, 71, 83; hunting ban, 77–80; and hunting of, 55, 68–80; in legend, story and fable, 45–8, 58–9, 61, 75–7; in literature and art, 10, 29, 36, 37, 46, 65, 68–9, 75–7, 84–5; mating and reproduction, 66–8; names and associated idioms, 56, 58, 69–70; opponents of hunting, 75–80; persecution and killing of, 55, 70–1, 72, 82–5; sensory abilities of, 61–4; sport hunting as invented tradition, 70–2; sport hunting, ritual and performance, 70–3, 55; taxonomy and physiology, 45, 48–57, 59–62, 66, 83; and urban world, 48, 57, 67, 80–6, 218; as vagabond hero, 75–6, 79–80, 83–4; wildlife biology and natural histories of, 56–7, 58
Francatelli, Charles Elme, 191
Freeman, E.A., 75
Frisch, Leopold, 50
Fudge, Erica, 3

Gabriel's Hounds, 264–5
Galilei, Galileo, 230–1
Gandy, Matthew, 84
Garnett, David, 76
Gay, John, 69
Gelert, 252, 256–7
Gessner, Conrad, 159–60, 207
Gibson, Alexander, 280
Goldsmith, Oliver, 55, 233–4
Goring, Alan, 134
Gosse, Philip, 133, 135
Gosse, Philip Henry, 279
Gould, Rupert, 299
Gould, Stephen, 50
Graham, Laurie, 90
Graham, Tommy, 279
Grassi, Giovannino de', 206
Gray, Hugh, 297
Great Yarmouth, 179–80, 182, 186, 187, 188, 189, 193, 194
Griffin, Emma, 78, 79
Grimm, Brothers, 30
Grotius, Hugo, 184
groundhog, 27
Guinefort, 257
Gunn, Neil, 185
Gurt Dog, 267
Gytrash, 263, 265

INDEX

Hadspen House (the Newt), 166
Haggard, Rider, 277
Haight, Amy, 19
Halliday, Scott Ron, 301
Haraway, Donna, 10
Hardy, Thomas, 102, 108
Hare, 30, 71
Harris, Steve, 142
Harrison, Paul, 276, 278, 280
Harrods Pet Kingdom, 42
Hatch, 254, 255
Hawkhurst Gang, 104
Hawkins, Benjamin Waterhouse, 292, 293
Hawkins, Thomas, 186, 290–1
Hayes, Nick, 75, 79
hedgehog, 6, 45–6; appreciation of, 35–41; association with the Devil, witches and magic, 25, 29, 30–1; conservation measures, 43–4; as culinary delicacy, 32–3, 40–1; declining numbers of, 14, 38–9, 43–4; feeding habits, 14, 18–19, 21–5, 33, 44; and fruit collection, 21, 23–6, 44, 64; future for, 14, 43–4; as garden favourite, 13–14, 21, 28, 43–4; and hibernation, 16, 20–1, 26–7; historical persecution of, 33–5; in legend, story and fable, 21–8, 29, 33–4, 29, 33–4; in literature and art, 23, 30, 33–9; mating and reproduction, 16, 19–20; medicinal uses of, 31–2; and milking cows, 21, 22–3, 33–4, 44; names and associated idioms, 28–9; and nocturnal habits, 14, 16, 18–19, 21; as pets, 41–2; practical uses of, 30–2; and rolling into a ball, 17–18, 19, 33; and road deaths, 38–9, 40; and self-anointing, 27–8; spines, 16–17, 30, 33; taxonomy and physiology, 14–21, 41–2; and weather forecasting, 21, 26–7
Hedgehog Preservation Society, 39
Heege, Richard, 192
Hemmington, Martin, 64, 81
Henderson, J. Scott, 77
Henderson, William, 264
Henry I, 99
Henry VI, 100
Henry VIII, 34, 255
herring, 6; and Cold War incident, 173–4; British shoals and territories, 176–7; decline of British industry, 194–5; and the Dutch trade, 181–2, 183–4; feeding strategies, 175; as food staple, 170, 178, 180–1, 185, 191–4, 196; and FRT noises, 172–3; future 195–6; habits and behaviour, 170–8; and herring 'lassies', 186–90; legends, stories and fable, 172, 178, 190; in literature and art, 183, 192; mating and reproduction, 176–8; movement and migrations, 174–7; names and associated idioms, 170; overfishing of, 195–6; place in British culture and landscape, 170, 178–90, 196; population numbers of, 171, 195–6; and the red herring, 191–2; and the Scottish industry, 183–90; taxonomy and physiology, 170–5, 190; trade and the 'grand fishery', 178–82; ways of cooking and preserving, 180, 192–4, 196

Herring, J.F., 69
Hibernaculum, 20, 26, 35, 43
hibernation, 16, 20–1, 26–7, 153, 156
Hicks, John, 277
Highland Clearances, 105, 185
Hirst, Damien, 92, 113
Hobsbawm, Eric, 70
Holkham Estate, 106
Holmes, John, 281
Holmes, Oliver Wendell, 215
homing pigeon, *see* Racing Homer
Hooke, Robert, 231–3, 243
Horne, Richard Henry, 256–7
Horsfall-Turner, J., 265
Hound Tor, 268–9
House, Charles Arthur, 127
Hughes, Ted, 10
Humanitarian League, 75
Humphreys, Mary Gay, 216
Humphries, Courtney, 116
Hunt Saboteurs Association, 77
Hunting with Hounds Act (2004), 79
hunting, of fox banned as sport, 77–80; as invented tradition, 70–2; opponents of, 75–80; ritual and performance code, 70–3
Hutchinson, Henry, 291
Huxley, Thomas Henry, 279

Imaizumi, Yoshinori, 280
Industrial Revolution, *see* industrialism
industrialism, 38–9, 110–1, 126–7, 147, 164–5, 209
International Commission on Zoological Nomenclature, 50

Jago Edge-Hill, William, 70
James I, 184
James, David, 299
James, Ronald, 281
Janiga, Marian, 119

Janssen, Zacharias, 230
Jehle, Robert, 151
Jerolmack, Colin, 139
Jesse, Edward, 252
Johnes, Martin, 130, 132
Johnson, Boris, 147, 148
Johnson, Owen, 162
Johnson, Richard, 119
Jones, D. Gwenaullt, 132
Jones, Jonathan, 232

Keogh, John, 32
Kerridge, Richard, 146, 155
Kipling, Rudyard, 30, 68
Kirby, William, 212
Knapp, James, 33
Konig, Charles, 286
Krulwich, Robert, 63

Lambton Worm, 274–5
landscape park, 72, 73, 108–9
Langland, William, 101
Larkin, Philip, 43
Latreille, Pierre Andre, 229
lawnmower, 43
League Against Cruel Sports, 77–8
Lee, Alexander, 132
Leonardo da Vinci, 156
Lewis-Stempel, John, 46, 47, 60
Lewis, Philip, 41
Linnaeus, Carl, 14, 50, 210, 225
Linssen, E.F., 218
lion, 7, 62, 65, 102
Livingstone, Ken, 140, 146–7
Loch Ness, 266
Loch Ness Investigation Bureau, 299
Loch Ness Monster, *see* Nessie
Lochner, Stefan, 206
Lockman, John, 183
Lockwood, Rachel, 84
Lofting, Hugh, 76
London Beard (pigeon), 127
Longleat, 7
Lovegrove, Roger, 33, 34, 47
Lovell, Robert, 32

INDEX

Lowestoft, 180, 186, 187, 188
Loxton, Daniel, 297
Lucas, Joseph, 127
Ludd, Ned, 110
Lumley, Reverend William, 128

McCannon, Olivia, 267
MacDonald, Mary, 188
Macfarlane, Alexander, 89
Mackrell, J., 69
McLean, T.L., 136
Magnus, Albertus, 229
Magnus, Olaus, 64
Mantell, Gideon, 286
Maplet, John, 16
Marsh, Richard, 217–18
Masefield, John, 68
Massive Attack (trip-hop artists), 219
Metal, Penny, 218
Meynell, Hugo, 72
microscope, 209, 230–3, 238, 243
Miller, John, 49
Mitchell, John, 170
Moffett, Thomas, 207–8, 238, 242
Mole, 15, 37
Monbiot, George, 114–15, 141
Monty Python, 40
Moore, John, 126
More, Thomas, 105
Morgawr (sea giant), 277–81
Morris, Pat, 16, 21, 28
Morton, John, 149, 151
Mosco, A. Rosemary, 121
Moss, Stephen, 154, 155
Mothy, James 268
Mr Tod, 36, 46, 65
Mrs Tiggy-Winkle, 13, 35–7
Mulder, Fox, 301
Mulvey, Laura, 84
Murray, Donald S., 175

National Homing Union, 130
National Pigeon Service, 135

Natural History Museum, 51, 219, 281, 291, 292, 298
nature, human captivation with, 9; human estrangement from, 8–9
Nessie, 295–302
New Labour, 78–80
New Leicester (sheep breed), 106
New Zealand, 20, 111
newt, 6, 14, 30; behaviour, habits and life cycle, 151–5; British species, 147–8, 148–50, 165–6; and conservation measures, 146, 147–8, 163–8; cultural perceptions of, 145–6, 155–63; as endangered species, 146, 163–8; future for, 167–8; habitat, 149–61, 160, 165; and importance of ponds, 164–8; legends, stories and fable, 155–63; in literature and art, 162; mating and reproduction, 145–6, 149, 154–5, 162; medicinal uses of, 161; names and associated idioms, 149, 156, 161, 163; natural histories of, 149–51, 159–61, 162; persecution of, 161–2; as pet, 146–7; population numbers, 151, 164–6, 167; taxonomy and physiology, 148–51, 160–1
Newton, Victor, 135
Norfolk Horn (sheep breed), 110
Norman, Mark, 270
Norwich Cropper (pigeon), 127

Offa, 95
Ogilvie, Brian, 206
Omand, Donald, 266
Orwell, George, 112
Osman, Major W.H., 135
Owen, Richard, 291

Padfoot, 263, 264
Pagel, Mark, 225
Penny, Thomas, 207
People's Trust for Endangered Species, 220
Pepys, Samuel, 125
pesticides, 14, 44
PETA, 141
Phillip, Arthur, 111
pig, 2, 10
pigeon, 7, 63, 66, 146; breeds, 117–18, 126–8, 130; cultural perceptions of, 116–18, 120, 121, 123, 126–8, 138–42; and domestication, 116, 123, 138–9, 253; and doves, 117–18, 119; eating habits, 122–3; ecological value of, 142; in literature and art, 121, 127, 133, 142; mating and reproduction, 121–2; as medieval meat economy, 123–6; medicinal uses of, 125; as messenger, 129–37; names and associated idioms, 117, 123, 124–5; as object of fancy, 126–8, 137–8; as pest, 118, 126, 138–42; place in culture and landscape of Britain, 117–18, 130–2, 142; population numbers, 120, 128; racing and sport, 130–2, 138; racing and working-class masculinity, 130–2; taxonomy and physiology, 116, 118–23, 128–9; in urban space, 118, 138–42; and war/military uses of, 121, 132–7
Pigeon Action Group, 141
Pigeon Alliance, 141
Pigeon Control Advisory Service, 142
Pigeon Service Special Section, 135–7

Pigeon Society, 128
Pike, Oliver, 57
Pink, Thomas, 73
Pink Floyd, 112
Pinny, Anna Maria, 285
Playfere, Thomas, 30
plesiosaur, 7; cultural perceptions of, 273–4, 291–4; extinction of, 283; legend, stories and fables, 274–81; in literature and art, 279, 288–95; and the Loch Ness mystery, 295–302; and Mary Anning, 284–8; public displays of, 292–5; taxonomy and physiology, 281–3, 286–8, 291; and Victorian fossil mania, 284–95
Pliny the Elder, 24, 95, 157, 159, 204
Plutarch, 26
ponds, importance of for wildlife, 43, 163–8, 200
Potter, Beatrix, 13, 35–7, 65
Poulsen, Bo, 183, 185
Power, Eileen, 97
Price, Lawrence, 26
Priddy Fair, 101
Pritchard, David, 257
Prothero, Donald, 297
Punch magazine, 217, 294–5
Punxsutawney Phil, 27
Pye, Robert, 75

Quorn Hunt, 72

Racing Homer (pigeon), 130–2
Rayner, Bernie, 141
Reagan, Romany, 269
Reuter, Paul Julius, 129
Reynard the Fox, 46, 65, 76, 77
Rines, Robert, 300
roads and road culture, 38, 40
Rochester Bestiary, 23–5

INDEX

Romans, 31, 32, 94, 95, 123, 129, 178, 179, 204, 227, 251, 255
Romanticism, and Romantic presentations of nature, 35, 37, 68, 76, 113, 121, 209, 256
Romany, 29, 33
Romney Marsh, 102
Roos, Karen, 166
Rothschild, Lionel (Walter), 234
Rothschild, Miriam, 224, 234–5, 239
Rothschild, Nathaniel (Charles), 234
Royal Bath and West of England Society, 107
Royal Lancashire Agricultural Society, 107
Royal Navy Pigeon Service, 133
RSPB, 147
RSPCA, 77
Russell, Harold, 228
Russell, John, 74
Rusty, 254, 255

St Andrews, Castle Combe, 100
St Mary Redcliffe, Bristol, 59
St Peter & Paul, Northleach, 97–8
St Tiggywinkles Wildlife Hospital, 40, 41, 235
Salamander, 147, 149, 153, 155–60, 161, 162, 167, 205
Salmon, William, 125
Salt, Henry, 75
Samuel, A.M., 172
Sartin, Paul, 267
Sassoon, Siegfried, 68
Save the Trafalgar Square Pigeons, 141
Scaliot, Mark, 242
Scarry, Richard, 37–8
Scofield, Paul, 283
Scott, Peter, 299, 300

Seahouses, Northumberland, 193
sea monsters, 275–81
Seldon, John, 184
Shakespeare, William, 30, 161, 229, 258
Sharples, Lauren, 264
sheep, 7, 26, 62, 123; breeds, 92, 93, 94, 106–9, 114–15; counting, 89–91, 115; and Crown taxation, 102–3; and ecosystem damage, 114–15; evolution and ancestry, 92–4, 253; fairs and shows, 99, 101–2, 107–8; futures, 114–15; and genetic modification, 92, 113–14; and Highland Clearances, 105; in legend, story and fable, 90–1, 101–2, 103, 105, 114; in literature and art, 101–3, 108–9, 112–13; in modern times, 109–11, 114–15; names and associated idioms, 91–2; and opposition to industrialization, 110–11; place in British landscape and culture, 91–2, 93–4, 97–100, 101,103, 108–9, 114–15; population numbers, 92, 96,97; rearing and management, 90, 93–4, 104–9, 253; and scientific agriculture, 104–9, 115; and smuggling, 103–4; taxonomy and physiology, 94–5; and wool trade, 94–5, 96–104
Shiels, Tony 'Doc', 278, 281
Shikama, Tokio, 280
shrew, 15
Simond, Paul-Louis, 238–9
Sinclair, Sir John, 106, 107
Sleepy Easton, 254–5
slug, 18, 39, 42, 168
Smith, Delia, 196
Smith, Dick King, 38–9
Smyth, Herbert Warington, 185

snake, 30, 147
Soay (sheep breed), 92–3, 114
Society for the Diffusion of Useful Knowledge, 108
Society for the Free British Fishery, 183
Society for the Improvement of British Wool, 107
Solinus, 178
Southdown (sheep breed), 106, 108–9
Speke the Headless, 254, 255, 258
Spence, William, 212
Spencer, William Robert, 256
Spenser, Edmund, 161–2
Spicer, George, 297
Spicer, Major John, 22
sport hunting, 55, 68–80
stag beetle, 6, 14; in British culture and landscape, 204–5, 215–18, 219; British habitat and range, 200, 218, 220; conservation measures, 200; decline, 200; devilish associations, 205; as fashion item, 215–18; future for, 219–20; legends, stories and fables, 203–4, 212–13; life cycle of, 200–1, 217; in literature and art, 206–7, 215–18; mating and reproduction, 201–3; medicinal uses of, 204, 208; names and associated idioms, 205; natural histories of, 205–8, 209–15; as pet, 213–15, 221; population and numbers, 200, 218, 220; taxonomy and physiology, 200–2, 203; and untidy gardens, 220; in urban areas, 219; and Victorian nature study, 209–12, 218
Star Carr, 253
Stein, Rick, 196

Stocker, Sue and Les, 40
Stoker, Bram, 266
Stonehenge, 29, 254
Stones, Nick, 261
Stow-on-the-Wold, 99, 101
Stringer, Arthur, 74
Stronsay Beast, 280
Surtees, Robert, 68
Swammerdam, Jan, 212
Swift, Jonathan, 232
Swinden, Henry, 179

Talbot, J.S., 56
Taylor, E.S., 262
Tehrani, Jamie, 275
Terrier, the, 10, 15, 63, 64, 74, 92, 93, 122, 199, 251, 259, 269
Terry, Ellen, 217
toad, 21, 27
Tomlin, Len, 246, 247
Tongue, Ruth, 266
Topsell, Edward, 18, 24–5, 26, 28, 31, 32, 159, 160, 161
tortoise, 30
Trafalgar Square, 140–1, 146
Treadmill Experiment, 120
Trollope, Anthony, 73
Trubshaw, Robert, 261
Tusser, Thomas, 107, 228
Twiti, William, 70
Tyson, Mike, 137

Uist Hedgehog Rescue, 42
urbanisation, 38–9, 43, 48, 57–8, 67, 80–6, 110–11, 115, 116, 118, 138–42, 181, 215, 218–19
Ure, George, 127
Uttley, Alison, 37

Van Leeuwenhoek, Antonie, 232
Van Zwanenberg, David, 241–2
Varro, 123
Vauxhall Pleasure Gardens, 126, 183
Vegetable Lamb of Tartary, 114

INDEX

Vermin Acts, 34, 70
Verne, Jules, 291
Vesey-Fitzgerald, Brian, 58, 61, 70
Victorian nature study, 126–8, 137–8, 209–12, 218
Viret, M. Peter, 18, 26

W.R.D., 23
Wade, James, 192
Wahlberg, Magnus, 173
Wake, David, 148
Wallen, Martin, 50, 53
Ward, Rowland, 298
Warmer, Joyce, 136
Warwick, Hugh, 37
Waterford, Marquis of, 69
Watkins-Pitchford, D.J., 76–7
Webb, Mrs Arthur, 196
Webb, Mary, 76
Wells, H.G., 217
Westerberg, Hakan, 173
Westwood, Brett, 154, 155
Wetherell, Marmaduke, 298
Weyhill Fair, 101, 102
Whiston, Kate, 128
White, Harold, 131
Whyte, Constance, 299
wild, in British culture, 7, 9, 43–4, 46, 47, 48, 74, 81, 84–5, 115, 141–2, 148, 259, 260, 263, 302; and rewilding, 9, 43–4, 114, 141–2, 148, 259, 220–1, 260, 263, 302
Wilde, Oscar, 75
Wildlife and Countryside Act (1981), 39, 163, 200

Wilkins, Harold, 279
Willett, Sam, 219
Wilson Robert Kenneth, 298
Wilson, Ben, 172
Wilson, Edward O., 9, 220
Wiltshire Horn (sheep breed), 110
Wiltshire Shearmen, 110–1
Wiltshire, Kathleen, 258
Wisht Hounds, 267–8
Wistman's Wood, 268
Woburn Abbey, 107
Wodehouse, P.G., 162
wolf, 56, 57, 65, 71, 72, 124, 253, 256–7, 260–1
Wood, J.G., 162
Wood, Reverend John George, 213–14, 221
Woodger, John, 193
wool churches, 97–8
Woolf, Virginia, 68–9, 252
Woolfson, Esther, 142
Woolley, Jonathan, 263
Worcester, William, 100
Wordsworth, William, 89
worm, 18, 25, 66
Wotton, Edward, 207

Yallop, Alfred William, 194
Yano, Michihiko, 280
Yellowstone National Park, 63
Yeltsin, Boris, 173
Yersin, Alexandre, 238
Yeth Hounds, 268
Youatt, William, 108

Zephaniah, Benjamin, 44